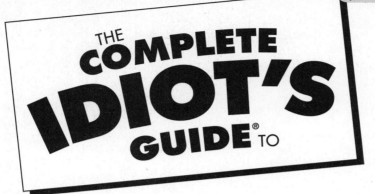

THE
COMPLETE IDIOT'S GUIDE® TO

Pleasing Your Man

by Eve Salinger

ALPHA

A member of Penguin Group (USA) Inc.

Dedicated to Gray, in appreciation of his profound patience, reliable sense of humor, and willingness to jump off a cliff with me from time to time.

ALPHA BOOKS

Published by the Penguin Group

Penguin Group (USA) Inc., 375 Hudson Street, New York, New York 10014, USA

Penguin Group (Canada), 90 Eglinton Avenue East, Suite 700, Toronto, Ontario M4P 2Y3, Canada (a division of Pearson Penguin Canada Inc.)

Penguin Books Ltd., 80 Strand, London WC2R 0RL, England

Penguin Ireland, 25 St. Stephen's Green, Dublin 2, Ireland (a division of Penguin Books Ltd.)

Penguin Group (Australia), 250 Camberwell Road, Camberwell, Victoria 3124, Australia (a division of Pearson Australia Group Pty. Ltd.)

Penguin Books India Pvt. Ltd., 11 Community Centre, Panchsheel Park, New Delhi—110 017, India

Penguin Group (NZ), 67 Apollo Drive, Rosedale, North Shore, Auckland 1311, New Zealand (a division of Pearson New Zealand Ltd.)

Penguin Books (South Africa) (Pty.) Ltd., 24 Sturdee Avenue, Rosebank, Johannesburg 2196, South Africa

Penguin Books Ltd., Registered Offices: 80 Strand, London WC2R 0RL, England

Copyright © 2005 by Eve Salinger

International Standard Book Number: 978-1-59257-365-3
Library of Congress Catalog Card Number: 2005925277

09 08   8 7 6 5 4 3

Interpretation of the printing code: The rightmost number of the first series of numbers is the year of the book's printing; the rightmost number of the second series of numbers is the number of the book's printing. For example, a printing code of 05-1 shows that the first printing occurred in 2005.

Printed in the United States of America

Note: This publication contains the opinions and ideas of its author. It is intended to provide helpful and informative material on the subject matter covered. It is sold with the understanding that the author and publisher are not engaged in rendering professional services in the book. If the reader requires personal assistance or advice, a competent professional should be consulted.

The author and publisher specifically disclaim any responsibility for any liability, loss, or risk, personal or otherwise, which is incurred as a consequence, directly or indirectly, of the use and application of any of the contents of this book.

Most Alpha books are available at special quantity discounts for bulk purchases for sales promotions, premiums, fund-raising, or educational use. Special books, or book excerpts, can also be created to fit specific needs.

For details, write: Special Markets, Alpha Books, 375 Hudson Street, New York, NY 10014.

Publisher: *Marie Butler-Knight*
Product Manager: *Phil Kitchel*
Senior Managing Editor: *Jennifer Bowles*
Acquisitions Editor: *Paul Dinas*
Development Editor: *Nancy D. Lewis*
Production Editor: *Janette Lynn*

Copy Editor: *Kelly D. Henthorne*
Illustrator: *Shannon Wheeler*
Cover/Book Designer: *Trina Wurst*
Indexer: *Julie Bess*
Layout: *Ayanna Lacey*
Proofreading: *Mary Hunt*

Contents at a Glance

Contents

Appendixes

Foreword

When it comes to relationships, there are an infinite number of things that we are not taught, yet are expected to know. Since the beginning of time, women have most often served as the relationship keepers, or the partner in a couple most responsible for making their marriages and other long-term love relationships work. As psychologists who specialize in relationship issues, we are always answering questions from highly intelligent women about what makes their men tick; and are often struck by the fact that there is so much embarrassment about asking. So think about a few of those things that you believe you "should" somehow know instinctively, but don't. You might have been able to get some—but most likely not all—of the answers to your most haunting questions by talking to friends or others in your life to which you had access. Moreover, throughout life, new questions will always arise. *The Complete Idiot's Guide to Pleasing Your Man* is packed with the wisdom you are seeking, which can be invaluable to both his well-being and yours. Consider it an outstanding source of *tutoring* about such issues as:

♦ Sex—not only how to do it but how to develop the right attitude.

♦ Learning all about his body and teaching him about yours.

♦ How to take care of him both physically and emotionally, both in and outside of the bedroom; and so much more.

The advice in this book will strike you as some of the things your mother should have told you, or perhaps did, but in the language of her generation. Eve Salinger brings it all up to date while filling in the gaps and treading where even the hippest mothers so often feared to go. She not only helps you learn what to do, but just as importantly, what to avoid in areas such as flirting, health, sex, and appearance—to name a few. So with *The Complete Idiot's Guide to Pleasing Your Man*, there never again has to be a conflict between keeping your mate happy and making your relationship ultra satisfying for yourself as well.

—Michael S. Broder, Ph.D., and Arlene Goldman, Ph.D.

Authors, *Secrets of Sexual Ecstasy*

Michael S. Broder, Ph.D., and Arlene Goldman, Ph.D., are psychologists, husband and wife, and co-authors of *Secrets of Sexual Ecstasy*. Dr. Broder's other books include *The Art of Living Single, The Art of Staying Together,* and *Can Your Relationship Be Saved?* They live and practice in Philadelphia, Pennsylvania.

Introduction

What kind of woman reads a book on how to please her man? A woman who senses that pleasing her man will put her in a position to create the kind of relationship she dreams of—one in which she herself is admired, desired, and pampered beyond her wildest dreams; a woman who knows that treating her man like a king will result in him treating her like a queen; a woman who, no doubt, knows something about pleasing her man already, but who is always eager for savvy and spicy ideas that will make her man feel appreciated and appreciative.

The Complete Idiot's Guide to Pleasing Your Man offers a cornucopia of advice and strategies for keeping men happy. In the spirit of good sense and good fun and in the interest of creating a greater number of happy couples, it encourages women to reconnect with the feminine instincts that have always made the world go round. Mother Nature gave all of us women the raw materials we need—in both body and mind. Now we just need to make the most of them and, boy, will our men be pleased that we did.

In this book you'll find inspiration, and from it, you'll gain the confidence you need to think of yourself as a girlfriend and lover—even if you've been married so long they've stopped making your wedding china pattern. A comprehensive, practical approach to all the aspects of pleasuring, *The Complete Idiot's Guide to Pleasing Your Man* will tell you all you need to know about taking care of your guy physically, mentally, and emotionally. Oh and, yes, it includes a few tricks (or more than a few) that you can have up your sleeve to really stir up his animal instincts from time to time. Finally, because this book specifically addresses man pleasing in committed relationships, it will help and encourage you to enhance monogamy by continually re-creating aspects of yourself and of your relationship.

So, read on. Enjoy what this book will do for you, what you will do for your man, and what he will ultimately do for you!

How This Book Is Organized

This book is divided into seven parts. Each will direct you through different aspects of pleasing your man.

Part 1, "Please Please Him," will offer an overview of what pleases and displeases men and what kind of women they find most pleasing of all. It will help you to understand why pleasing your man—and making him your number one priority—is in your best interests. It will also inspire you to please your man not by trying to be like someone else, but by being your best, most authentic self.

Part 2, "Be a Girlfriend," offers tips for looking gorgeous in the natural way that men adore, as well as for flaunting your fabulousness with some first-rate flirting techniques. It also covers the "do's" and "don'ts" of long-term relationship etiquette.

Part 3, "Be a Temptress," helps you set the stage for romance by revealing the truth about what inspires desire. It offers advice on how to build anticipation with the world's greatest aphrodisiac—the mind—and how to create the perfect home environment for loving. Finally, it helps you prepare your man's body, as well as his mind, through sensual touch.

Part 4, "Be a Spice Girl," is as advertised: spicy. This naughty-but-nice section of the book offers instruction on some common and some less-than-common sexual positions, as well as in the art of oral loving. The how-to's of spicy sex talk rounds out this section.

Part 5, "Mixing It Up," takes sex a bit further still, adding notes of adventure and excitement to ensure that your man—and you—will nearly faint with pleasure. Learn to incorporate fantasy and role-playing into your love life. And learn to boost his ego and his ardor by letting him please you.

Part 6, "Emotions in Motion," provides guidelines for interacting with your guy in the realm of feelings. It explains the ways in which guy talk differs from girl talk and tells you how to read a man's monosyllables and body signals. It also offers rules for coping with your man and as he copes with life's setbacks and with the realities of growing older.

Part 7, "A Man for All Seasons," offers tips for keeping your man healthy, fit, hot, handsome, and totally committed—so that you can have him around for many, many years to come.

Pleasing Sidebars

To add zing to this book and make it even more pleasing, sidebars have been sprinkled throughout. Within them are all kinds of titillating tidbits. There are four types of sidebars:

Tantalizing Terms

There are so many ways to say pleasing things. These sidebars define terms related to man pleasing that are mentioned in the book.

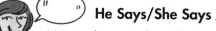

He Says/She Says

Men and women have lots to say on this subject. These sidebars contain advice and anecdotes from people who have pleased and been pleased.

Teasers & Pleasers

Because you can always please your man just a little bit more, these sidebars are chock full of additional tips, temptations, and tidbits of information.

Uh-Oh's and No-No's

You don't want any of your pleasing techniques to go awry. When would-be pleasers contain little pitfalls, look to these sidebars for counsel and cautions.

Acknowledgments

Profound thanks to my tireless research assistant and gal pal, Jean Arlea, to my dear editor, Paul Dinas (whom I will always aim to please), and to Nancy Lewis, Janette Lynn, and Kelly D. Henthorne who patiently combed through this manuscript and offered countless valuable suggestions for enhancing it.

Trademarks

All terms mentioned in this book that are known to be or are suspected of being trademarks or service marks have been appropriately capitalized. Alpha Books and Penguin Group (USA) Inc. cannot attest to the accuracy of this information. Use of a term in this book should not be regarded as affecting the validity of any trademark or service mark.

Part 1

Please Please Him

The Beatles sang, "Please please me like I please you." Does your man please you? I hope so! And I certainly think so—or you wouldn't be reading this. But the truth is that the *more* you please him, the more you will please one another, and the stronger your relationship will get.

In this part of the book, I'll introduce you to the art of man pleasing by taking a look at what men really want and debunking some myths on that subject. I'll discuss the connection between using your feminine instincts and perpetuating a solid, long-term relationship. You'll be inspired to enhance what Mother Nature already gave you. And you'll begin to identify opportunities to please your guy by letting him know how very important he is to you.

Chapter 1

Profile of a Satisfied Man

In This Chapter

- The conflicting roles men play
- Five key things a man needs from a woman
- Female archetypes men adore
- Things a pleased man will do for you
- Things a pleased man won't do *to* you

The world is not always kind to men these days. But with a pleasing woman at his side, a man is able to handle whatever comes his way. A solid relationship can compensate for just about any obstacle the world puts in a man's path. When his partner knows how to treat him right, he'll show that he's got the right stuff. In return, he'll treat her right.

What does it mean to please a man? If you look up the verb "to please" in a thesaurus, some of the synonyms you'll find are "satisfy," "gratify," "make happy," "delight," "thrill," and even "entertain." Get ready to do it all, to have fun and gain confidence along the way, and to reap many exciting rewards as a result.

It's Tough to Be a Guy

Once upon a time all that society asked of a man was that he go off into the forest, wrestle a wild boar or a wayward ox, and bring his prize home for dinner. Any modern guy will tell you that those sound like the good ole days. At least everyone's expectations were clear.

These days little boar wrestling is required, and dinner can be picked up at a drive-thru. But what our culture asks of men is a far more complicated matter.

Changing social norms have resulted in a societal view of men that's filled with confusing and conflicting expectations. For example:

◆ We want our men to be *macho*, yet we want them to be sensitive.

◆ We want them to be aggressive, yet accommodating.

◆ We want them to be ambitious in their careers while always putting their families first.

◆ We want them to be good boys … with a hint of roguish devil.

◆ We want them to be strong and stoic—but open and emotional.

Tantalizing Terms

The word **macho** is derived from the Spanish, where it is used as a noun meaning "virile man." As an English adjective, it means "strongly masculine."

The way the mass media portrays the ideal man, most guys worry that they will come up short even if they are a cross between Arnold Schwarzenegger, Dr. Phil, Brad Pitt, and Spiderman.

So, what's a guy to do? If he complains, the world at large can be unsympathetic. After all, he needs to *take things like a man*. However, if a guy is lucky, he's got someone like you in his corner. With you to give him what he needs, he can be and do just about anything he chooses to.

What a Woman Can Do for Her Man

We've heard it a million times. So many men who consider themselves successful and fulfilled attribute their good fortune to the fact that they found the right woman.

By honoring his woman in this way, a man isn't denying his own skills, hard work, and determination. But he *is* acknowledging the invaluable contribution his partner made by activating those qualities inside him. The ways in which a woman shows her love and commitment can serve as catalysts for the energies that will bring out the best in her man.

Life is challenging, and it's easy to become distracted from doing the things that matter most—no matter how much we want to. So it never hurts to keep a Big Five checklist in mind:

- ◆ **A** Is for Acceptance
- ◆ **E** Is for Excitement
- ◆ **I** Is for Inspiration
- ◆ **O** Is for Ogling
- ◆ **U** Is for Understanding

A handy mnemonic device for remembering the Big Five is to remember the five vowels: A, E, I, O, U.

A Is for Acceptance

A man will be all he can be when he is validated for who he is. He knows he's not perfect and that no sensible woman will imagine he is. That's the point: He needs to be loved for his flaws and eccentricities as much as for anything else.

E Is for Excitement

A man needs his woman to bring zest into his life—to continually thrill and stimulate him by renewing herself and their romantic relationship in creative ways. Monogamy should definitely not rule out variety and novelty. The sensual and sexual excitement a woman instills in a man can keep him enthusiastic, curious, and vital throughout the years.

CAUTION

Uh-Oh's and No-No's

Don't think a man is less interested in or capable of being excited by a woman with whom he has a long-term relationship. Keep him curious about what delights might be in store.

I Is for Inspiration

Since the dawn of time, women have inspired men to pursue quests, to explore the world, to triumph in battle. Helen of Troy alone had a "face that launched a thousand ships." Although not every man will undertake an epic journey or a mythic mission, every man needs his own Helen—to encourage him, to motivate him, to say, "Go for it."

He Says/She Says

"When I quit my job and started a business 10 years ago everyone told me I was crazy—except my wife. It was her support that made me go forward and make it a success, despite the odds and the obstacles."
—Edward, 40

O Is for Ogling

The word "ogle" comes to us from an old German verb meaning "to eye." It implies "to eye with desire." Although they might not express it out loud as often as women do, men relish being admired and desired by their partners. A man doesn't just want to be excited by his woman; he wants to know that she finds him exciting as well.

U Is for Understanding

Men don't always find it easy to say what's on their minds. In general, boys are not rewarded for speaking with emotion while they're growing up, and the habit of keeping some things inside can last a lifetime. But even the most "strong and silent" type wants someone near him to know the real him.

A man wants his woman to intuit his feelings—even if he can hide them from everyone else. He wants her to empathize with him. He doesn't expect her to always agree with him, but he does want to know she understands and respects his point of view.

Women Men Dream of: Adored Archetypes

We often hear that men prefer certain types of women more than others, but what they really prefer are *women who make them feel good about themselves*. It's true that over the course of human history, men have shown that they are drawn to certain female archetypes—classic ideals of womanhood:

- The Good Mother
- The Sensual Girl/Woman

- ◆ The Muse
- ◆ The Bawdy Bad Girl
- ◆ The Good Sport

Notice in the descriptive sections that follow, however, that each adored archetype symbolizes an aspect of the womanly sustenance for which men long.

The Good Mother

"Men really just want their mothers," is a simplistic misconception. It doesn't tell the entire story of what men need. But men *do* crave certain aspects of maternal care in their relationships. This is only natural, because a loving mother is the first woman to give a male the gift of unconditional acceptance.

Mothers have many ways of letting their sons know that they believe in them. The very way they look at their boys acknowledges how special they think they are. Such positive regard gives a boy the feeling that Mom can recognize in him things no one else may yet be able to see. No wonder men long to re-create this dynamic later in life.

A celebrated relationship in which the good mother ideal played a large role was that between former First Lady Nancy Reagan and her husband, President Ronald Reagan. During the course of the president's every public appearance, his devoted bride could be seen looking at him with a rapturous gaze that vividly communicated how much she thought of him and how completely she approved of everything about him.

Keep in mind, however, that mothering one's man can be overdone. A man wants a woman to re-create his mother's tender loving care, but he doesn't want her to treat him like a helpless infant. The good mother archetype is one aspect of men's overall ideal, but so is the exciting, enticing woman who makes them feel very much a man.

CAUTION

Uh-Oh's and No-No's

Men crave maternal-type acceptance, but too much mothering is smothering. Accept and adore him, but don't baby him or boss him.

The Sensual Girl/Woman

Women turn men on—thank goodness. The mere glimpse of a sexy, provocative woman can jolt a man out of the doldrums and elevate his, er, mood. Happily, men can be excited and rejuvenated by women with all sorts of different physical characteristics—but the one thing all exciting women have in common is their ability to surprise a guy and keep his curiosity piqued. That's why the girl/woman archetype is so powerful. It combines a woman's sensuality and sexuality with the freshness, innocence, and boundless energy of youth.

Who could possibly embody the exciting girl/woman archetype better than the immortal Marilyn Monroe? Her voluptuous body, delicate features, and "come hither" voice combined the qualities of both lost little girl and woman of the world. Marilyn captivated men around the globe, and her image remains one of the most powerful symbols of knockout sensuality.

Happily, there's a little bit of the vibrant and alluring girl/woman in every female. Every woman has the capability of conjuring—and offering to her man—fresh new delights.

The Muse

In Greek mythology, the *Muses* were the nine goddesses who inspired artists and men of science to excel at their pursuits. They represent man's deep-seated longing for a divine wellspring of ideas and incentive. Not much has changed in modern times: Every man wants an inspiring woman to be his "goddess."

> **Tantalizing Terms**
>
> The name **muse** is related to the English word "mind," and means "memory" or "reminder." Ancient poets, having no written texts to rely on, had to call on their *muse* in order to recite the lines they had authored.

Inspiration can take many forms. A woman can cheer her man on, give him the energy to persist when he's about to give up, utter just the right words at the right time, and reassure him that he's got what it takes. She can be a sounding board for ideas he dare not reveal to anyone else just yet. And she can be a great brainstorming partner.

The Bawdy Bad Girl

Whether it's Mae West or Madonna, men have always appreciated a woman who is upfront about her full-out appreciation and admiration of men. This archetypal woman is good at being "bad"—in the best sense of the word. She's playful, outspoken, unconventional, and funny. What man could resist the forthrightness and self-confidence—not to mention the wry deadpan humor—in Mae West's immortal bad girl line, "Is that a pistol in your pocket, or are you just happy to see me?"

The bawdy bad girl type is a head-turner who likes—and gets—oodles of male attention. She enthusiastically returns it in kind. When a man rates an ogling look from a playful bad girl, he can feel like she's undressing him with her eyes.

He Says/She Says

"Nothing gives me an emotional boost like than when my girlfriend gives me a once-over and a wolf whistle. It makes me feel like Mel Gibson. Talk about making my day."
—Sam, 27

The bawdy bad girl walks the walk and talks the talk of eroticism. Needless to say, she loves sex and knows that it can and should be great fun. She's nobody's pushover though. Alongside her playfulness, she's a discriminating lady.

The Good Sport

The good sport is a gal pal. Men value her for her chipper, game-for-anything attitude. They see her as a co-adventurer and, very importantly, as an understanding confidante. She's someone with whom a man can share the good times and the not so good, and laugh about it all later. When all's said and done, every man wants and needs a true friend like her.

June Allyson and Dorothy Lamour (of Bob Hope and Bing Crosby road movie fame) first typified the on-screen good sport persona. They played characters that were at once easygoing and outgoing. They were always willing to commiserate and ready to share a joke. Later, Terri Garr and Sandra Bullock also played such roles to perfection.

Y Is for ... You

Although each of these archetypes represents an aspect of womanhood that men love, each man—like each woman—is a unique individual. Clearly, your guy picked you from among all the women he has ever met because you have the capacity to represent the best of all wonderful women to him while still being uniquely yourself.

But are you using your full capacity to give your man the things that will make him the best man he can be? Test yourself to identify areas where your loving attitude could stand a brush-up.

How Pleased Is My Man?

On a scale from 1 (not at all) to 5 (a great deal) how much of each of these good feelings do you think you give your man? Check yourself by writing down an example of a *recent* time when you gave him this feeling.

1. Acceptance. I accept my man and validate him for who he is.

    1 2 3 4 5

    Example: _____

    _____

    _____

2. Excitement. I keep things interesting in the romance department.

    1 2 3 4 5

    Example: _____

    _____

    _____

3. Inspiration. I show that I am my man's greatest fan and cheerleader.

    1 2 3 4 5

    Example: _____

    _____

    _____

4. Ogling. I show my man that I find him attractive and desirable.

    1 2 3 4 5

    Example: _____

    _____

    _____

5. Understanding. I listen well and show respect for my man's point of view.

1 2 3 4 5

Example: _____

_____

_____

Add them all up. What was your score?

5—10 Start focusing more about how you can express your love.

11—15 You're trying, but you've got a ways to go.

16—20 Keep up the things you're doing.

21—25 Bravo!

Here's a great way to start improving your score. In any of the five areas where you were unable to give an example, go back and write something you *could* do to help fill in the gaps. You can start with something very simple, like making one small comment or gesture. For instance:

◆ If you can't think of the last time you made him feel accepted, remind yourself to praise your man for one of the many admirable things he does.

◆ If you can't think of the last time you excited him, think of something surprising you can do to appeal to his sensual side—like whispering something provocative in his ear in a public place.

◆ If you can't think of the last time you inspired him, remind yourself to say, "You can do it, honey," the next time you see him feeling frustrated.

◆ If you can't think of the last time you ogled him, look for an opportunity to compliment his appearance and let him know he turns you on.

◆ If you can't think of the last time you showed understanding, make it a point to listen carefully when he's in the mood to open up—but don't give him advice, just tell him you can understand how he feels. (Think about how many times you wanted him to "just listen" and not try to "fix it.")

◆ If you can't think of any practical and simple strategies right now, don't worry. This book is full of ideas to help you along your way.

Keep reading and come back to update your "How Pleased Is My Man" list at any time.

What a Satisfied Man Will Do

The rewards of pleasing your man and keeping him satisfied are many. A satisfied man will put his woman on a pedestal where she belongs. He will cherish and adore her. In countless little ways he might show his devotion and desire every day.

A satisfied man will …

- Sing your praises
- Be loyal and true
- Be generous
- Be chivalrous
- Share the remote
- Call you when he's running late
- Call you just to say, "Hi"
- Be gracious to your mother
- Put the toilet seat down (occasionally)
- Remember your birthday (most of the time)
- Carry the heaviest suitcase (even though it's never his)
- Whistle at you when you're in your swimsuit (or birthday suit)
- Put your photo on his screensaver
- Go to a "chick flick" with you
- Lend you his sweater when it's chilly
- Make time for the two of you
- Snuggle with you
- Play footsie under the dinner table
- Share his dreams with you
- Confide his hopes to you
- Give you the most wonderful smile
- Make you laugh

- Slay a dragon for you (or at least defend you to a rude store clerk)

- Remind you he wouldn't trade you for the world

Some satisfied men have taken their loving devotion to their women so far that they make history in the process. They have fought duels to the death to defend a woman's honor. They have sailed the seven seas to bring her untold treasures. The smitten Duke of Windsor actually gave up the British throne to wed Wallis Simpson, saying "I have found it impossible to carry on … without the help and support of the woman I love."

Your man will most likely never have an opportunity to renounce a kingship for you. And dueling has been deemed somewhat hazardous to one's health. Nevertheless, a man who is pleased with his woman will do all manner of majestic and magnanimous things. Best of all, he'll do them gladly—without ever needing to be asked, let along nagged.

What a Satisfied Man Won't Do

Happily, there are some things a satisfied man won't do. He won't be a bore or a boor. He won't neglect or reject you. He won't let you forget how much you matter.

A satisfied man won't …

- Call out for Shania Twain in his sleep

- Think that an iron or toaster oven makes a good gift

- Forget whether you prefer silver or gold

- Pretend that cubic zirconium is "as good as diamonds"

- Ask you to "hold it in" on a long car ride

- Hog the quilt on a cold night

- Tell you that you look great "for your age"

- Forget to hold the door open for you

- Interrupt you for call waiting (too often)

- Make fun of you for being on a diet

- Keep a goatee that you find too scratchy

- Let the fire go out
- Go to bed mad at you
- Eat the chocolate ice cream and leave the vanilla
- Take you for granted

Will a satisfied man be perfect? Of course not. Will he slip up some of the time? Well, yes, because—like you—he's only human. A satisfied man won't morph into a superhero. He won't scale tall buildings in a single bound. But he will be the very best man be can be. Because that's what you deserve.

The Least You Need to Know

- Society today expects men to assume multiple, conflicting roles—and to never complain.
- A woman can bring out the best in her man by providing him with emotional sustenance, sensual delights, and good old-fashioned fun.
- A man is content when his woman accepts him, excites him, inspires him, ogles and admires him, and truly understands him.
- A satisfied man will hold his woman in the highest esteem and never take her for granted.
- A satisfied man won't be perfect, but with his woman's help he will be the best man he can be.

Chapter 2

Profile of a Pleasing Woman

In This Chapter

- ◆ Why man pleasing is a lost art
- ◆ The win/win of pleasing your man
- ◆ Displeasing female types
- ◆ Find out whether you're a man pleaser
- ◆ The significance of sex
- ◆ Using what Mother Nature gave you

A woman who knows how to please a man will create the relationship she dreams of. She will be admired, desired, pampered, and indulged beyond her wildest fantasies. It's a fact of life, therefore, that a woman who understands the art of giving pleasure is a woman empowered.

In our mixed-up world, however, many of us have come to believe the opposite. We associate pleasing a man with sacrificing ourselves. Nothing could be further from the truth—and it's time to straighten out the mix up.

The good news is that every woman has the natural capacity to entice, enthrall, and care for her man—and to reap the many rewards that ensue.

What's more, she can do this all while pleasing herself and taking good care of herself. All it takes to begin is an open mind and a positive attitude.

The Lost Art of Man Pleasing

Once upon a time, not so very long ago, there would have been little need for a book such as this. Traditionally, a little girl began learning the art of pleasing men at her mother's knee. Through direct advice and indirect observation, girls on their way to womanhood received lessons in everything from batting their eyes and tossing their hair to flashing an irresistible smile at just the right moment.

They learned …

- ◆ how to flirt, flatter, and dote.
- ◆ how to treat a man like a man, showing him genuine appreciation for all he did.
- ◆ when it was a good idea to talk, when it was a good idea to listen, and when it was a good idea to stop the talk and just conjure up some really good lovin'.

These blossoming young women turned their smitten suitors to putty in their savvy female hands. And when they paired off, two by two, everyone involved recognized the truth behind the adage, "Man is the head of the family, woman the neck that turns the head."

All in all, this was a pretty good system. But suddenly, everything changed. With the advent of the Women's Movement in the 1970s, doing anything for the purpose of pleasing a man became politically incorrect. Mothers balked at the idea that their daughters should focus their energies on anything other than excelling at academics and athletics, winning in the workplace, and otherwise pursuing worldly success. Now don't get me wrong: It's well and good that women can do such things with all the same freedoms as their male counterparts. But in pursuing these goals, we females threw out the proverbial baby with the bathwater.

Today, the pendulum is swinging the other way. Women who truly want it "all" recognize that solid long-term relationships can be attained by adding the art of man pleasing to their other accomplishments. We understand that pleasing a man does not require an attitude of surrender, submissiveness, or subordination. It does require a willingness to revel in being female—and there's nothing wrong with that.

No matter what a woman's philosophy or politics, no matter if she considers herself "liberated" or "old fashioned," or just a practical gal who enjoys having a good guy around, she will enhance her life by reconnecting with womanly knowledge that has always made the world go round.

A Win/Win Situation

A woman who works at pleasing her man—hard enough to read a whole book on the subject—is heading for a win/win situation. The result of her pleasing will be that her man will be eager to please her right back. He will reward her efforts, and then some.

A woman smart enough to please her man is practicing enlightened self-interest. That's because the things she does to nurture her man also nurture her relationship. Within the context of a strong, loving, ever-exciting long-term partnership, each person becomes more than he or she otherwise would become alone. A man becomes a better man with the help of his woman; a woman becomes a better woman with the help of her man.

Pleasing your man and strengthening your relationship is largely a matter of attitude. We create the outcome we want by believing in our hearts that certain things will happen. The power of belief is exceptionally strong.

Teasers & Pleasers

Ordinary self-interest asks, "What you can do for me?" Enlightened self-interest asks, "What can I do for all of us?" Everyone's a winner.

The process of pleasing your man begins with your conviction that he is worth it. Your belief in his worthiness translates into treating him well. Day by day, you do little things to show how much you accept and admire him. When he's down, you cheer him up. When he's about to give up, you encourage him. When he makes a little blunder, you get over it and move on.

Now your man's attitude about himself begins to improve. Secure in your high opinion of him, his self-doubts diminish. Because you have instilled in him the most positive expectations for himself, he will begin to behave in ways that continually prove he merits your positive attentions. Watch him as he comes to predict his own success and rises to each and every occasion. He has benefited from your *self-fulfilling prophecy*.

Tantalizing Terms

A **self-fulfilling prophecy** means that when we expect someone to act a certain way, they tend to act out our expectations. Expect the best of someone, and that's what you get.

If you want to better understand the power of the self-fulfilling prophecy, there are many examples of it in literature. In *My Fair Lady*, based on the play *Pygmalion*, an upper-class professor transforms a cockney flower girl into an elegant lady. He does so because he recognizes the elegant lady inside her and treats her as such.

In the following tale, *The Princess and the Troll*, the self-fulfilling prophecy works magic:

> *Once upon a time there was a troll who fell in love with a beautiful princess. Like all trolls he was a bit rough around the edges. So he donned a mask and masqueraded as a handsome prince. The two wed, and the princess treated her husband with love and kindness. Soon, the troll realized that looking the part of a prince was not enough. He began to act like a prince worthy of a princess. He was noble, generous, and gracious to all. The princess and her husband lived happily.*
>
> *One day, a traveler from the troll's village came to the court. He told the princess her husband's true identity. "You are wrong, sir," said the princess. But the troll felt he could hide no longer. He took of his mask and underneath was … a handsome, noble, and gracious prince.*

Although this story is a fairy tale, its lesson could not be more real. It also could not be more relevant. The way a man is treated affects how he acts; the way a man acts determines what he will become.

What Men Don't Want

Unfortunately, some women think that the best way to get a man to "behave" is to manipulate him. We may boss him, complain at him, and make all kinds of demands of him. All he needs to do to "improve," we think, is see the light—in other words, to see that he is wrong and we are right.

Sometimes these tactics *do* get a man to give in. But, whether we realize it or not, they are also causing him to give up. A man who is mistreated will no longer believe in himself or in his relationship. He may go through the motions, but his heart won't be in it.

Certain styles of man manipulation are especially counter-productive, for example:

- The Nag
- The Whiner

◆ The Scorekeeper

◆ The Pressure Cooker

◆ The Martyr

Although they may seem to get a man to "toe the line" in the short-term, they'll be relationship threatening in the long run. These styles are annoying irritators. They're not pleasers, they're anti-pleasers.

The Nag

The Nag knows what needs to be done and wants it done on her timetable. She hounds, pesters, and persists—no matter what—in "reminding" her man of his duties. Often, the focus of nagging is something important to the person doing the nagging, but not to the person being nagged. But even if the nag has a valid point (yes, the trash does need to go out on trash night or sit around for another week), being right doesn't justify nagging.

Nagging is a very prevalent style in familial relationships, but it's rarely found elsewhere. It wouldn't be acceptable in social situations where we're trying to sustain friendships, and it's certainly never done when we're just getting to know a man and trying to attract him. Besides being irritating, nagging is often ineffective. A man who is nagged may resist doing what he is "supposed to" as a way of indicating his annoyance. The cycle perpetuates, and no one is pleased.

> **CAUTION**
> **Uh-Oh's and No-No's**
> Studies show that women do more than two thirds of nagging in families. The most common kind of nagging concerns household chores.

The Whiner

Unlike the bossy Nag, the Whiner tries to get what she wants by sounding pitiful. The unspoken message she gives her man is "Can't you see you're making me miserable?" Whining may spur a man into action more effectively than nagging—simply because it is so maddening that a guy will do almost anything to put a stop to it. The long-term effect, however, will be to create frustration. Whining also seriously saps the romance out of a relationship, because it's such an unattractive behavior. It's impossible to flirt and whine simultaneously. (*Caution:* Do not try this at home!)

The Scorekeeper

The Scorekeeper knows exactly whose turn it is to clear the dishes, pick up the dry cleaning, and drive the kids to soccer practice. It's as if she has a workflow chart emblazoned on the inside of her forehead. Although the Scorekeeper thinks she is being fair, she is not being gracious or kind. She's also not being very smart. The best way to get a man to want to do something for you is when you spontaneously and sincerely do something nice for him.

He Says/She Says

"I once broke up with a live-in girlfriend who insisted on keeping track of which of us spent a penny on anything for the household or on going out together. I didn't care about the financial aspect of it one way or the other, but her obsession with 'fairness' drove me crazy. I believe that in a good relationship, things just even out."
—Mario, 35

The Pressure Cooker

The Pressure Cooker always expects her man to do more than he's doing, earn more than he's earning, and work harder than he's already working. She's continually comparing her man to other men and letting him know where he comes up short. Although she wants more, more, more, she will get less of what really counts. Her man will lose confidence in himself because he knows his woman is dissatisfied with him.

The Martyr

The Martyr often starts out as a Nag. She'll make a request like, "Please take the laundry down to the basement." If nothing happens, she'll ask, "Did you hear me?" If that reminder is ignored, she'll sigh loudly and exclaim "Never mind, I'll do it myself!" Then the Martyr will make a great show of lugging the laundry, all the while lamenting her sorry lot in life. No man likes a Martyr's melodrama but, hey, if she's so willing to do everything herself, maybe he'll just let her. After all, she seems to be enjoying rehearsing for that Academy Award performance.

Are You a Man-Pleaser?

There's one simple, underlying reason why all the styles you just read about are antipleasers. They all fail to take into account the truth behind the wise but simple saying, "You can catch more flies with honey than you can with vinegar." Men want to do things for women who are sweet to them, who genuinely like and appreciate them, and who are willing to forgive them when they occasionally mess up and prove they're just regular fallible human beings.

Are you prone to be a pleaser or an anti-pleaser? Take this quiz and find out.

Am I a Man Pleaser?

On a scale from 1 (strongly disagree) to 5 (strongly agree), rate how you feel about the following statements:

1. I like men and enjoy their company.

   1 2 3 4 5

2. Men have deeper feelings than they may let on.

   1 2 3 4 5

3. The man in my life is great the way he is.

   1 2 3 4 5

4. The man in my life tries his best to make me happy.

   1 2 3 4 5

5. My guy and I often laugh together.

   1 2 3 4 5

6. I enjoy spending time alone with my man.

   1 2 3 4 5

7. My man opens up to me emotionally.

   1 2 3 4 5

8. I am easy-going and don't harp on my man's imperfections.

   1 2 3 4 5

9. I like to keep our sex life interesting.

   1 2 3 4 5

10. I enjoy making love.

    1 2 3 4 5

Add up your score.

10—20 You don't think all that highly of men. Give a guy a break!

21—30 Your mixed feelings are showing.

31—40 You're got tremendous pleasing potential.

41—50 Wow!

Now go back and take a second look at any of the questions you answered with a 1 or 2. Make a mental note of the statements you disagree with. Any such numbers reveal a negative attitude about men in general, about the current state of your relationship, or about your evaluation of your own potential. Remember, attitude is all-important! You can't change an attitude overnight, but you can stay alert to your areas of negativity. As you go on reading this book, many of your attitudes should begin to shift gradually and naturally. Take this quiz again when you're done and see!

How Important Is Sex?

You no doubt noticed that the last few questions of the *Am I a Man Pleaser?* quiz concerned sex. If you've browsed through this book's table of contents, you've probably also noticed that a lot of this book will be devoted to sensuality and sexuality. At this point some of you may be wondering, "How much of pleasing a man boils down to pleasing him in bed?"

It would be a mistake to think that sex is all there is to pleasing a man. Even the most sexually dynamic male gets downright bored with a relationship that offers nothing more than physical satisfaction. Every aspect of the male-female relationship should be cultivated and continually improved upon in order to hold a man's interest and enthusiasm. On the other hand, the benefits of enhancing your man's sexual pleasure—and your own—shouldn't be underestimated.

Teasers & Pleasers

Brain chemicals released during sex include *endorphins*, *serotonin*, and *encephalin*. These chemicals are all linked to feelings of relaxation and a sense of well-being.

Sexual attraction plays a profound role in male-female relationships. Its possibilities entice us the moment we meet and, when things are as they should be, they persist decades later. A strong sexual bond with a man is a surefire pleaser for reasons both obvious and subtle:

♦ Good sex is good fun—it simply feels great.

♦ Sex relieves physical, mental, and emotional tension.

- Sex burns calories and can help keep you fit!

- Having good sex makes a man feel manly.

- Having good sex makes a woman feel womanly, which men love.

- Having sex with a man reassures him that you find him attractive.

- A powerful sexual connection solidifies the emotional bond between two people.

- Good sex can help avoid infidelity—sexually satisfied partners are less likely to stray.

The long and the short of it is that men like sex, and a woman determined to please her man should get as good at it as she possibly can. She should also get good at being sexy. Although the act of sex certainly won't consume the majority of time in a relationship, the *promise* of sex can last all day.

Follow Your Feminine Instincts

Even if you weren't raised learning how to please a man, doing so will be easier than you might imagine. That's because you have a really great lady on your side: Mother Nature. Mother Nature wants men and women to get along. She designed the world that way. Mating is an essential part of nearly every life and, like most creatures, we spend an overwhelming amount of time and energy advertising our availability for mating and assessing members of the opposite sex to see whether or not they would make suitable future mates.

Unlike many of the earth's creatures, however, most humans decide at some point to mate for life. More than 90 percent of the world's people marry at some point in their lives. Mother Nature's behind that, too, because having two adults around is better for a family's survival and success. From a strictly biological point of view, men could go on mating with new women indefinitely, but confirmed bachelorhood is rare. Most men stay with the women they love and make lives together as long as that monogamous relationship sufficiently meets their needs.

That's why good old Mother Nature gave women the brains and the bodies to keep men happily hanging around.

Pheromones, Hormones, and Other Moans

One thing Mother Nature appears to have given women and men is pheromones. Pheromones are natural scents that, although undetectable to the conscious mind, serve as powerful forces of sexual attraction. Pheromones are produced by glands near a person's armpits, nipples, and groin. Although research is inconclusive, they're probably detected by something called the VNO (vomeronasal organ), a small cavity in the nose. You don't have control over your pheromones (although, as you'll read in Chapter 9, you can use scents to enhance sensuality), but they are an example of just how intricately Mother Nature has planned out the many steps of the mating dance.

Tantalizing Terms

A **hormone** is a chemical substance produced in the body's endocrine glands. Its function is to stimulate or regulate metabolism. Derived from the Greek language, the word literally means it means "to excite" or "to stir up."

Hormones—chemical substances secreted into the bloodstream by glands—are also part of Mother Nature's design. Many hormones are directly involved in sex. When we feel sexual attraction, nerve endings in the hypothalamus—a pea-sized structure in the brain—notify the pituitary gland to send hormones to the sex glands. The sex glands then produce more hormones (estrogen, progesterone, and testosterone). You're now further aroused. Your heart beats faster, muscles tense, and you experience a pleasant, tingly sensation.

In addition to overtly sexual behaviors, hormones affect many gender-related behaviors. In fact, there is evidence that hormones impact brain organization early in life, and that they create differences in male and female brains. Certainly the environment has an impact on the behavioral traits we develop, but from the start, the environment is acting on brains wired differently in girls and boys by male and female sex hormones.

Gender-related differences in the brain have an impact on childhood play behaviors, with boys manifesting more aggressive play and girls engaging in more nurturing play. These biological and psychological predispositions tend to continue into adulthood, giving rise to specialized skills. Skills that women appear to have a natural bent for include care giving, communication, and cooperation. This is not to say that men are not capable of caring, cooperating, or communicating, nor is it to imply that women can't do the things that men do. But Mother Nature seems to have given women some extra relationship-building and relationship-sustaining tools in our tool belts. Good for Her, and good for us.

Yin and Yang Energies

In addition to different hormones, Mother Nature also gave women and men fundamentally different, but complementary, energies. An ancient Chinese philosophy—still widely referred to today—describes these energies as *yin* and *yang*. According to this philosophy, everything in the entire world is comprised of female and male energies. The combination of yin and yang makes for harmony in the universe. The two balance each other perfectly, like night (yin) and day (yang), and have a mutually dependent relationship.

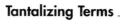

Tantalizing Terms

Yin and **yang** are words from the Chinese Taoist tradition. Yin energy, which represents the female, is necessary to balance yang energy, which represents the male.

Chinese sages used the yin-yang theory to explain some important features of the relationships between opposites. They recognized that the normal, healthy, existence of everything in nature depends on the mutual enhancement and beneficial interaction of opposite forces—hot and cold, light and dark, growth and diminishment. They also noticed that yin attracts, nourishes, and sustains yang, and vice versa. The greater the difference, the greater the attraction.

When it comes to man and woman, the implications of yin and yang are clear. The two genders are different—physically and emotionally—but the unity of their opposites is meant to be.

So, *vive la difference*. You and your man are wonderfully unalike in many ways. That's how it ought to be. Celebrate your natural differences; don't fight them. Embrace your natural female energy and tap your feminine instincts to the fullest. Doing so will help you achieve harmony with the man you love.

The Least You Need to Know

- Pleasing a man does not require being subservient or submissive.

- A woman who knows how to please a man will enjoy superior treatment in her relationship—it's a win/win proposition.

- Treat a man like he's wonderful, and he will be—that's a self-fulfilling prophecy.

- Pleasing women don't nag, whine, keep score, pressure a man, or play the martyr.

- Sex isn't everything, but it's important; its role in a relationship shouldn't be underestimated.

- Don't fight Mother Nature—she has given you what you need to please your man.

Chapter 3

Using Art, Not Artifice

In This Chapter

- The importance of being sincere
- Fake behaviors that don't work
- Choosing to be your best self
- The power of positive reinforcement
- Expressing appreciation
- Overcoming emotional obstacles to pleasing your man

In the first two chapters, you've read a lot about the kinds of attitudes and behaviors that men find attractive and the kinds that turn them off. But don't make the mistake of seeking a shortcut to pleasing your man by pretending to feel things you don't feel, behaving in ways that don't suit your personality, or trying to be someone you're not.

Your man doesn't want you to be a fake. Pretenses, ploys, and tricks are the biggest turn-offs of all. Your guy loves the real you, not an artificial you. He just wants you to be the best you that *you* can be. As this chapter will show, making your man happy is a question of art, not artifice.

Being Authentic and Sincere

One day, a woman I'll call Ann decided that from now on she was going to make a full-out attempt to increase the romantic passion and intimacy in her marriage. She made this decision in the aftermath of an argument she and her husband, Bob, had had the night before. The argument, like so many others, had begun when Ann presented Bob with a laundry list of complaints about his lack of communication, his reluctance to help around the house, and his disinterest in making love. Bob had stormed out for his Thursday night softball game with the guys, despite the fact that Ann made it clear she disapproved. While he was gone, Ann set up the sofa bed for Bob in the living room.

But the next day, Ann decided it was time to turn over a new leaf. She was going to take responsibility for improving her relationship. She arranged for the kids to spend the evening with a neighbor. She went out and bought herself a gorgeous plunging-neckline silk negligee, unlike anything she'd ever owned. She placed bouquets of roses throughout the house and put two porterhouse steaks—her husband's favorite meal—on the grill. She poured champagne and loaded the CD player with romantic classics. She put on her makeup and her nightgown, reclined on a chaise lounge and waited for her husband to come in from a hard day at the office.

When Bob came through the front door, he almost turned around and walked right back out. He was certain he was in the wrong house. When Ann threw her arms around him, told him he was the most wonderful husband in the world, and promised everything in their relationship was going to be perfect from now on, he seriously wondered whether aliens had abducted his real wife and left this bizarre stranger in her place.

Ann's sudden transformation had an effect opposite from what she had planned. Bob did not respond the way she'd anticipated. Instead, he grew quiet. He said he hoped things would improve, but she shouldn't have made all the fuss. The "perfect" evening fizzled. Ann and Bob sat in front of the television and ate their steaks in silence.

The truth was that Ann had gone over the top. A romantic evening is a wonderful thing, but by itself, it's not an indicator that a woman's attitudes are going to alter. Ann would have been better off if she'd worked on changing some of her negative patterns and talked honestly with Bob before presenting him with a totally atypical scenario for which he was emotionally unprepared.

Ann had good intentions, but she also had unrealistic expectations of herself *and* of her man. Bob couldn't just pretend that the way his wife had been treating him had been a bad dream. He sensed that Ann's 180-degree change in attitude couldn't last because it did not deem to reflect the real her. Her actions seemed artificial.

A real man does not want a fake woman. He wants a woman who is authentic and sincere. He wants a woman he can trust. If a woman genuinely treats him better, it will be much appreciated. But if she is faking it, he'll know … and he won't be pleased.

While you work on enhancing your man's satisfaction level, don't forget to keep yourself honest. Check in with yourself on a regular basis and evaluate: Am I faking it, or am I making it real? The following are some examples of each:

- Faking it: Inviting his mom for dinner, then saying mean things about her under your breath.

  Making it: Inviting his mom to dinner and finding something you actually like about her.

- Faking it: Saying you're not mad when he makes a mistake and then giving him the silent treatment.

  Making it: Forgiving him for his mistakes.

- Faking it: Asking him to pick what movie to see and then sighing all through it.

  Making it: Suggesting a movie you think you'll both enjoy.

- Faking it: Cooking his favorite food but not eating it yourself because "it's not healthy."

  Making it: Finding healthy ways to cook his favorite foods.

- Faking it: Planning a sexy evening when you're really not in the mood for sex.

  Making it: Letting him know when you're in the mood by flirting and enticing.

- Faking it: Telling him his tie looks great when you think it looks awful.

  Making it: Buying him some fabulous new ties.

- Faking it: Telling him he's not putting on weight when he obviously is.

  Making it: Getting both of you involved in fun fitness activities.

- Faking it: Making embroidered tool cozies for his basement workshop to show you respect his space   .

  Making it: Leaving his tools and workshop alone.

- Faking it: Trying to talk him out of being grumpy.

  Making it: Respecting his feelings and accepting that everyone has moods.

- Faking it: Spending lots and lots of time and money on your appearance so you'll look great for him.

  Making it: Spending some of your time and money on him.

- Faking it: Telling him you really like his guy friends when you don't.

  Making it: Being a good sport about him spending time with friends you don't like.

- Faking it: Pretending not to be upset if he forgets a birthday or anniversary.

  Making it: Providing subtle reminders ahead of time so he can save face.

- Faking it: Insisting he tell you exactly what's on his mind.

  Making it: Letting him know you're available to talk when he wants to.

- Faking it: Pretending you don't care when he falls asleep in front of the TV at night.

  Making it: Giving him a good reason to stay awake.

- Faking it: Never forgetting Valentine's Day.

  Making it: Never forgetting the date you first met.

- Faking it: Kissing him passionately in public to show you care.

  Making it: Kissing him passionately in private.

If too many things of the "faking it" examples seem like things you do, let this list serve as a "look out" list for you. When you feel that you are preoccupied with putting on appearances, look out! Stop trying to pull the wool over everyone's eyes—most of all your man's. And never lie about what makes you happy. Instead, figure out a way to make both of you content.

Let Him Bring Out Your Best

In any good relationship, it's important to be yourself. But just which "self" should you be? We all have multiple selves. That doesn't mean we have "split personalities" or any other kind of psychological disorder. It simply means that we all are capable of a wide range of behavior.

If you think about it for a moment, you know that on certain days and on some occasions, you are your very best self. You feel alive and alert and have a good attitude that can't be easily shaken. When you feel like this, you have a natural charisma. Others are attracted to your positive energy and outlook. When they approach you, they find that their instincts were correct—you are just as much fun to be with as they had imagined!

On the other hand, there are days when you are gloomy and withdrawn. You are unreceptive to the world around you. Your mood and outlook are negative. Consequently, people tend to stay away. If they do approach you, they're not rewarded for their efforts. You're just not very good company.

Think back. When you and your man were first getting together, which self did you display most often? Your best self, of course. And his pleasure at seeing you at your best brought out your good qualities even more.

Now, your relationship is in a more mature phase. You may actually have forgotten what it feels like to put your best foot forward. Use the checklist that follows to indicate where you fall on the scales of opposing traits *when you are at your best*:

Glum	1 ___ 2 ___ 3 ___ 4 ___ 5 ___	Cheerful
Cranky	1 ___ 2 ___ 3 ___ 4 ___ 5 ___	Calm
Bored	1 ___ 2 ___ 3 ___ 4 ___ 5 ___	Curious
Dull	1 ___ 2 ___ 3 ___ 4 ___ 5 ___	Engaging
Lethargic	1 ___ 2 ___ 3 ___ 4 ___ 5 ___	Energetic
Difficult	1 ___ 2 ___ 3 ___ 4 ___ 5 ___	Easygoing
Selfish	1 ___ 2 ___ 3 ___ 4 ___ 5 ___	Generous
Pessimistic	1 ___ 2 ___ 3 ___ 4 ___ 5 ___	Optimistic
Rude	1 ___ 2 ___ 3 ___ 4 ___ 5 ___	Considerate

Reserved	1 __ 2 __ 3 __ 4 __ 5 __	Outgoing
Unaffectionate	1 __ 2 __ 3 __ 4 __ 5 __	Affectionate
Standoffish	1 __ 2 __ 3 __ 4 __ 5 __	Flirtatious
Unappreciative	1 __ 2 __ 3 __ 4 __ 5 __	Appreciative

He Says/She Says

"Everybody has days when things go wrong, and I'm no exception. But I've learned that it's my reactions to things that make the difference in how I feel. I can't control what happens, but I can control how I respond."
—Marcy, 35

This checklist should be a portrait of your most positive self. Choosing to be this self on a daily basis is like choosing which hat to wear. Why choose one that's unflattering? Of course there will be days that are more stressful than others—days when it's harder to keep your proverbial hat on your head. How you feel isn't always a choice, although you can choose what to do about it. The more positive the place from which you begin your day, the easier it is to recover from setbacks.

Set your standards high. Make a conscious choice to shoot for the top. Being your best self is a great gift that you can give your man—and yourself.

The Art of Appreciation

All of the items on the "best self" list are important, but right now is a good time to spend some additional time on the final item: being unappreciative versus being appreciative. When we are being courted, we are very apt to notice every little thing that our man does for us—because we are actively looking for evidence that he cares about us. If he carries a heavy package for us, or offers to pick us up at the airport, we can hardly say thank you enough.

Sadly, in long-term relationships we begin to take for granted the things our men routinely do to make our lives better in ways both large and small. Showing appreciation is a habit we fall out of. We tell ourselves we can always do it another time down the road. Why wait? Almost nothing is more certain to immediately alter the chemistry of a relationship for the better than getting back into the habit of offering praise and acknowledgment on a routine basis.

The Power of Positive Reinforcement

When a man realizes that his efforts are being noticed and approved of, his mood and attitude will be uplifted. And because his efforts are being rewarded with gratitude, he will actually take pleasure in doing even more things that are praiseworthy. That's what is known as positive reinforcement.

Positive reinforcement is a cornerstone of behavioral psychology. Simply put, it refers to the fact that behavior that gets rewarded gets repeated. When it comes to men, you'll find that they enjoy receiving praise and acknowledgment from their partners so much that they will not only repeat what earned them your gratitude in the first place, but also look for ways to do even more. This is another example of a win/win strategy for pleasing your man.

If you've gotten out of the habit of expressing appreciation to your guy, here are a few tips to get the habit restarted:

- Be on the lookout for things for which to thank him. Our brains are wired to notice problems. We look for things that are wrong and things that need fixing. If we flip a light switch and no light comes on, we may complain that the bulb needs replacing. With a little effort, however, we can also start to notice things that are going right. If we later flip the same light switch and the light comes on, we shouldn't neglect to thank the person who changed the bulb.

- Never mix praise with demands. If you're expressing appreciation, keep that sentiment pure. Don't dilute praise by adding a tag line about what else your man could be doing.

> **CAUTION**
>
> **Uh-Oh's and No-No's**
>
> Praising your man is reinforcing. If you give thanks for a little, you will receive a lot. But avoid sending mixed messages. Never follow a "thank you" with a criticism or a demand.

- Repeat good things you hear. If your girlfriend complimented your husband's good looks, or your brother told you what a great game of tennis he played, pass those compliments along. Everyone loves the bearer of good news, and your man will feel doubly complimented when you are the compliment messenger.

Always remember that it is as important to be genuine and sincere in your praise as it is to be so in everything else you do. There's no need to conjure up artificial reasons to acknowledge your man. Simply open your eyes to the obvious.

Ways to Say Thank You

Believe it or not, some of us may feel a little shy about saying thank you. As with any habit we've lost, regaining it may take practice. What could be nicer, though, than practicing being grateful?

One way to say thank you is to be very specific. When you notice something your man has done for you, mention exactly what it is he did and tell him exactly why you appreciate it. For example:

◆ Thanks for getting takeout food tonight. I love it when we have extra time, because we don't have to cook and clean up. You made my night.

◆ Thanks for picking up the kids today. I really would have had a hard time catching up at work if I'd missed that meeting. I appreciate it.

◆ Thanks for talking to my mom when she called. She loves it when you chat with her. You made two women very happy.

◆ Thanks for taking my car through the car wash. I always mean to do that and seem to forget. I love that you remember for me.

◆ Thanks for cheering me up. You always know how to make me laugh. You changed my entire mood.

Now, use the space that follows to practice some of your own compliments.

1. _____

_____

_____

2. _____

_____

_____

3. _____

_____

_____

4. _____

_____

_____

5. _____

_____

_____

Another way to say thank you is to simply reaffirm your general sense of appreciation. Doing this every once in a while is relationship enhancing. It's also a really pleasant surprise if you walk up to your man, give him a hug, and say something like, "Thanks for being there for me—I appreciate everything you do," or "I'm so glad you're in my life—you always make me smile."

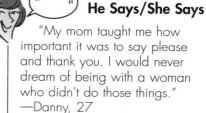 **He Says/She Says**

"My mom taught me how important it was to say please and thank you. I would never dream of being with a woman who didn't do those things."
—Danny, 27

Do I Deserve a Great Guy?

Some women have a more challenging time than others feeling authentic in their relationships. They believe they may risk losing everything unless they "put on a good act." Likewise, some women find it more difficult than others to express genuine and sincere appreciation. They feel like no matter how hard they try, something in their relationship is always amiss. They focus on the negative. When we resist being ourselves, and when we find little for which to be grateful, we create obstacles to satisfying relationships.

Perhaps you feel that something is blocking you from being the person you would like to be and the woman your man would like to see. Consider that one or more of the following issues may be the cause:

♦ You come from a family where your emotional needs weren't met. Unfortunately, children get accustomed to the emotional climate in their original families, whatever it may be. For you, feeling deprived of the love you deserve may be such a familiar scenario that you are re-creating it without meaning to do so.

◆ Your dad did not treat you the way you wished he had. Although you may not have consciously chosen a man who reminds you of your father, women sometimes try to "work out" difficult father-daughter relationships by repeating troublesome behavior patterns with their partners.

◆ Deep down you expect to be rejected. In Chapter 2, you read about self-fulfilling prophecies. What we expect to happen often does. If you anticipate rejection, you may be setting things up so that you do the rejecting first.

◆ You don't know how to nurture yourself. It's hard to please others when you don't know how to make yourself content. That's putting the cart before the horse.

◆ You feel guilty about being happy. If your friends or family members are stuck in unhappy relationships, you might feel as though you have no right to be an exception. Misery loves company!

◆ Your self-esteem is very low. Lack of self-confidence may lead you to believe that, no matter what you do, no man could ever find you as pleasing as he might find someone else. These negative comparisons preoccupy you and discourage you.

◆ You don't feel secure unless you are "in control." You are uncomfortable with the idea that pleasing a man does not mean manipulating him.

◆ You feel like a fraud. You think a really good guy will see through you, so you end up with men whose attentions you don't really value.

◆ You are drawn to unfixable problems. Believe it or not, frustration and misery can be addictive. There's a part of you that gets a "fix" from unhappiness, and perhaps from the attention that being unhappy seems to earn you.

◆ You prefer fantasy to reality. You are so busy dreaming of the "perfect" man and the "perfect" relationship that it is hard for you to recognize the things you already have and work on enhancing them.

Uh-Oh's and No-No's

Sometimes the issues that interfere with your personal fulfillment in relationships merit professional intervention. If interpersonal problems are recurring, you may wish to consider individual or couples therapy, classes, or workshops.

If any of these sound familiar, you may secretly hold the belief that you just don't deserve a great guy and a great relationship. Until you believe that you deserve something you won't be able to achieve it. You'll keep getting in your own way.

But don't give up! It is never too late to address these issues. It is never impossible to break out of a negative pattern. Change begins with your sincere desire for that change to take place.

The first step, once again, lies in being honest—this time with yourself. Recognize what may be standing in your way and resolve to get past it. Tell yourself that *the real you* does deserve a great guy and a wonderful long-term partnership. Reaffirm this daily. You'll be amazed at what can happen when you believe in the power of your authentic self.

The Least You Need to Know

- ◆ Don't be a fake; your man will sense it and resent it.

- ◆ Being our best self is an active choice that each of us can make every day.

- ◆ Positive reinforcement is a win/win strategy—behaviors that get rewarded get repeated.

- ◆ There are many ways to say thank you, but what's most important is that your man knows you appreciate him.

- ◆ Some women need to work on letting themselves believe they deserve a great guy and a great relationship.

Chapter 4

He's Your Number One

In This Chapter

- ◆ Letting your man know you care
- ◆ Having spontaneous versus scheduled sex
- ◆ Understanding the importance of guy time
- ◆ Respecting a guy's domain
- ◆ Picking guy gifts for any—or no—occasion

You know your man is important to you. I know it, too, because if he weren't, you wouldn't be reading this book. But does *he* know much you care? Your first instinct may be to say, "Of course." But don't be so certain. In the hectic swirl of day-to-day life, it can be all too easy to lose sight of what—and who—really matters. This chapter will help you remind your guy that he's your number one.

Why He's Your Priority

It may strike some of you as totally impractical to say that a woman should make her man her topmost priority. How can you do this in light of all the other demands that your work, your family, your community, and society in general put upon you? *Hey,* you might think, *if I don't put myself first at least some of the time, who will?*

Now here's the part where I remind you that pleasing your man is a win/win proposition and a matter of enlightened self-interest. I say a woman should put her man first. I also say a man ought to put his woman first. When the first dynamic is in place, the second follows just like night follows day. *Who will put you first?* He will, of course—that is, if you are able to keep your priorities in perspective.

Making your guy your top priority does not mean catering to his whims 24/7. It doesn't mean you should be his valet—not any more than he should be your butler. What it does involve is adopting an attitude of consideration.

When you and your guy first got together, you were probably always thinking about what activities he enjoyed, where he liked to go, what he liked to eat, whom he wanted to socialize with, and so on. You probably also did lots of little favors for him—and it was really your pleasure to do so. Has anything changed? Be honest.

How Often Do You Put Him First?

On a scale from 1 (never) to 5 (quite often), how often do you do the following for your man?]

1. I serve his favorite foods.

   1 2 3 4 5

2. I accompany him to his favorite restaurant.

   1 2 3 4 5

3. I try new activities he wants to try.

   1 2 3 4 5

4. I ask his opinion about which movie we'll see.

   1 2 3 4 5

5. I invite his family over.

   1 2 3 4 5

6. I invite his friends over.

   1 2 3 4 5

7. I make his friends and family feel welcome when they come.

   1 2 3 4 5

8. I do a chore that is supposed to be his responsibility.

   1 2 3 4 5

9. I buy or make him a gift in the absence of a special occasion.

   1 2 3 4 5

10. I plan surprises and celebrations for him when an occasion is upcoming.

   1 2 3 4 5

Add it all up. How did you do?

10—20 Start thinking more about what your man likes and wants.

21—30 You're getting there, but you're not there yet.

31—40 You're very thoughtful. Keep it up.

41—50 You're extremely considerate!

Notice that in this quiz, a high score doesn't mean you "always" put your man's preferences before your own, only that you are frequently unselfish. The corollary to this will be that he will be considerate of your preferences as well.

A Matter of Time

Another thing that mattered when you were first getting together with your man was making it a priority to spend time with him. This certainly wasn't something you felt obligated to do; spending time with one another was fun. No matter how busy you were with other things, somehow or other everything else in your life got accomplished *even though* you devoted hours to doing things with and for your guy.

You say your life is even busier and more complicated now, and you're probably right. After you and your guy became a couple and started building a life together, there were more social obligations, family obligations (*especially* if you have children), more financial considerations, and more household responsibilities.

But what happened to having an old-fashioned good time? In fact, what happened to hanging out together at all? Do you have any idea how much time you do—or don't—spend with your man and what you two do with the time you spend? The following chart will help you keep track for a week.

Day	Hours Spent Together	What You Did
Monday	_____	_____
		_____
		_____
Tuesday	_____	_____
		_____
		_____
Wednesday	_____	_____
		_____
		_____
Thursday	_____	_____
		_____
		_____
Friday	_____	_____
		_____
		_____
Saturday	_____	_____
		_____
		_____
Sunday	_____	_____
		_____
		_____

Add up your joint waking hours. Now, deduct from those hours the following:

- Time spent together but focused totally on your kids

- Time spent together when you were really thinking about work

- Time when you made a public appearance as a couple but were each mainly socializing separately

The time remaining counts as quality couple time. Amazingly, you might find that it is practically nonexistent. In any case, I'll bet it's shockingly less than you had imagined.

Now it's time to do something about it. The sections that follow will give you ideas on dealing with work, kids, and social obligations.

Dealing With Work

Work is important for many reasons. Work makes people feel useful and valued. A job well done is a source of pride and personal fulfillment. As a practical matter, work also generates income, and every couple needs revenue to turn their dreams into reality.

All this makes it very easy—too easy, in fact—to default to work as a reason for not spending time with your partner. Some people can actually become addicted to work, the way they can to a drug. Since we, as a society, strongly value the work ethic, it's sometimes difficult to recognize this as the problem that it can be.

Even if neither of you is a workaholic, balancing work with one's private life is becoming increasingly difficult as the whole world speeds up and as technology allows communications from the workplace to intrude more and more into the home realm. Even if you are not literally taking work home with you, you might still be bringing home leftover emotional residue from the workday. This negative spillover from work can be intensely preoccupying.

If work or work-related emotions are sapping the quality time you and your man spend together, ask yourself a key question:

Just what is it you're working for? When all is said and done, no one has ever devoted their last gasping words to the wish, "If only I'd spent more of my life working."

> **CAUTION**
> ### Uh-Oh's and No-No's
> Are you becoming a workaholic? If you find it difficult *not* to work and sometimes use work as an escape from other parts of your life, you could be at risk of addiction. Time off is healthy and essential.

Dealing With Kids

There's no denying that caring for children is a 24/7 commitment. But children have not yet learned about setting limits—and that is why adults have to set them.

If you and your man have rarely been alone since children became a part of your lives, let me implant two key words into your mind—well, okay, one hyphenated word: *baby-sitter*.

Baby-sitters don't have to be an expensive indulgence. If you're lucky enough to live near either set of parents in your extended family, keep in mind how absolutely thrilled grandparents might be to spend time with their grandchildren. If your family isn't nearby, consider swapping kid-watching duty with other couples in the same situation as you. Trade off a few hours once a week, and make four people really happy—not to mention the kids, who will enjoy being together after they get used to the arrangement.

If your kids are very little, consider having a sitter take care of them after they fall asleep. If your children are older, here's another magic word: *sleepover*. It's a party in which kids get to spend the whole night at a friend's house. The following week, you and your kids can reciprocate and play hosts. Now everyone has an entire night to play.

It's all too easy to say you feel guilty about leaving the kids. But, as a responsible parent, try to take a larger view about what's really in the children's best interests. When you and your man are happy and satisfied, the kids can't help but thrive because they have healthy role models.

Dealing With Social Obligations

When you become a couple, it seems people can't wait to invite you both along to a variety of social gatherings and special events. At first it feels great to be recognized as a twosome about town. Social life, however, can start to be a drain on private time spent in one another's company.

Although there's nothing wrong with maintaining an active social life, once again balance is key. If accepting and reciprocating social invitations starts to seriously infringe on one-to-one time, cut back. Just say no.

Teasers & Pleasers

If you add one quality hour a week of time with your man, that adds up to 52 hours per year—the equivalent of more than two full days and nights.

Instead of socializing with hordes of friends or relations, do something simple together. Go to a bookstore and browse. Sit in the backyard and watch a sunset. No one is suggesting that you never socialize again. Maintaining friendships and a social network is very important. Just be somewhat selective. You can't please all of the people all of the time—not if you're really trying to please the man you love.

To Schedule Sex, Or Not

It's important to take the time to plan things with your man, be it taking in a movie to taking a vacation. But should sex be planned? Although scheduling sex is frequently suggested as a remedy to a lackluster love life, many women feel there is something unnatural about it.

Sure, spontaneous sex is fantastic. But let's look at some of the things that can interfere with it:

1. **Fatigue.** Both physical and mental exhaustion can sap your sex drive.

2. **Over-commitment.** Too many obligations are competing for your attention.

3. **Guilt.** There must be something else you should be doing.

4. **Unsynchronized schedules.** He's getting up when you're falling asleep.

5. **Lack of privacy.** Kid, cats, dogs, all think your bedroom is open for business 24/7.

6. **Interruptions.** If it's not the kids, it's the phone, the fax, the pager, the doorbell.

7. **Worry.** A particular problem or concern is preoccupying one or both of you.

8. **Stress.** Generalized free-floating anxiety can be hard to turn off, even in the absence of a specific, immediate challenge.

9. **Doubt.** Sure, *you* want to do it, but what if your partner is too busy with other matters?

10. **Procrastination.** Oh, what the heck, you can put it off until tomorrow, or the next night, or the next.

With so many potential distracters, it's a good idea to schedule passion on your calendar in advance at least every once in a while. Then you can have the additional fun of focusing on your "appointment" ahead of time. Your passion and excitement can only build.

He Says/She Says

My husband and I had a really hard time trying to schedule romantic encounters until we started thinking about things a bit more creatively. Since we're both morning people, it dawned on us that we could set our alarm clocks a half hour early once or twice a week. Now we both go off to work wearing a smile.
—Larissa, 36

Guy Time for Guy Stuff

Although it's important to spend time together, it's also important to remember that it's not wise to give your guy the idea that you and he should be joined at the hip. Independence is just as important to men as the interdependence they have with their mates. In short, guys need time to be guys. Paradoxical as it may seem, one wonderful way to show your guy he merits your attention and affection is to leave him alone some of the time. (Besides, when you give him a chance to notice he misses you, he'll see the truth in the old adage, "Absence makes the heart grow fonder.")

A Man's Gotta Do What a Man's Gotta Do

When you were first dating your man, you probably never complained when he went off with his pals and did guy things. If he went out to play softball, you wished him and his team good luck. If he went fishing, you might have packed him a lunch, "oohed" and "ahhed" over his catch, and cheerfully listened to his fish stories about the ones that got away. Maybe you weren't crazy about your beau choosing to spend time away from you, but you were supportive. Instinctively, you knew that guy-type activities enhanced his feelings of virility and masculinity. You also realized that it would paint you in a bad light if you deprived him of such pursuits. You knew enough not to be a party-pooper. Besides, his going off to do guy stuff left you free to do girl stuff.

Somehow, this kind of support and understanding can vanish when a man becomes "yours." The guy-type pursuits that seemed so boyish and charming now seem like inconveniences. What does he mean he wants to go off golfing when the lawn needs mowing? Why does he choose bowling with the boys over staying home with you every single Thursday night? Doesn't he love you anymore?

He Says/She Says

I love the evenings that my husband plays basketball with the guys. I order in Chinese, read, and relax. Then he comes home really jazzed, and we usually have a great end to the night.
—Candy, 31

Relax. First of all, keep in mind that he's probably not spending any more time with the guys now than before you were a couple—perhaps less. You might have just slipped into the habit of trying to control his entire social agenda. You might also have slipped into the habit of insecurity—interpreting your man's absences as indications that you can't be all things to him at all times. You know what? *You can't be, and you should not try to be.* How would you like it if your guy mandated that you could never hang out with your girlfriends again? It's unthinkable, isn't it? Well, he needs to bond with members of his gender just as badly as you do—and he may have fewer opportunities.

Encourage your man to do guy stuff with the guys. He'll feel understood and appreciated instead of hen-pecked and frustrated. He'll come home to you happy, energized, and a manlier man than when he left.

A Man's Domain

Even when your man is at home with you, he needs a certain amount of guy space. There are several areas of your living space that need to be respected as a man's domain. These areas are easy to identify because they form the outer perimeter of your domicile.

It's in a man's nature to stand guard between his kin and the outside world. Because of this, men have always felt comfortable on the periphery of their home turf. In the days of antiquity, while women tended the fires, men looked afar to see what was on the horizon. In medieval times, while women sat near the hearth and made a home, men mounted turrets and looked to defend the outskirts of their lands. Some might assert that men got to have all the adventure; some might think it was wiser to huddle near warmth than, say, hang around a dank and dangerous moat waiting for hordes of barbarians. But in any case, men seem to have an affinity for outer edges. In the modern home, this translates into three areas that are clearly the manly realm. Invade them at your own risk—or, better yet, don't invade them at all.

1. **The garage.** It's got cars, car stuff, bins and tins full of nuts, bolts, and screws. It's got drills, saws, heavy-duty power cords, and assorted lawn-care machinery. It smells kind of funky, and there are oil stains all over the floor. What could be a more perfect masculine environment?

2. **The backyard.** Its trees and shrubs remind him on some visceral level of the primeval forest where early man stalked and hunted his prey. Better yet, it's got a grill—or should have one—so the prey can be prepared for dinner. Even if you and your man take turns preparing food in the kitchen, a pleasing woman recognizes that outdoor cooking is strictly a manly endeavor. Searing skewered meat or fish over a fire provides a deep-seated primordial gratification for most guys.

3. **The basement.** It might be a little dark and dank, but the basement is a place where a guy can really descend into elemental guyhood. The basement has got lots of the same cool stuff as the garage, plus room for all your guy's mystery

boxes (the ones he hasn't unpacked in three or four moves but insists he can't throw away). If your man's really lucky—and you're a really good sport—he might expand his basement domain to include a game room, a large-screen TV, and a wet bar. Maybe he hasn't gotten around to it yet, but a man can dream ….

A woman can show how strongly she believes in putting her man first by respecting the sanctity of her guy's key domains. Resist the temptation to clean up your guy's areas. Don't spray them with air freshener. Don't make him frilly curtains for the garage. Eat with enthusiasm whatever it is that comes off that outdoor grill—even the mystery meat. Most of all, when your guy is doing guy things in his guy space, try not to interrupt him any more than is absolutely necessary. A man is so happy in his garage, his backyard, and his basement that you'll often hear him whistling or humming. That's a good sign. Don't ask what he's doing that fills him with so much glee. Just let him be.

Great Guy Gifts

Buying an appropriate guy gift for your man is another way to show you are making him your priority. The right gift says "I know who you are." It also says, "I want you to enjoy being who you are."

Women often say men are difficult to buy gifts for. It's true that men are not usually as skillful as we are at dropping hints concerning gifts they'd like to receive. The following list of popular male gift preferences is meant to provide some ideas. But you know your guy better than anyone. See whether you can mentally put yourself in his shoes and imagine what item might make his life a little more enjoyable, comfortable, or convenient than it is today.

1. **Tools.** Tools make guys feel confident about their ability to get any job done. In truth, tackling any job is easier when one has the proper tools to do it. Guys like all kinds of tools, but power tools—with their high-volume sound effects and their vague air of danger—provide a special adrenaline rush. Men also appreciate tools that are hard to find and that serve a very specific purpose. They'll show them off to their pals the same way you might show off the perfect pair of dress shoes.

2. **Electronics.** Make your guy your own Inspector Gadget by getting him the latest in a never-ending supply of high-tech devices. Portable audio devices, DVD

burners, handheld computers, digital cameras, wireless headphones, and hand-held massagers (for when you're not around to do the job) are just a few of the many possibilities.

3. **Sporting Goods.** Whatever his favorite sport may be—from golfing or tennis to fishing or hunting—rest assured that there is a certain kind of equipment he covets. Whatever it is, he is certain it will enhance his abilities tenfold. If you don't know what it is, ask one of his buddies. They'll be only too happy to tell you. They'll also reinforce what a wonderful woman you are for asking.

4. **Tickets.** Go online and order him tickets for a sporting event or concert he really wants to see. Remember, it needn't be something you want to see. In fact, you don't even have to go with him. Tell him to invite one of the guys along (you don't really want to go to a monster truck rally anyway, do you?), and you'll really score some pleasing points.

5. **Music, DVDs, and Books.** As with ticket purchases, keep his tastes foremost in mind. Get him a copy of his favorite action movie. Let him listen to all the music you don't like on that portable audio device you already got him. As for books, a general rule of thumb is that men read fewer novels than women do. Think about biographies, books about history and science, and how-to tomes.

6. **Watches.** Men don't wear much jewelry, but most feel the watch they wear should not only do an impeccable job of keeping time but also make a statement about them. A watch, therefore, is a practical tool, a status symbol, and a piece of adornment. Watches are available in any price range, but you don't need to spend a fortune to meet all these criteria. When in doubt, opt for precision and clean, elegant contours.

CAUTION

Uh-Oh's and No-No's

Beware cheap knock-offs of expensive designer watches. They usually don't keep proper time for long. Better to buy a reliable, affordable watch that's the real McCoy.

7. **Cologne.** Here's an area where a guy can assuredly use a second opinion. It's always difficult to know what smells good on us, especially because when we try on colognes in stores we sample the scent immediately—before it's had time to react with our unique body chemistries. If your guy doesn't already have a favorite cologne, help him identify one by trial and error. Spray on a sample, wait an hour or so, then give him your honest opinion. He'll thank you, and the research will be fun for you both.

Teasers & Pleasers

A pleasing alternative to beer, stout is not only flavorful but also loaded with healthful antioxidants. In addition, its high concentration of B-1 vitamins can lessen the risk of clogged arteries.

8. **For the Drinking Man.** If your man enjoys imbibing in spirits now and then, there are number of gifts related to enhancing the pleasure. Consider accessories for that bar he's building—or dreaming of building—in the basement. Think about the perfect glasses for his ideal beverage (from wine to martinis to Bloody Marys). If beer's his thing, look into services that will provide a monthly sampling of exotic microbrews, imports, and variations on the beer theme, such as ales and stouts.

9. **Leather Goods.** There's something inherently manly about the feel and the smell of good leather. Consider jackets, boots, briefcases, or laptop cases if your budget is on the high end. Wallets, gloves, or belts make great gifts if you're going for something less extravagant.

10. **Clothing.** Your guy might like to buy the basics for himself. But many men are unlikely to splurge on something a little special. Apparel he might not ever think to buy for himself but might well relish includes sheepskin slippers, silk robes, and cashmere scarves or socks. When he dons any of these sensual, comforting items, he'll feel like he's being given a warm, loving hug.

A thoughtful gift can be given for a special occasion or for no reason whatsoever. If you're feeling especially creative, invent an occasion that shows you care. What could be more pleasing than being surprised with a *Thanks for Taking Out the Trash* gift or an *I Like Your Smile* gift?

The Least You Need to Know

- ◆ Putting your man first means always taking his needs into consideration.

- ◆ Remember to make time for one another—don't let obligations crowd out fun.

- ◆ Scheduling sex from time to time ensures you will connect and gives you both the fun of looking forward to it.

- ◆ While time together is important, guy time and guy space will reinvigorate your manly man.

- ◆ To identify the right gift for your guy, put yourself in his shoes—or maybe his sheepskin slippers.

Part 2

Be a Girlfriend

Remember what it was like when you were in the early stages of being your guy's girlfriend? How would he have described you? I'll bet some words that come to mind are "pretty," "fun," "flirtatious," and "sweet." Now think about how your "new boyfriend" responded to you back then. I'll bet he was eager, attentive, and a real gentleman.

In this section, you'll find tips for looking naturally great in the way men appreciate, and for bringing the art of flirting back into your relationship. You'll also find guidance for re-establishing "best behavior" patterns that we all adopt when we're in courtship mode where neatness—and sweetness—count.

5

Simply Gorgeous

In This Chapter

- The sense men rely on most
- The ideal level of beauty maintenance
- Secrets of lifelong weight control and fitness
- Radiant skin, luscious lips, and bright eyes
- Staying silky smooth and self-confident

Men are visual creatures. They are apt to be more absorbed by what they see than by any other sense. It probably seems to you that your man is always looking at something: a ballgame on television, an action movie, a shiny new car passing by on the street, and—of course—an attractive woman. Well, all of that is the way it should be—especially the part about looking at women.

Men like to watch women walk down the street, relax on the beach, drive past them in a convertible. They have a penchant for posters, wall calendars, and magazines that feature fabulous females. It's all good. If your man enjoys letting his eyes linger on a beautiful lady, be happy. Mother Nature designed things that way. The fact is that girl watching is what keeps men feeling alive and aroused.

Ideally, of course, you want to be the attractive female that your man enjoys looking at most. Even if he sees you every day, you want him to be excited by the very sight of you. In this chapter, you'll learn how to make that goal a reality—not by trying to look like someone else, but by looking like your best self: simply gorgeous.

Maintaining the Magic

Most women relish the thought of their men being so pleased by their appearance that the men long to drop everything else and gaze at them adoringly. But for many women this seems like a distant daydream. Sometimes we recall how our man used to ogle us and we sigh, as if we think recreating that time is a lost cause.

It's not.

The truth is there's nothing your man would like better than to imagine you as his calendar girl. But sadly, we might be discouraging this dynamic without meaning to.

Teasers & Pleasers

The outside of the body is a reflection of what goes on inside. A calming daily routine such as 15 or 20 minutes of yoga or tai chi will help you to achieve an inner and outer glow. Doing it over time will have an amazing cumulative effect.

After we become settled in a relationship, we might unconsciously begin to pay less attention to our own looks and spend a lot less time and effort on fitness, grooming, and beauty regimes than we used to when they were a regular part of our lives. When it comes to our personal appearance, we say we are just too busy and preoccupied, or that we are "fighting a losing battle."

On the other hand, some of us might go to the other extreme. We can become so anxious about losing our looks—and perhaps of losing our men because of this—that we might overcompensate by obsessing on appearing flawless all the time. Unfortunately, this can put men off. Remember, there is nothing pleasing about a woman who appears to be trying too hard. And there is certainly nothing pleasing about looking fake or feeling uncomfortable.

Do you fall into one of these categories, or are you perhaps the happy medium—a woman who enjoys maintaining her attractiveness without making herself—and her guy—crazy? Take the following quiz to find out.

Are You High, Low, or Medium Maintenance?

1. I spend at least a half an hour styling my hair:

    Never / Some Days / Most Days / Daily

2. I will not leave the house if I feel I don't look perfect:

    Never / Some Days / Most Days / Daily

3. I keep my man waiting while I primp:

    Never / Some Days / Most Days / Daily

4. I inspect and touch up my fingernails:

    Never / Some Days / Most Days / Daily

5. I try on several outfits before making up my mind:

    Never / Some Days / Most Days / Daily

6. I apply full make-up:

    Never / Some Days / Most Days / Daily

7. I flip through beauty and fashion magazines:

    Never / Some Days / Most Days / Daily

8. I buy, or think of buying, a new cosmetic or beauty product:

    Never / Some Days / Most Days / Daily

9. I expect my man to notice and compliment my looks:

    Never / Some Days / Most Days / Daily

To compute your score, give yourself the following:

1 point for each Never

2 points for each Some Days

3 points for each Most Days

4 points for each Daily

If you scored:

10—19   You are a low maintenance type. Consider revitalizing your interest in your physical appearance. It can revitalize the magic in your relationship.

20—34   You are a medium maintenance type. You take good care of yourself without losing perspective.

35—40   You are a high maintenance gal. Although it's great that you're concerned with looking fabulous, you can go overboard. A man can easily grow impatient with a woman who spends so much time paying attention to herself that she has little time left for him.

To best please your man—and yourself—with the way you look, cultivate the happy medium attitude. Every woman interested in keeping her man's attention on her should be concerned with her appearance and develop habits that lead to good looks. But don't overdo it.

> **CAUTION**
>
> **Uh-Oh's and No-No's**
>
> Don't lose all those lovely curves! 80 percent of men like their women curvy, and only seven percent prefer waif-like bodies.

Remember, pleasing a man is about art, not artifice. The best way to be gorgeous is to be "simply" gorgeous. Concentrate on being your freshest, best looking, and most self-confident—not trying to achieve some unattainable face and figure.

Feeling Fit

It's sometimes been said that being happy in a relationship and staying in shape simply don't go together. Both women and men tend to gain weight when they are in committed relationships. Women actually do it faster, putting more weight on in the short run after they marry or move in with a man.

Does feeling emotionally comfortable lead to indulging in comfort foods? That could certainly be part of the reason. Tired of keeping in shape while "on the market," some of us might overeat out of sheer relief after we are in a committed relationship. But there are other relationship-related reasons for putting on the pounds as well. We love to cook for our man. We feel we should eat what he does, or risk being impolite. We spend more time cocooning at home in front of the TV and less time being active. The excuses seem endless, and so does the tendency to put on the pounds.

Now things get even more complicated. Women in relationships put on more weight than their single counterparts, but studies show that this is also the group that tends to diet most. However, "diets" that involve temporary, drastic nutritional changes, such as the elimination of an entire food category like fats or carbohydrates, don't work as a permanent weight loss solution. Besides, the dieting mindset can lead a woman to feel bad about herself if she falls short of achieving a supermodel body. All body shapes can be gorgeous and sexy. Your man must like your body type, or he wouldn't have been attracted to you in the first place.

Keeping in shape really means keeping your natural body shape within the range of appropriate weight for your height, as well as keeping your body firm and your spirit energized through activity. If you've put on some post-relationship body baggage, it doesn't take a rocket scientist to see the solution: eat less and exercise more.

Less Is Best

No matter which way you slice it, 3,500 calories equals one pound of body weight. If you consume 3,500 more than you burn in, say, the course of week, you will gain one pound a week. If you burn 3,500 calories more than you consume in that same time period, you will lose a pound week.

Here are some simple strategies for cutting back on calories consumed:

- Never eat leftovers while cleaning up—put all dirty dishes immediately into hot, sudsy water.

- Don't keep food in any room except the kitchen.

- Don't keep cookies out on the counters or put food in see-through containers.

- Don't buy junk food—neither you or your man need it.

- Serve yourself on a smaller plate.

- If you really crave something, have a bite or two—but that's all.

- Pinpoint your cravings: You might feel like you want barbecued spare ribs when you are really just craving barbeque sauce.

CAUTION **Uh-Oh's and No-No's**

Don't fall into the trap of matching your man mouthful for mouthful in his eating habits. Chances are he is bigger than you are. Let's keep it that way! Allocate your portions proportionally.

15-L

♦ Keep cut up veggies in the fridge where you can easily see them and reach them.

♦ If you crave candy, try fruit instead (try keeping some seedless grapes in the freezer for a special treat).

♦ Use whole grains (such as brown rice, whole wheat bread), which are high in fiber and make you feel fuller than processed flour products, such as white rice, pasta, and white bread.

♦ Eat organic foods, which are free of hormones, pesticides, and harsh fertilizers (they satisfy because they have superior taste).

♦ Eat slowly, putting your utensils down between bites.

Tantalizing Terms

Nutritional sociologists define couples as **eating units**. Their dietary choices and exercise habits are mutually influential. Couples who support each other in eating healthfully and exercising regularly will contribute to the health of one another and to the health of their relationship.

♦ Save up calories for special occasions so you can splurge on a fancy dinner, a wedding, or a vacation.

♦ Work with your partner to make sensible meal and snack choices. When a couple joins together, the food preferences and eating habits of each individual affect those of the other. (The formal term for this is called an *eating unit*.)

Above all, think positive. Weight loss and weight management can be a challenge, but a challenge is not a bad thing. Surround yourself with success stories, and remind yourself daily: "If they can do it, I can do it."

Move It to Lose It

Now we come to the other side of the equation. Any good weight management program should include some physical exercise. Obviously, exercise burns calories. But it also builds self-confidence, boosts energy, and keeps us mentally sharp. Any woman willing to take the few simple steps that stand between her and fitness will soon begin to feel better, and the improvement will reflect itself in every facet of her existence, including her relationship with her man.

When it comes to planning an exercise regime of activities like aerobics, jogging, swimming, and many other exercises, it's wise to discuss the options with your doctor. Take his or her advice in planning your goals and how best to achieve them. Remember the happy medium here as well. Pick an exercise level that makes sense for you given what shape you're now in and what you've been doing. If you've been more or less sedentary for years, don't attempt a mini-marathon or join an advanced kickboxing class right off the bat.

Teasers & Pleasers

Stay off that scale, with the help of BMI. BMI stands for Body Mass Index—a better way to determine how close you are to a healthy weight. This calculation takes your height into account and assigns you a number in a health risk index.

Your BMI is calculated by dividing your weight by your height squared (in meters). The resulting number determines what category you fall into. No need to do the math. Just Type BMI into a Web search engine and you'll find numerous sites featuring automatic calculators.

Here are some simple strategies for incorporating more movement into your life without unnecessary pain and strain:

- ◆ Walk. It's one of the best exercises there is, and you don't need any special equipment or training. In fact, suggest a walk with your man after dinner—instead of snacking in front of the television.

- ◆ Dance while you work around the house, using headphones and some of your favorite up-tempo tunes.

- ◆ Take up a sport: consider tennis, racquetball, basketball, or another fast-paced competitive endeavor. As adults, we don't have much access to neighborhood pick-up games, but investigate local Ys, parks, and community centers.

- ◆ If you have no place to leave the kids while you work out, make them part of your workout by playing tag, kicking a soccer ball around, or jogging with the little one in a stroller.

- ◆ Exercise in small time increments—because research shows that 10 minutes of exercise here and there will help you almost as much as longer, less frequent workouts. (Aim for at least 200 minutes a week—that's about half an hour a day.)

- If you hate to work out alone, join a class or get a friend to work out with you.

- If you feel self-conscious exercising in front of others, use exercise videos and try a solitary stress-reducing walk or run.

- If you're using exercise equipment at a gym, have a trainer walk you through the paces the first few times to lessen the chance of injury.

- Regardless of what exercise you choose, stretch before and after, holding each stretch—without bouncing—for a minimum of 20 seconds to maximize its benefit.

- Have sex when you feel like eating: It burns calories and takes the mind off food for a while.

Exercise and eating habit changes are not meant to be band-aid solutions. Before you begin a regimen of healthy eating and working out, ask yourself this question: How long can I go on like this? The answer should be, "Forever." If you can't imagine sticking with your new behaviors even after you reach the weight you want to be, you should try something else. Going on and off the same plan again and again is a no-win situation.

He Says/She Says

"One day, in a parking lot, I had a revelation about getting more exercise. I realized how much time I spent driving in circles trying to get a spot closest to the store where I was going. It would take me less time to park further away and walk, and then I would be burning calories. I started doing this everywhere, and I bought a pedometer to tell me how much farther I was walking. I got in a couple of miles a week that way." —Dina, 35

A Radiant Face

As much as they appreciate a good body, men love to look at a lovely female face. What they want to see there can be best summed up in one word: radiance. Your face should be a reflection of your inner warmth and vivacity. It needn't be a flawlessly symmetrical work of art, and it shouldn't be masked with a great deal of make-up. Men do not like the look of an overly made-up woman, and often say they think women tend to wear too many cosmetics.

Men start out their lives gazing into the face of a woman they love. It's only natural that they should continue to get pleasure from letting their eyes linger on the female visage. To please your man, you naturally want your face to look lovely. But you should also try to get it to look lovely naturally. These skin care tips will help:

- Drink lots of water (six to eight 8-ounce glasses a day), which hydrates your skin from within and improves skin texture and quality.

- Eat a sensible, well-balanced diet—low in sweets and saturated fats—to avoid blemishes.

- Keep exercising because skin is nourished by the blood and oxygen, and a good workout stimulates circulation and helps skin absorb nutrients and grow new cells at a faster rate.

- Use sunscreen, which will shield your skin from disease and keep it from developing dark sun spots.

- Avoid using soap, which contains alkali that breaks up the top layer of skin, allowing moisture to escape. (If you must use soap on occasion, avoid those with added disinfectants or perfumes.)

- If you've got a limited budget for skincare products, spend it on a good cleanser, toner, and moisturizer.

Well cared-for skin is simply gorgeous on its own and does not require lots of make-up coverage. Whatever make-up you do wear, be sure to remove it before bed. It clogs up your pores. Besides, men don't appreciate waking up to the sight of a pillowcase smeared with foundation, blush, and mascara.

He Says/She Says

"I know my wife thought more make-up made her look more glamorous and youthful. Her girlfriends reinforced that by complimenting her when she used a new shade of eye shadow. But to me, women like the look of make-up on each other more than men like it. Recently my wife and I went on a camping trip and she wore no make-up at all. I kept telling her how great she looked, and suggested she cut back on her make-up once we got home. She did, and I tell her all the time she looks so young and lovely to me."

—Louis, 40

Lip Service

When it comes to being simply gorgeous for your man, lips are an especially important facial feature. Lips are noticed all of the time because they move as we speak.

They are also noticed because even if you don't say a word out loud, lips can eloquently suggest, "Wouldn't you like to kiss me?"

Even though men don't like their women to wear lots of makeup, lipstick is often the one exception. Once upon a time, a woman would never dream of leaving the house without her lipstick on—even if she wore no other makeup at all. Then came a time lipstick was not deemed so essential. Happily, the tide is turning again. Great lips are back!

Some women are going all out for luscious lips, with collagen implants and tattooed lip outlines. That might well be in excess of what you need. These quick tips for lips will help you keep your lips lovingly luscious:

- Use lip balm daily, since cracked, dry lips are a turn-off and feel awful.

- Slick your balm on generously, but be sure to let it dry before applying lip liner.

- Get a natural shade of lip liner and carefully draw around the rim of your lips, and blend the edges with a sponge applicator.

- To make your lipstick last longer, gently color in the entire top and bottom lip with a pencil coating after you do the rims.

- When applying lipstick avoid anything very dark or very light.

- Always top your lipstick with gloss.

- Keep duplicate lipsticks and glosses at home and in your purse so you can re-apply as needed.

Lip care is easy and relatively inexpensive. A new shade of lipstick is a very affordable way to perk up your mood and give you an instant sense of renewal. Get ready, get set, and pucker up.

CAUTION

Uh-Oh's and No-No's _____

Instant lip-plumping products that contain ingredients like menthol and ginger have gotten mixed reviews. Tests do show they can increase lip fullness by a small percentage, but many women say the effect is extremely brief and that the chilling sensation on the lips is unpleasant. If you don't like the feel of such products, forget about them. You won't radiate a "kiss me" message if you're uncomfortable.

Bright Eyes

Eyes are the other facial feature that can send "come hither" messages. When you and your man look at each other he should feel your eyes are a window into the real you. Go easy on the make-up, but make sure your eyes look their best and their brightest by doing the following:

- Get enough rest: Fatigue shows itself in dark circles under the eyes, which even the best concealer won't camouflage completely.

- Limit alcohol: Overdoing it leads to red eyes and more dark circles.

- Refresh your eyes routinely: Apply cucumber slices or potato slices to closed lids for fifteen minutes.

- Avoid eye infections: Remove eye make-up before bed and throw out old eye make-up after six months.

A note to eyeglass wearers: As you certainly know by now, guys do make passes at girls who wear glasses. Just frame your eyes well. Even if you wear glasses just for reading, take the time to find frames that flatter the shape of your face and that don't make your eyes seem smaller. And if you wear contacts, don't over wear your contact lenses, or you will redden your eyes and risk potential corneal damage.

Teasers & Pleasers _____

Tweezing and shaping your eyebrows is a must. Well-defined and nicely arched brows make the eyes seem larger and can almost serve as a mini face-lift. Believe it or not, the best place to get a good close-up view for this handiwork is in your car. Pull down the driver's side visor and use the lighted mirror. No, not while you're driving!

Smooth as Silk

As we know, men love to look. But looking is often a prelude to touching. So don't forget the "simply gorgeous" aspect of pleasing your man's tactile sense.

What does a man want to experience when he touches his woman? As one man put it, "The sensation of touching warm silk." Staying soft to the touch from head to toe is a sure-fire turn on. As soon as your man brushes up against you, even accidentally, he'll want to keep going, and going, and going.

Hair Affair

For soft hair, a conditioner is in order. Pay attention to your hair type when purchasing a conditioner (people with thick hair require different varieties than those with fine hair, for example). Also be aware of the special features and uses of various conditioner types.

- Moisturizers are concentrated with humectants—compounds that attract and hold moisture into the hair.

- Reconstructors normally contain protein, such as human hair keratin protein, which strengthens the hair.

- Acidifiers will compact the cuticle layer of the hair and create shine and bounce (most detanglers are acidifiers).

- Glossers contain very light oils derived from silicone, which reflect light when used in small amounts—and also control the "frizzies."

- Thermal protectors safeguard the hair against heat damage from blow-drying, curling irons, or hot rollers.

- Oils (E.F.A.s) are needed by those who treat their hair with chemicals (such as color or perm chemicals). They transform dry and porous hair into soft, pliable hair.

Toe Glow

Imagine this scenario: You get into bed on a chilly winter night and rub your tootsies up against your man for warmth. "Ouch," he says, "are you wearing sandpaper slippers?"

Now imagine this scenario: You get into bed on a chilly winter night and rub your tootsies up against your man and he says, "Mmm, honey, your feet feel like butter."

Although many of us tend to give short shrift to our feet in our beauty regimes, many men actually find the female foot a highly erotic zone. With a little TLC, feet—like the rest of you—can be simply gorgeous.

Don't worry if you can't spare the time or the money for a professional pedicure. You can create a foot spa at home that can pamper and revitalize in seven simple steps. At least once a week:

1. Soak your feet for 10 to 15 minutes and pat dry.

2. Clip toenails straight across, or wait until feet are completely dry and use an emery board.

3. Using pumice stone, remove any rough areas.

4. Massage cuticle area with a little oil or moisturizer.

5. Gently push back cuticles.

6. Apply foot lotion and massage into each foot.

7. Remove any excess lotion.

> **Teasers & Pleasers**
>
> Recipe For Silky Smooth Feet: Mix 1 cup of lemon juice (or Real Lemon juice), cinnamon (for scent), 2 tablespoons (or less) olive oil, ¼ cup of milk, and enough water to fill a basin. Soak feet for at least 15 minutes. Your feet will emerge fragrant, refreshed, and satiny.

If you wish to apply polish to your toes—men tend to love this detail more than polished fingernails—put a small amount of polish on your brush and paint one stroke down the center of your nail. Your brush should hold just enough color to accomplish this. Stroke the sides of the nail and you are done. Wait until polish is dry to the touch and then apply a clear topcoat to add life to your pedicure and protect your nails.

Go ahead, take off the sneakers and sweat socks and slip your feet into a sexy pair of strappy sandals.

The Great Shave Debate

Men appreciate a silky feel to all of a woman's skin, and that means making a commitment to hair removal for underarms, legs, and the bikini area. Depending on where you tend to grow hair, you may also wish to consider removing growth from arms, back, or facial areas.

But how to do it? There are—and have been throughout history—innumerable methods of hair removal. For example, in a "sugaring" technique that originated in Egypt, a paste made primarily of sugar was applied to the surface of the skin and then removed, taking the hair along with it. In "threading," an ancient method of hair removal still used in many countries in the Middle East as well as India and Pakistan, 100 percent cotton thread is twisted and rolled along the surface of the skin entwining the hair in the thread, which is then lifted out from the follicle. Today, we have high-tech (and costly) methods such as electrolysis and laser hair removal. And, of course, there is always shaving and waxing—each of which has its diehard advocates.

How you remove hair is a matter of personal preference and aesthetics, as well as time and cost factors. The following table illustrates which methods are suitable for which body areas and tells—on average—how long each treatment lasts.

Method	Duration	Suitable Body Areas
Electrolysis	Permanent (after numerous treatments)	Face, underarms, arms, Legs, back, bikini line
Laser	Permanent/Semi-permanent	Face, underarms, arms, legs, back, bikini line
Depilatories	2 weeks	Underarms, arms, legs, bikini line
Shaving	3 days	Underarms, legs, bikini line
Sugaring	3 to 6 weeks	Face, underarms, arms, legs, back, bikini line
Threading	3 weeks	Facial areas only (eyebrows, upper lip, chin)
Tweezers	3 to 8 weeks	Eyebrows, chin
Waxing	3 to 6 weeks	Facial areas, underarms, arms, legs, back, bikini line

Lately, many women wish to consider going beyond the bikini line and removing most or all of their genital hair via waxing or shaving. Although this is certainly a hot trend, if you're doing it to please your man, it's best to ask him first whether he thinks this would be an exciting idea. Some men find it extremely arousing, especially since shaved pubic hair has long been a staple in X-rated movies. On the other hand, your man might prefer you to maintain a more natural look in this regard. That said, if there are no objections, it might be titillating for you both if you change your look down below, even if only temporarily.

Teasers & Pleasers

Referring to genital hair removal, the terms Brazilian waxing and Hollywood waxing are often used interchangeably. Specifically, the term *Brazilian waxing* refers to partial genital hair removal, often leaving a strip of hair, *Hollywood waxing* refers to total genital hair removal.

Owning It

After you have made up your mind to be simply gorgeous, it's important that you cultivate a gorgeous attitude. Certainly any of us can look around at the images of women on television, in movies, in magazines, and in catalogues and advertisements, and be critical of ourselves as compared to those women. But such negative thoughts will sap your vitality and take the spring out of your step.

Uh-Oh's and No-No's

Never fuss with your appearance in public. Repeatedly pulling out a pocket mirror to check your hair or lipstick communicates that you feel unsure of yourself and that you are too high maintenance. Better to court the windblown look and tolerate the occasional smudge than to call negative attention to yourself in this way. If you are looking for flaws, others will, too.

Besides, let me tell you a very important secret: Even those women don't look like those women. Models and actresses will be the first to admit that their images are airbrushed, that they are pinned and sewn into their clothes, and that lighting plays an enormous role in the way they come across on camera. Portraying an illusion is part of their jobs, and they accept it as such, but it should not be what you're about. You are all about the art of being the best possible you.

The Least You Need to Know

- ◆ Men are visually oriented and are aroused by what they see.
- ◆ Girl watching is healthy—and you can be the girl he watches.

◆ Time spent on beauty maintenance is important, but it doesn't pay to overdo it.

◆ Men prefer a fresh, natural look to an overly made-up and fussy appearance.

◆ Don't try to look like someone you're not; artifice and imitation detract from your natural allure.

Chapter 6

The Flirt Factor

In This Chapter

- ◆ Why flirting still works in committed relationships
- ◆ The body language of flirting
- ◆ The verbal language of flirting
- ◆ How to avoid flirting missteps
- ◆ Flirting and self-confidence

To flirt is to say you like and admire someone. To flirt is also to hint of the promise of things to come. Flirting is a basic impulse, part of human nature. It is a universal and essential aspect of human interaction. Anthropological research shows that flirting is to be found, in some form, in all cultures and societies around the world.

Most of us flirt instinctively when we spy a future prospect for a relationship or when we are just beginning to date and court. Sadly, however, after we are in a committed relationship, we often let the art of flirting flounder.

But abandoning flirtatiousness is a terrible idea, a symptom of the sort of complacency that can do a relationship in. Keeping flirting alive keeps fun, sauciness, and a bit of mystery in a relationship. Besides, for a woman to flirt with a man is good for his ego and his libido—not to mention hers.

Foreplay All Day

Flirting takes a great many forms. Certainly it can consist of outright sexual innuendo. If your man comes in from working in the yard covered in perspiration and you stroke him on the cheek and say, "Baby, you look sooooo hot. Who's my handyman with such handy tools?"—well, that's a pretty clear sexy flirt. It's a good one, too! It will not only inspire your man to do a good job on the yard work but also make him eager to shower up afterward, put on a dash of cologne, and get snuggly.

But blatant innuendos, titillating as they are, can—and should—be supplemented by a whole repertoire of other kinds of flirting, including:

- Flattering your man

- Laughing at his jokes

- Getting him to laugh

- Asking him questions to show your interest in his interests

- Making a romantic gesture (like picking him a flower)

- Grooming him (like straightening his tie)

- Being physically affectionate (like giving him a spontaneous hug or peck on the cheek)

- Pampering him (like fluffing his pillow or rubbing his aching feet)

- Creating something for him (like writing a card, knitting a sweater, making up a silly song)

Teasers & Pleasers

Sharing a laugh with someone creates an emotional bond. Always be on the lookout for an opportunity to share a laugh with your man. This communicates that you're on the same wavelength. Besides, laughter is relaxing, and a laughing face always looks sexy.

In fact, there are so many ways to flirt with your man I bet you can easily work some flirtation into each and every day. Watch and see the result. The flirtier the day, the more romantic the night.

Body Talk

One key thing to know about flirting is that you can accomplish a great deal of it without saying a word. Body language is a critical part of flirtatiousness. With gestures, posture, and facial expressions—particularly eye and mouth movement—a woman can communicate to her man that she finds him appealing and is engaged by him romantically, physically, emotionally, and mentally.

Body language is a prime means of communication among humans in all situations. In fact, researchers in the field of body language—also known as kinesics—estimate that up to 70 percent of what we communicate is nonverbal.

All you need do to prove to yourself that everyone communicates with their bodies is to look around in different settings and situations. Can you tell who is the most impatient person on line at the supermarket by their grimace and tapping toes? Can you tell who is the most bored person at the meeting by their slumped posture and blank stare? Of course you can.

Now start observing the couples around you. Look at men and women dining together at a restaurant. Can you distinguish a couple who is dating from one who has a long-term relationship? Unfortunately, you usually can because the long-term couple is not leaning toward one another, not touching, not making eye contact. But that's not going to be you and your man, is it? Because you are going to actively practice flirting with your body and using body talk to communicate interest rather than indifference.

Sure, much of how we communicate nonverbally is below our level of consciousness. Our body language can, and often does, run on autopilot. However, anyone can learn to use body language consciously and to communicate very clearly with it.

> **Teasers & Pleasers**
>
> According to some evolutionary psychologists, flirting may be the foundation of human creativity. They say our intelligence, our versatile language, and our entire complex civilizations are the equivalents of the peacock's tail: a courtship device evolved to attract and retain sexual partners. Everything from art to rocket science might be merely a side effect of the essential desire and need to charm.

The Casual Touch

When we are interested in and attracted to someone, we want to make physical contact with them. I'm not talking about groping, but about subtle, sensual touches.

Notice how people in blossoming relationships always seem on the lookout for reasons to connect physically, even in seemingly offhand, casual ways. No matter how long you've been together, your man will be pleased when you start to look for opportunities to reach out and touch him.

- Brush up against him—just a tiny grazing—as you walk by.

- Give him a pat of encouragement—in the form a series of light touches on the back, the upper arm, or the wrist—when you sense he needs a boost.

- Give him a brief shoulder massage when you sense he is tense.

- Make a nice comment about something he's wearing and touch the part of his body he's wearing it on.

Remember, touching is most flirtatious—that is most a promise of things to come—when it is subtle and gentle. Don't manhandle your man. And don't blatantly fondle your man in public, as it will only embarrass him. (Think how you would feel if the tables were turned.)

Pleasing Postures

Your posture can also play a pivotal role in flirting with your man. Posture can be used to indicate your level of attentiveness to someone as well as whether or not you are open to advances from them.

In general, females tend to adopt different body postures than males. Men tend to adopt postures that make them appear taller, larger, and more impressive. They often place their hands in their pockets and jut out their elbows, which serves to enlarge the chest. They might also lean one hand above shoulder height on a wall to appear taller and more imposing. Be aware that when your man does this he is signaling his masculinity.

Unlike males, we females tend to adopt postures that make us look more petite and demure, such as drawing their knees toward the body when seated. We also adopt postures that draw attention to physical attributes that are attractive to males, such as arching our backs to display our breasts, or crossing and recrossing our legs to draw attention to them and to the genital area.

CAUTION

Uh-Oh's and No-No's

When mirroring your man, keep feminine decorum in mind. For example, if you're in a short skirt, don't mirror a man's open-legged sitting stance. When in doubt, opt for the lady-like choice.

See whether you can catch yourself doing these things, and then see whether you can do them a little more often, to signal your overall femininity. Now, let's get a bit more personal. To particularly please your man with your postures, consciously add these stances to your flirting repertoire:

- Mirroring posture. When two people are attracted to one another, they adopt what researchers call "postural congruence" or "postural echoes." This means they unconsciously adopt the same ways of arranging and holding their bodies. Mirror-image postural echoes—where one person's left side reflects the other person's right side—are the strongest indication of harmony and rapport between any pair. When you consciously arrange your body and limbs to mirror your man's (for example, leaning forward with your left arm on the table when he is leaning forward with his right arm on the table) you will create a feeling of harmony and like-mindedness. Experiments have shown that although people are not consciously aware of someone deliberately mirroring their postures, they will evaluate a person who does this very favorably.

- Listening posture. Studies consistently show that we are overwhelmingly attracted to people whom we feel listen to us closely. With our body talk we can clearly put forth the message, 'I'm listening to you. I think what you have to say is fascinating and important." To show you're listening, lean in, nod, and make eye contact. Make sure your arms are unfolded (crossed arms say you are closed off to a speaker's words) and that your hands are unclenched (clenching indicates tension). Never wring your hands or tap your feet while your man is speaking.

By the way, even when you're not consciously using your body stance to flirt, be sure to mind your posture. Stand tall; don't slump. The latter projects insecurity and tends to make one nearly invisible. The former says you are pleased with who you are—and, thus, pleasing to be with. What's more, correcting your posture can improve your mood.

Teasers & Pleasers

Communication researchers have found that nodding can be used to regulate conversations. Making single, brief nods while your partner is speaking acts as a simple sign of attentiveness, which keeps the speaker speaking. Double nods will change the rate at which the other person speaks, usually speeding up the flow. Triple nods or single, slow nods often interrupt the flow altogether, confusing speakers and discouraging them from continuing. So, if you want to express interest and keep your man chatting with you, stick to brief, single nods.

Bedroom Eyes

Countless poets—including Lord Byron, Shakespeare, and Elizabeth Barrett Browning—have written about the soulful, captivating power of a woman's eyes. Countless actresses—from Greta Garbo to Bette Davis to Elizabeth Taylor—have been revered for the expressiveness they can convey with a mere glance. Even if we're not poetically inclined, we all instinctively understand that eyes are indeed the windows to our inner selves.

Of course, it isn't just how one's eyes appear, but what one does with them that counts. When it comes to sending powerful messages of love, longing, and seductiveness, the eyes have it. Have you turned your eyes flirtatiously on your man lately? If not, try:

◆ The wink. Winking—the brief closing and opening of one eyelid—is a very clear flirting signal. Winking is especially fun and effective in public situations where it can be used to broadcast a secret, private signal across a crowded room. Next time you're at a party or other big event with your guy, catch his eye and give him a quick wink. You might hear later how it actually gave him goose bumps.

◆ The peek-a-boo gaze. This is a grown-up version of the game we play with babies. Catch your man's eye, then cast your eyes downward, then make eye contact again, and then glance downward again. This conveys that you are drawn to your man but also that you are a bit shy and demure about your feelings.

◆ The once-over. Let your eyes take in your man's body. Then cast them, in turn, on his eyes, his lips, and his eyes once more. This says, "I'd love to be touching you and kissing you right now."

Speaking of eyes that speak of love: Dilated pupils are a sign of romantic attraction. Our pupils enlarge naturally when we want to see more of something. Our eyes also dilate in low light, such as candlelight. So break out the candles to make your eyes say "I'm yours."

CAUTION

Uh-Oh's and No-No's _____

Some people aren't comfortable with winking. They fear looking like they have a piece of lint caught in their eye. Some people tend to overdo their winks, and come off looking a bit scrunchy-faced. If either of these types sounds like you, try practicing in a mirror. If you watch people flirt in the movies, you'll learn all kinds of winking styles that can really send strong messages.

The Sensual Smile

"Beauty is power, a smile is its sword." So wrote British novelist and playwright Charles Reade—and how very right he was. More than any "beauty treatment" a smile makes a woman's face look lovely. And more than any other nonverbal behavior, it sends a message of positive regard.

There are all kinds of smiles, from full-out toothy grins to swift, subtle upturns of the lips. The most important thing of all, however, is that a smile be genuine. Most people can intuitively sense when we're truly smiling, as opposed to faking it. That's because a simulated smile doesn't involve the muscles around the eyes in the way a genuine one does.

How to create a genuine smile? Easy. Just think of something pleasant or funny and let the rest happen naturally. Then turn your smile on your guy. For added pizzazz, remember these two variations:

- The over-the-shoulder smile. Look over your shoulder … and smile at him. This asymmetrical position signals that you find him intriguing.

- The appraisal smile. Look him over from head to toe, nod with approval, and then flash him your most winning smile.

In addition to smiling, there are other ways the mouth can be used flirtatiously. Using your tongue to wet your lips can be very enticing. So can drawing attention to your lips by placing your finger beside them. Some women flirt by gently nibbling and sucking on an object, like a pen, and moving it in and out of their mouths. That can work if you keep it very subtle. You don't want to come off as a caricature of a flirt.

He Says/She Says _____

"I used to be self-conscious about my smile, and so I smiled rarely. Then one day my husband said, 'You never smile at me anymore.' It hadn't occurred to me that he took my lack of smiling personally. After that, I had a tooth whitening treatment and felt comfortable smiling again. I can't tell you how much better my husband responds to me now."
—Cathy, 35

Sweet Nothings

Talk, of course, is another important flirting element. Flirtatious talk has the same goal as flirtatious nonverbal behavior—to express interest in the other person. So bear in mind that when talking to flirt you want to use your words to show that you are riveted by your man.

The good news is that, unlike when flirting with a stranger, it's fairly easy to come up with an "opening line" for beginning a flirtatious conversation with your man. Since you two are a couple, you already have many things in common. Bring up a private joke or a shared memory you both find amusing. Initiate a conversation on one of his favorite topics, or simply tell him something about himself you know he likes to hear.

When you initiate a flirtatious conversation with your man—one that says, "I like you. Let's have some fun."—be prepared to …

- ◆ Be playful.
- ◆ Be flattering.
- ◆ Be funny.
- ◆ Ask questions that allow him to show his expertise.
- ◆ Listen to his responses attentively. Don't just wait for your turn to talk.

Remember, in a serious relationship, there's plenty of time for serious conversation. But flirting and weighty or mundane subjects do not mix.

So be prepared not to …

- ◆ Talk about household chores.
- ◆ Talk about the kids.

- Bring up sore subjects.

- Whine or complain.

- Make demands.

Although it can, and should, look effortless and spontaneous, verbal flirting requires following the unwritten laws of etiquette that govern all fluent conversation. Flirtatious banter involves taking turns in the dialogue, shifting gears if things get awkward, and encouraging the other person to speak by showing signs of nonverbal attention.

Sighs and Whispers

Of course, almost anything you say can sound flirtatious if you say it in a soft, breathy whisper. Think of women like Marilyn Monroe and Jackie Kennedy Onassis. They could read a grocery list aloud to a man, and he'd melt.

If you're feeling flirty but can't think of exactly what to say to your man, go for a simple, "Hi, honey" or "How are you doing, baby?" in your sexiest tone. Don't mumble, murmur.

Teasers & Pleasers

Thanks to the wonders of technology you can use your voice for impromptu flirting anytime, anywhere. See Chapter 13 for some ideas about sexy phone chats.

Terms of Endearment

One way of keeping a flirtatious note in almost all your talk is to refer to your man by a pet name. Of course, there are generic pet names that many of us often call the ones we love, such as these:

- Honey

- Sweetie

- Baby

- Darling

- Sugar

These are wonderful terms of endearment. Even more intimate and flirtatious, however, is to come up with a name that only you, and no one else, calls your man.

Of course, I can't recommend a special, personal nickname for you to call your man. You have to come up with it—that's what makes it so personal. Such names often are inspired by a unique trait—be it a physical trait or a personality trait—or out of someone's particular love of an activity. Usually they bubble up at the spur of the moment and, if they feel right, they just "stick." If you just stay open to the idea, I'm certain a special nickname will occur to you. When it's established, you'll be reaffirming your special bond each and every time you use it.

Dress to Flirt

Whether flirting with your body, with words, or both, dressing so as to offer a hint of provocative promise is always a surefire man pleaser. But, remember, the key word here is "hint." Successful flirty dressing always reveals something, but it also always leaves something to a man's imagination, so that he can have fun by mentally filling in the blanks.

Avoiding Extremes

A woman who hides under piles of clothing is hardly dressing flirtatiously. An abundance of clothing may be practical at times—say, if you and your guy are going dog-sledding or ice fishing—but it hardy says, "Come hither, big boy." When you dress with flirting in mind—which should be often—avoid the following:

- Baggy sweaters
- Extremely loose-fitting pants
- Shapeless sweats
- Sack-type dresses

On the other hand, a woman who reveals too much skin, or whose clothes fit too tightly, is undermining her flirtatious statement by making it too forthrightly. Besides, she might get her man wondering whether she's trying to attract someone other than him. And that's not a very pleasing thought! So also avoid the following:

- Necklines so low you're in danger of letting it all hang out
- Skirts so short you can't sit in them

◆ Clothing so snug it reveals underwear lines or love handles

◆ See-through anything without undergarments

Sometime soon, when you're home alone, conduct a "flirt alert" inspection in your closet. Be honest. Do you have too-big Papa Bear clothes you hide behind? Do you have extra snug Baby Bear clothes that give too much away? Relegate them to the back of the closet or, better yet, give them away. Now Mama Bear will have only the best-fitting in-betweens from which to choose.

Wink With Your Wardrobe

Want to really flirt with what you wear? Think about creating a kind of "wink" with your wardrobe. A few simple tricks will gain his interest and stimulate the mind's eye:

◆ Create the illusion of longer, thinner legs with high, skinny heels.

◆ Make the most of a small bosom with flattering necklines such as halter necks and cross-your-heart styles.

◆ Wear something with lots of buttons down the front and leave just enough of them open to suggest the merest hint of what lies beneath.

◆ Give the subtle illusion of deeper cleavage by blending bronzer between your breasts.

◆ Accentuate your curves by wearing clothing that is cut on the bias (diagonal lines across the weave of the fabric). This can give you a better fit and a softer drape.

◆ Accentuate your waistline by wearing blouses or shirts that nip in at the bodice and fan out at the waist.

Don't be afraid to experiment with different looks. In fact, mixing up your style of dress can be provocative in and of itself. Whenever you try something new—even so much as a hat or scarf—that makes you feel sexy and flirty—you will prompt your man to take a second look. Remember, we are all attracted to variety and novelty.

Teasers & Pleasers _____

Show off your waist as much as possible. Women with figures men rate extremely pleasing have in common a waist-to-hip ratio of between .6 and .7. For example, a 24-inch waist and a 36-inch hip (.667) or a 28-inch waist and a 40-inch hip (.7). Women with many different body types share this proportion. They include Sophia Loren, Twiggy, Kate Moss, and Marilyn Monroe. Even the statue of Venus de Milo fits this shapely formula.

The Anti-Flirts

As with most things, there are a few important caveats when it comes to flirting. If you keep these simple warnings in mind, you'll please your man by exercising your flirtatious powers at the right time in the right way, for the best possible results. Ignore these anti-flirts at your own risk. They are to romance what a cold shower is to passion.

Bad Timing

Although flirting is great for adding spice to the average, humdrum day, there are some days and some situations when it's fine to be there for your guy in a compassionate, caring way, but inappropriate to actively flirt. For example…

- If he's really sad

- If he's really mad

- If he's preoccupied with a pressing problem

- If he's worried, fearful, or anxious

He Says/She Says _____

"I love it when my wife occasionally gives me a little goose on the behind as I walk by. But I had to ask her never to do that in front of my mom. You know, there are some things a guy's mom should never see!"
—Brian, 33

You should also hold off flirting for a while if he's preoccupied with friends or "guy stuff." Remember, it's important for guys to have their space and time for macho activities. If you try to actively flirt with your man while he's, say, watching Monday Night Football with his pals, he could feel like you're unfairly competing for his attentions.

Be especially sensitive to timing as well if there are people around—like his parents or his boss—who make your guy feel self-conscious. There's a time and a place for everything, and part of good relationship manners is to be aware of such dynamics.

Mixed Signals

If you're going to flirt, make sure that you're not just doing it perfunctorily to cover up a bad mood. Flirting indicates that you want to connect emotionally with your man. If you wink and smile, but then roll your eyes and turn away, he'll feel confused and rejected. Better to wait for a later opportunity to flirt if your heart's not in it.

Too Hard to Get

One of the myths about flirting is that playing hard to get is an irresistible tactic. Although maintaining some elements of mystery and coyness are alluring, total unavailability quickly becomes a discouraging bore. The point of flirting with your man is—eventually—to seal the deal. So although some teasing is pleasing, following a flirt fest with a rebuff of your man's advances is unfair and counterproductive.

The Seductiveness of Self-Confidence

Being generous with your flirting is one of the best relationship investments you will ever make. But let's face it: It's hard to make someone else feel good about himself when you're not feeling good about yourself. Besides, self-confidence, in and of itself, is sexy and alluring.

As women in a culture that perpetuates the illusion of eternal youth, physical perfection, and ultimate achievement, we often tend to be more self-critical than self-confident. Many of us set standards for ourselves that are unrealistic and then feel blue when we don't meet those standards. This hurts us, and it hurts our relationships. On the other hand, when we focus on the positive in ourselves, we enhance our own appeal and are predisposed to see positive attributes in our men—who, after all, picked us in the first place.

Self-Esteem Boosters

Everyone needs a confidence boost sometimes. The best person to get it from is ... you! Here are some techniques to help you derive self-confidence not by comparing yourself to other people, but by being what psychologists call "inner-directed" and validating your special qualities from within.

◆ Stop negative self-talk. How many times a day do you chastise yourself for imperfections? It's time you start paying attention to those negative messages you send yourself so that you can begin to actively dispute them. Check yourself every time you have a thought such as, "If only I were more this or less that." Immediately counter such thoughts with positive affirmations, like, "I'm great just the way I am." After a while you'll stop being your own worst critic and begin to train yourself to automatically think more positively.

◆ Set and meet realistic goals. Unable to complete a triathlon or scale mount Kilimanjaro? Join the club. Now, what will you be able to do in the next day, week, and month that will represent an accomplishment that will make you feel proud of yourself? Map it out for yourself in bite-sized, attainable pieces. Tell someone close to you that you're going to do it (this will help you not to slack off). Then go ahead and do it!

◆ Allow yourself to take in praise. Most of us can recall in great detail negative comments that have been made to us. But when someone says something positive about us, we tend to dismiss it. When someone thanks us for something kind or generous that we've done, we say, "Oh, it was nothing." When someone compliments us—for example, by saying we look great—we actually argue with them, offering a rebuttal such as "Oh, no. I've gained five pounds and my hair is nothing but split ends." From now on, give yourself permission to accept praise gracefully. When someone says something nice about you, say, "Thank you." Then repeat the praise to yourself in the first person ("I do look wonderful today").

Remember, it's easy to default to a negative self-opinion. We all do it some of the time. Today is the day to begin actively being positive. The more you practice, the simpler it will become and more natural it will feel.

Flattering Yourself

For an added boost to your self-confidence, and to put you in a flirtatious mood, take an opportunity to flatter and flirt with yourself. Yes, that's right—with yourself. Flirting is about admiration, appreciation, and acknowledgment. Fill in the following lists to begin acknowledging yourself.

I'm very good at doing many things, including:

1. _____
2. _____
3. _____

In my life I've accomplished many things, including:

1. _____
2. _____
3. _____

I'm a great companion and lover for my guy for many reasons, including:

1. _____
2. _____
3. _____

Now take your lists, look at yourself in a full-length mirror, and read them aloud. As you read, smile. And when you're done, give yourself an affectionate wink. Now you're really ready to go forth and flirt.

The Least You Need to Know

- Flirting is an instinctive and very constructive human behavior; it's a way of connecting from the heart and acknowledging someone—as well as lots of fun.

- A great deal of flirting can be accomplished without uttering a single word.

- Flirtatious talk is focused on making the other person feel admired and understood.

- Dressing to flirt requires leaving something to your man's imagination.

- Good flirting requires good timing and sensitivity.

- Successful flirting goes hand in hand with feeling good about yourself.

Chapter 7

Don't Forget Etiquette

In This Chapter

- Why "sweetness counts" in long-term relationships
- Things your man shouldn't see or hear
- Bedroom etiquette
- Managing your moods and PMS
- The golden rule of etiquette

Every relationship has a honeymoon—an initial phase of courtship when everyone involved is as sweet as honey. During early dating and courtship we don't have to be told to suppress inappropriate behaviors or to pull it together despite a grumpy mood. We know that when we let it all hang out—physically, verbally, or emotionally—we are probably not in our most appealing mode. Let's face it. We just might scare someone off.

After we're together for a while, however, things can start to slip. We are not nearly as careful about being courteous and considerate of our partners. Soon, we commit breaches of etiquette on a regular basis. Our men might pretend not to notice but, believe me, they do.

However, when a woman makes it her business to restore etiquette to her relationships, she will not only please her man but also inspire him to do likewise. The entire caliber of the relationship will be uplifted.

This chapter will help you to restore your early level of sweetness and consideration to your relationship and remind your man of what a lady you really are.

On Your Best Behavior

Imagine this scenario: A woman comes home from work, having stopped at the supermarket on the way. She's not in the best mood. Her day was stressful; the market was crowded; and some guy nearly backed into her in the parking lot. She opens the door to her house and slams it behind her. She loudly plops two bags of groceries down on the kitchen counter and lets out a swear word. She looks at her husband, who's watching TV and says, "Here's your groceries." Then she pops open a can of soda and drinks the beverage straight from the can. Sitting down across from her husband, she complains, "Can't you get up and unpack the groceries, or do I have to do that, too?" Later, with her husband in earshot, she complains on the phone to a girlfriend that he never does anything around the house.

Now imagine this scenario: The same woman comes home, having had the same frustrations in her day. Realizing she's not in a great mood, she takes 10 calming breaths before she goes inside. She brings in one bag of groceries, leaving the other in the trunk. "Hi, honey," she says as she notices her husband sitting in front of the TV. She places the bag of groceries on the kitchen counter and calls out, "I'm getting a soda. Can I get one for you?" "Sure, thanks," he says. She pours two sodas into glasses and brings one over to him. She sits beside him as she sips her drink. "Gosh what a day," she exclaims. "I'm exhausted. How was your day?" After hearing about her man's day and recounting hers, she mentions there's another bag of groceries in the car and asks nicely if he wouldn't mind helping her with it. Her guy says "Sure thing," gets to his feet and carries the groceries inside.

Does the first scenario seem like something that might happen at your house? Does the second seem like something you'd want to happen? If you think it's far-fetched that a man entranced by television would get up to carry a bag of groceries inside for his wife, think again. No miracle was at work here and no manipulation—simply some courtesy on the woman's part. By treating her man better, she got treated better in return.

Think of the differences between what the woman did and did not do in the first and second scenarios. Now try writing some of them down:

1. _____

   _____

2. _____

   _____

3. _____

   _____

4. _____

   _____

5. _____

   _____

Did you notice that she got her bad mood under control and greeted her husband pleasantly? She offered him a soda when she got one for herself. She poured her soda into a glass and sipped it, as opposed to gulping it from a can. She inquired about her man's day. Now think of what she did not do: She did not slam doors or bang things and didn't use foul language. She didn't demean her husband either to his face or to someone else while he listened on. All in all, she was kind and polite, and her actions paid off.

Good manners and a sweet attitude are among the most underestimated tools when it comes to keeping relationships on track and romance thriving. That's because they tend to generate instant reciprocity. It's hard not to be nice to someone who is being nice to you. Try it and find out for yourself.

Ten Things a Man Should Never See

When it comes to etiquette between men and women, one of the main things to keep in mind is that there are certain things a man should never see you do. This is true no matter how long you two have been together as a couple.

Subjecting a man to certain sights will prove a turn-off. It will also be considered just plain rude. Here are the top 10 visual taboos—activities a woman should never do in the presence of her man:

10. Don't let him see you in hair rollers or with any kind of "beauty cream" piled on your face. Plan ahead so your beauty prep work is only on your face and never "in" his face. To parade around in this mode says, "I don't care how I look when you're the only one here."

9. Don't weigh yourself. This is a process better done in private, especially if you believe it might lead you to feel frustrated or cranky. Besides, he doesn't care what the number on the scale says—nor should he.

8. Don't stand naked in front of the mirror and sigh. This is an unattractive behavior because it communicates that you don't feel comfortable with yourself. It's also impolite to appear so self-absorbed in front of your man. Let him be the judge of what he sees.

7. Don't use the toilet. Closing the bathroom door takes but a second and is one of the most worthwhile time investments you will ever make. No one needs to be privy to you in the privy.

6. Don't use or display feminine hygiene products. Men tend to feel uncomfortable and embarrassed when women tend to their feminine health and hygiene needs in front of them. They want you to be fresh and clean, but they don't need to know the details.

5. Don't eat or drink from containers. Use silverware, plates, and glasses, please. It's unladylike to chug orange juice or scrape ice cream from the carton. Treat yourself better, and he will feel better treated.

4. Don't wear undergarments with tears and holes in them. This is not only unbecoming but sends the message that you don't think enough of him to mend your ways. (The one exception to this rule is if you are specifically dressing in peek-a-boo lingerie.)

He Says/She Says

"One of the things that attracted me to my fiancé was how much class she had. Watching her whenever I took her out to dinner, I actually learned quite a few things about table manners. She never had a doubt about which fork to use or how to pass the salt properly. I thought it was charming. I would hate if she lost that after we were married."

—Pete, 33

3. Don't tug on your underwear. If you have a wedgie or if you feel that your bra is slipping, it's easy enough to excuse yourself for some quick repair work behind closed doors.

2. Don't flirt with another man. As we know, flirting with your man is a terrific way to please him. But if he sees you flirting with another, his feelings could be mortally wounded.

1. Don't roll your eyes or grimace at him. Even if he says or does something objectionable, don't compound the problem. And as impolite as this behavior is in private, if you make a face at him in public, he'll be mortified.

Take a look at this list and see how many of these politeness infractions you may be guilty of. If you vow to eliminate even one such behavior per week until they're all extinguished, you will be amazed how much pain you'll avoid and how much pleasure you'll generate. A little decorum goes a long way toward preserving your dignity and showing respect for your man and your relationship.

Ten Things a Man Should Never Hear

I know you want to please all of your man's senses. So, just as there are things a man should never see, it won't surprise you to know that there are certain things he ought never to hear. Here are the top 10 aural taboos to steer clear of:

10. Don't ask him whether you look fat. What good can possibly come of this? He'll feel put on the spot, and whatever answer he gives will feel somehow wrong to you both.

9. Don't dwell on your faults. This is a tedious, self-involved subject. We all have flaws, but pointing them out to your man won't make them go away. Work on what you need to and stay positive.

8. Don't dwell on his faults. Attacking him is disrespectful and will only serve to exacerbate whatever you feel his issues are.

7. Don't criticize his family. Even if he complains about them, he really doesn't want to hear it from you. That's especially true where his mom is concerned.

6. Don't fight with your mother. Men complain all the time about being subjected to the same heated mother-daughter battles over and over. It grates on their nerves, and it can make your man feel like he's irrelevant.

5. Don't belch or otherwise expel gas. You may protest that sometimes you can't control it but think back to when you were courting. Somehow you controlled it then. If you know there are foods that make you gassy, do your best to stay away from them. If that's not possible, take an anti-gas food enzyme, such as Beano, when you eat them.

4. Don't use foul language. Nothing is so unbecoming as a woman with a mouth full of swear words. Practice substituting "shoot" and "fudge" for other epithets. (Some off-color talk during sex, however, is another matter. See Chapter 13.)

3. Don't be sarcastic. A bitter, edgy tone of voice is hurtful and offensive. Always resist the temptation to be clever at his expense.

2. Don't complain about him to others. It's amazing how many women will rant about their man in the third person when he's standing right beside them. What could be more embarrassing?

1. Don't yell. The screaming banshee persona is frightening, and men quickly learn to tune you out when you raise your voice.

Are you guilty of any of these slips in etiquette? If so, begin to edit yourself. It's certainly not always easy to muster up the self-control needed to change what might have become a long-ingrained habit. little by little, though, you will get there if you remain mindful.

Composure and Exposure

When it comes to matters of physical intimacy, rules of etiquette are also mandatory. In fact, tact is often never more explicitly called for than in matters of sex.

Some men have rather famously observed that they would like a woman who is "a lady in the living room but not in the bedroom." But by this, they mean only that they want a woman who is uninhibited about sexuality. They certainly do not mean that a woman's thoughtfulness and consideration should be checked at the bedroom door. Anything but!

Manners in Bed

Sexual etiquette lapses are all too common in long-term relationships. In fact, lack of tact and consideration in the bedroom can be one of the main reasons that some couples begin to lose interest in their sex life.

A woman can do many impolite things to her man in bed. Do you know the score when it comes to sexual etiquette? Answer these questions and see:

◆ Have you ever told your man he compares unfavorably to a previous lover?

Often / Sometimes / Never

◆ Have you ever told him you fantasize about someone else when you have sex with him?

Often / Sometimes / Never

◆ Have you ever criticized your partner's body when he is naked?

Often / Sometimes / Never

◆ Have you ever implied that his penis is too small?

Often / Sometimes / Never

◆ Have you ever asked him "What do you think you're doing?" or "Where'd you get that?" when he tries something new?

Often / Sometimes / Never

◆ Do you give him marching orders instead of seductively asking for what you want?

Often / Sometimes / Never

◆ Do you ever stop sexual activity after you have an orgasm but before he does?

Often / Sometimes / Never

◆ Have you ever insisted on pillow talk afterward even when he was falling asleep?

Often / Sometimes / Never

◆ Have you ever told him you discussed the sex in your relationship with other people?'

Often / Sometimes / Never

◆ Have you ever told him his sex drive was too low?

Often / Sometimes / Never

◆ Have you ever told him his sex drive was too high?

Often / Sometimes / Never

If you've answered "Often" to or even "Sometimes" to any of these questions, it's time for a sexual etiquette overhaul. Although you can't undo what's been done, you can certainly prevent such gaffes from happening again.

Putting your man down by making unfavorable comparisons, sharing fantasies about others, or in any way belittling his body is inexcusably rude—not to mention completely self-defeating. Such sexual *faux pas* will deflate his ego and possibly some of his other parts as well. The same goes for discouraging his sexual curiosity and creativity, harshly correcting his technique in mid-lovemaking, browbeating him for what you want, or being selfish about your gratification.

As for post-lovemaking etiquette, if your man—like many others—is inclined to drift off into a satisfied slumber after sex, so be it. This is not the time to force a conversation.

Sharing with your man that you discuss your sex life with others will embarrass him and make him self-conscious. Trust me, self-consciousness is not a trait you want to induce in your lover.

Admonishing a man for wanting too little sex or too much may end up confusing and alienating him so that he wants none of it. If he seems less interested in sex than you are, see what creative things you can do to get him more interested. If he is much more interested in sex than you are, understand that it may be one of the only ways he feels comfortable connecting.

You both can work on enhancing intimacy in other areas, for example, by undertaking new activities together. You might also ask yourself if there is something within yourself that is preventing you from enjoying sex as much as you might. Finally, keep in mind that the frequency with which a couple has sex tends to wax and wane throughout the course of a long-term relationship. Allow such matters the time to self-correct before becoming overly intent on "fixing" them. Graciousness works as well between the sheets as well as it does anywhere else. Be considerate of your partner's feelings. Be aware of his needs. And remember to say please and thank you.

Too Much Information

An important thing to keep in mind is that in the sexual realm, being polite does not always mean being totally, brutally honest. Be careful not to volunteer too many graphic specifics about sexual relations you might have had before you met your current lover. Even if he does inquire, observe how your man reacts to your responses. Temper them accordingly if you notice your man is becoming uncomfortable.

He Says/She Says

"I once broke up with a woman that I really cared for when she told me about her sexual past, and it turned out she had a long, torrid relationship with a guy I went to high school with. I'd always thought this guy was a compete moron. She told me how great sex had been with him. Well, that was more than I could stand to know."
—Stan, 29

Be aware, too, that there are certain questions a woman simply should not ask a man. I know you're curious, but there are times when you need to remain that way. Among the top questions never to ask your guy are:

♦ Do you ever imagine doing it with (my friend, my sister, etc.)?

♦ Do you ever have dreams where you're doing it with other women?

♦ Do you wish you could do it with me and another woman at the same time?

♦ Whom besides me do you think about when you masturbate?

Here are three excellent reasons not to ask these questions of your man:

1. They will almost certainly embarrass and fluster him.

2. They are likely to tempt him to give you a dishonest answer.

3. If he gives you an honest answer, you are likely to be upset and possibly start an argument.

Yes, guys fantasize about all kinds of women. That's the truth, but you do not need "the whole truth and nothing but the truth." Ladies, give a guy a break and leave him some measure of privacy.

Uh-Oh's and No-No's

Asking your man how many women he has slept with is a no-win question. If he mentions a high number, you might think he's a player. If he says a low number, you might worry that he's inexperienced. Steer clear of the numbers game and focus on the quality of your lovemaking, not his quantity of previous lovers.

Managing Your Moods

Everyone gets into a bad mood once in a while—and some of us more often than that. Life is filled with frustrations and disappointments, and our tolerance level for these things can vary from day to day, depending on how we're feeling internally.

Okay, but does that mean you have to subject your man to your mood? If you do, you'll just spread your bad mood around, which isn't a pleasing strategy by any measure.

Once again, I'm going to ask you to remember when you and your man first got together. For the most part, your bad moods would dissipate at the very thought of seeing him, wouldn't they? If you found yourself holding onto any vestige of crankiness, you'd just take yourself in hand and say: "Well, this won't do. He won't be pleased to see me in this frame of mind."

Teasers & Pleasers

Studies consistently show that acquiring stress management skills results in higher self-esteem, a greater sense of control, and better coping skills.

The challenge now that you are a real couple is to continue to manage your moods in his presence. Talk about a win/win endeavor. This challenge will not only spare your man glimpses of you at less than your best, but also will help you by affording you an incentive to learn to manage your moods.

Physical Calming

Many studies confirm that one of the very best ways to change a bad mood is to exercise. You needn't do anything fancy or get any special equipment. A brisk walk has been shown to reduce tension significantly.

The old adage about counting to 10 also works well for a quick calm-down. A nice embellishment of this technique is to close your eyes and picture a birthday cake with 10 candles. Count backward from 10 to 1 and as you do, mentally picture yourself blowing out each candle. As each candle is extinguished, feel your stress, anger, and frustration dissipate.

Spiritual Calming

For many people, one of the most effective ways to relieve stress is through quiet reflection or meditation. If this interests you, it's best to take a little time each day—early morning is often most conducive—to develop such a practice.

Studies by Herbert Benson, M.D., associate professor of medicine at the Mind/Body Medical Institute of Harvard Medical School, have found that as little as 20 minutes a day devoted to quietly focusing on a soothing phrase (such as the word "one" or "peace") or a calming image (like waves gently breaking) can lower blood pressure, reduce pain, and lessen the debilitating effects of stress.

If 20 minutes seems too long to begin with, start with 10, or even 5, and work your way up. Don't worry if your mind wanders, as that's perfectly natural. When you notice your thoughts straying, simply refocus on your word or image.

Emotional Calming

Another effective stress-management tool is sharing your anxieties with those who are supportive of you. Johns Hopkins University studies show that social support can have a profound effect on lessening the effects of stress. Sharing your concerns with someone you trust provides the relaxing benefits of social contact and serves to reinforce the feeling that you are not alone in feeling overwhelmed from time to time.

Your Time of the Month

What if you're usually pretty calm, but for a few days or so every month you become incredibly cranky, oversensitive, and insensitive to your man's feelings? You snap at him; you burst into tears when he makes any little comment; and as for sex—forget about it! Then your period starts and, presto, you're fine. If this sounds familiar, you are hardly alone.

According to the American College of Obstetrics and Gynecology, about 85 percent of menstruating women report one or more symptoms of premenstrual syndrome (PMS)—an umbrella term for the physical, psychological, and emotional symptoms that can occur seven to ten days before the menstrual cycle. Emotional and mental symptoms can include irritability, depression, crying spells, loss of libido, low energy, and difficulty concentrating.

Uh-Oh's and No-No's

Doctors suspect that PMS sufferers may experience chocolate cravings because chocolate is fairly rich in magnesium. The problem is that chocolate, laden with sugar, can worsen mood swings. Magnesium naturally occurs in many beans, almonds, greens, and salmon.

He Says/She Says

"I used to feel I was blindsided by my wife's PMS moods, because I never kept track of when to anticipate them—and neither did she. Then she started tracking her time, and now she gives me fair warning. I've learned not to personalize her moods for these few days a month."
—Robert, 35

You might think being susceptible to PMS dooms you to being on a monthly roller coaster until menopause. It's true that there is no magic "cure." However, you can do many things to help control PMS rather than letting it control you:

- Choose a diet low in red meats, fatty and salty foods, and refined sugars.

- Avoid caffeine and alcohol.

- Eat small, frequent meals to avoid a drop in blood sugar.

- Take B complex vitamins as well as calcium and magnesium.

- If you smoke, quit.

- If you still don't exercise, start.

- Look into herbal supplements such as evening primrose oil, which helps maintain a good hormonal balance by providing chemical messengers called prostaglandins.

Don't forget to keep track of when your time of the month is coming up. The calendar can provide a clear indication as to whether irritability is part of premenstrual syndrome. It's also a source of valuable history for your doctor. Besides, just being aware that you are vulnerable to mood swings can make you less volatile.

The Golden Rule of Etiquette

Ultimately what relationship etiquette all boils down to is this: Do unto the man in your life as you would have him do unto you. Be sweet, be thoughtful, and mind your manners.

If you are having any difficulty doing this, just pretend that your man is someone you only recently met. Ironically, we so often think twice about what we dare and dare not do in front of recent acquaintances. Why not extend the same courtesy to your partner?

Will there be times when you slip up? Sure. Nobody's perfect. Because slips are inevitable, it's a good idea to be extra sweet when you can. On days when you are able to put in just a little extra effort, try one—or more—of these special little ways to say, "I love you":

- Bring him coffee in bed.

- Gas up his car—then have it washed.

- Pack him a special lunch for work or have his favorite takeout lunch sent to him.

- Ask for his advice.

- Agree to go camping with him.

- If you usually complain when he plays golf, don't.

- Bring him a cold drink when he's doing yard work.

- Praise anything he cooks to the hilt, no matter how it tastes.

- Stock the fridge with his favorite beer before the big game.

- Make a tape of a TV show he's missing but would love to watch later.

- Tape a love note to his bathroom mirror or his windshield.

- Hide a pair of your sexiest panties in his briefcase or glove compartment.

- Surprise him with a book on his favorite subject—and you read it, too.

- E-mail him a digital photo of yourself wearing a big smile.

- Grab his hand as you walk into a party.

- Put a blanket on him when he falls asleep on the sofa.

Doing such things on a regular basis will create a reservoir of good feeling. It's like creating an etiquette savings account—a safety cushion for those times when one or both of you get a bit preoccupied. If your man is often reassured that you care for him and respect him, he'll reassure you that he feels the same—even on your occasional cranky days.

The Least You Need to Know

- Good manners should be sustained beyond courtship; don't let time and familiarity breed discourtesy.

- Respect your own privacy and his—some things should not be seen or heard, and some questions shouldn't be asked.

- Learning mood management boosts self-esteem—and keeps you from treating your man inappropriately.

- Finding little ways to say "I love you" builds up a wellspring of mutual good feeling and respect.

- When in doubt, just do unto your man as you would have him do unto you.

Part 3

Be a Temptress

Ah, temptation. What will a man do when he's enticed by an irresistible woman? He'll slay dragons and do battle with kings. He'll sail tall ships across stormy seas. He'll even come home from work early once in awhile and stay awake after dinner!

This part of the book offers step-by-step instruction in the subtle, age-old art of seduction. You'll learn why great sex begins in the ultimate sex organ—the mind. You'll learn to create a relaxed, pampering, sexy home environment that says, "Love me, lover." And you'll discover how to top off the mental stimulation of your man with the physical stimulation of sensual touch—and seal it with a kiss.

Chapter 8

Aphrodisiacs and the Mind

In This Chapter

- The most significant sex organ
- Stoking your man's mental desire
- Calming your man's greatest sexual fears
- The myth and magic of aphrodisiacs
- The placebo effect and desire

Many folk stories and fairy tales revolve around magic love potions—substances so powerful they can create instant, intense yearning. If you were in possession of one, would you use it on your man? It could be fun to try. But before you do, know that you already possess everything you need to make your man weak in the knees with desire.

Great Sex Is in the Mind

The brain has sometimes been called the most powerful sex organ. That's because the brain regulates so many of the hormonal responses and other bodily reactions that go into the physical act of sex. But while the brain may be the biggest sex organ, it is the mind—our very consciousness—that is the most significant. We say sex is often "on the mind," but the truth is that sex is *in* the mind. The brain prompts the body to achieve its goals, but those goals are determined by our dreams and desires.

"Desire is the very essence of man," is how philosopher Benedict Spinoza put it. Albert Einstein said, "Feeling and longing are the motivating forces behind all human endeavor." The woman who really wants to delight and captivate her man will heed these words—because desire, longing, and yearning are the seeds from which forests of pleasure can grow.

Tantalizing Terms

An **aphrodisiac** is anything that arouses or intensifies sexual desire and enhances sexual performance. Aphrodisiacs are named for Aphrodite, the Greek goodness of sexual love and beauty.

We've all heard tell of *aphrodisiacs*, but what many of us don't realize is that we do not need to search high and low to find a root, bark, or berry that is a tangible aphrodisiac. Each of us can become the equivalent of a sexual sorceress by harnessing our primal feminine power and instincts.

Yes, we can accrue a good deal of sexual knowledge. We can master many techniques and positions. We can even experiment with some delectable edibles that just might boost lovers' passions. All of these matters will be covered in this guide. But before we do this, let's understand the most essential fundamentals of male desire, for example, a man loves …

- A plan
- The hunt
- To dream
- A lover

These fundamentals constitute not mere sexual knowledge but underlying sexual wisdom.

A Man Loves a Plan

Builders by nature, men have always constructed domiciles from modest huts to skyscrapers. The most enjoyable part is the planning. Men love to think about what goes where and how it will all work when it comes together. The same is true with love and lovemaking. Always make sure that your man has something to look forward to.

A Man Loves the Hunt

Men are also born hunters. They are programmed to chase down what they want. The modern world has relieved men of the need to hunt down prey for dinner, but their mindset is still the same.

When it comes to women, men are very aware of the truth in the adage, "a man chases a woman until she catches him." Nevertheless, they relish their inborn urge to chase. It is a woman's prerogative to assist them in what can be a very exciting game. Even in a long-term committed relationship, the man must be given the feeling that there is a bit of fun to be had in stalking and prowling. Should you allow yourself to be "caught?" Of course. (Once in a while, you can even switch roles and be the huntress.) But, remember: hunters tend to value most the prey that can be a bit elusive.

Teasers & Pleasers

For a fun change of pace, you can turn a man's hunting instinct into an enticing game. Prepare a "treasure hunt" map and a series of clues that lead to a fabulous prize at the end of the quest: you, all soft and sexy and ready for love.

A Man Loves to Dream

All men have dreams. They thrive on visions of the future and how they would like to shape it. Talk to your man about his vision, his passion. Encourage him to shoot for the stars. Nothing will energize him more and keep him more interested in building that future with you.

A Man Loves a Lover

Nothing sparks a man's yearning like simply being in the presence of a woman who loves loving. When your glances, your touches, your words convey the overall impression that you are smoldering, he will continually simmer with desire. What fun it will be for both of you to turn up the heat.

Building His Confidence

A woman who wants to please her man should also be aware of the one thing most likely to snuff out desire—that is, a man's lack of confidence. A man's lack of faith in himself is the consummate anti-aphrodisiac.

We know it's tough to be a guy and that men have many vulnerabilities. When it comes to sex, however, we might just assume they are self-assured and always up for "getting some." The truth is that men have many concerns about their sexual prowess, for example:

◆ Fears about size

◆ Fear about performance

◆ Fear about aging

A pleasing woman will know how to alleviate each.

The Size Fear

It's highly unlikely that you've ever been inside a men's locker room. Me neither. But my sources assure me that one of the main activities that goes on there is men covertly checking out each other's genitals. They're comparing penis sizes, the same as when they were little boys and actually got out rulers to see whose was bigger.

As it turns out, there's always likely to be some guy around with a bigger penis—the same way there's always somebody in the ladies locker room that is going to have bigger, firmer breasts than we do. The result, sadly, is that almost all men feel somewhat concerned that their penises aren't big enough.

In reality, the locker room is a poor venue for comparing male organs. There is a far greater variance is the sizes of nonerect penises than there is in erect ones. The person in the best position to evaluate your man's penis size is you. But a word to the wise: Don't.

Never make a direct remark about the size of your man's member. No comparison, positive or negative, will win you points or curb his doubts. Even if directly asked, don't take the bait. Praise his penis for the pleasure it gives you. Then, prove it.

The Performance Fear

Will I get hard enough? Will I last long enough? What if I don't "get it up" at all? Men often wonder about such things even when their sex life is going swimmingly. If there is a bump in the road such as temporary erectile dysfunction, they can really come unglued.

Virtually every man has difficulty achieving or maintaining an erection at one time or another. Causes for temporary erectile difficulties include medical conditions (high blood pressure, diabetes, recovery from surgery), anxiety or depression, medications, recreational drugs, and over-indulgence in alcohol. But when it comes to impotence, the worst confidence buster is fear of impotence. A vicious cycle can set in if that fear takes over.

If—or rather when—your man experiences a temporary lapse in this area, he will likely be much more worried about it than you will. But your denying or ignoring it won't help. Telling him not to think about it is like telling someone not to think about purple elephants. Purple elephants will be all they can think about after those words are uttered. Let your man know that you under-stand his concern. Talk to him about it with sensitivity. If he wants to discuss possible causes, let him talk and speculate but don't let him get down on himself. If the problem per-sists, encourage him to visit his doctor to see whether there is an underlying condition. (See Chapter 19 for advice on getting your man to go to the doctor.)

> **CAUTION**   **Uh-Oh's and No-No's**
>
> Do not equate a man's temporary impotence with a lack of attractiveness on your part. That's taking an issue of his and making it all about you. Besides, the implication that he has hurt your feelings will make him make even more upset than he already is. Guilt is not an aphrodisiac.

The Aging Fear

Everyone—male and female alike—has a fear of aging. Our culture celebrates youth to such a large extent that it's nearly impossible not to associate growing older with a loss of vitality and personal attractiveness. Men also equate it with a loss of virility. They think that growing older will mean that sooner or later they will be unable to function in bed.

Happily, this is not the case. Even at 60, 70, and 80 years of age, most people can lead active, satisfying sex lives. But citing studies to your man won't assuage his fears. In fact they may just reaffirm the fact that, yes, you agree he is getting old. Instead of quoting statistics, reaffirm how attractive and desirable you find him. Do this not just in words, but also with actions. Nothing can take a man's mind off the fear of not having sex than, well, having some sex. Talk about a confidence builder!

Are There "Real" Aphrodisiacs?

Now it's time to address the question I know is on your minds. Do actual aphrodisiac substances exist, or are they simply myths? After all, a shortcut to desire now and then would be convenient, wouldn't it?

The list of supposed sexual stimulants is long and varied. Such a list can also resemble a recipe for a nice witch's brew. Among the substances said to boost the libido are goat eyes, deer sperm, frog legs, rhinoceros horn, toad skin, and the notorious *Spanish fly*. Assorted spices (like cardamom, cloves, and saffron) and herbs (such as yohimbe, which comes from the bark of West Africa's tree of the same name) are also frequently mentioned.

> **Tantalizing Terms**
>
> **Spanish fly** (cantharides) is a substance made from pulverized emerald-green beetles found in southern Europe. Spanish fly mimics arousal—badly—by irritating the urogenital tract and causing the genitals to burn, itch, and swell. Side effects can include pain, nausea, and vomiting. In some cases, Spanish fly has proved lethal.
>
> The word **ginseng** means "man root," and the plant's reputation as an aphrodisiac probably arises from its marked similarity to the male anatomy. For centuries, ginseng has been looked on as an energizing and rejuvenating agent in China, India, Korea, Indochina, and Tibet. Although there have been some experiments reporting a sexual response in animals treated with ginseng, there is no evidence that it has an impact on human sexuality. For us, ginseng has a mild stimulant action like that of coffee.

According to the Food and Drug Administration, the reputed sexual effects of so-called aphrodisiacs are based only in folklore, not fact. In 1989, the agency declared it found no scientific proof that any over-the-counter aphrodisiacs stimulate sexual function. Furthermore, buyers beware: some of the more exotic substances, such as Spanish fly and Chan Su (a topical drug made from the skin of a Chinese toad) can prove fatal.

So how did all this folklore evolve? In many ways, the myths follow a kind of home-spun logic. Certain animals are known for their prolific procreativity, so parts of those animals were imagined to be love aids. Spicy foods, such as chilies and curries, were probably confused for libido-enhancers because they raised the heart rate and induced sweating. Objects resembling the genitals (like oysters and *ginseng* root) were said to have an impact on the genitals.

Food for Love

Despite what Western science or regulatory agencies have to say, many people have offered up anecdotal evidence that supports the use of certain foods as romance boosters. Although there's no hard evidence to prove they impact the libido *per se*, many of them are quite healthy to eat. Experts agree that what's good for your overall health is probably good for your sex life, too. Being in better physical condition can certainly lead to better sexual performance. So there's no harm—and lots of fun romantic potential—in tempting your man with some of these edibles. Go ahead and experiment of you like!

Garlic

This seems like a food people should avoid if their aim is to get up close and personal. But garlic has a long history of use as a sexual stimulant, and was used as such by Egyptians, Greeks, Romans, Chinese, Japanese, and others around the world for this purpose. As Hippocrates noted, and as modern nutritionists agree, garlic has many healing properties. It also appears to stimulate the taste buds, making the rest of a meal even more appetizing. Bottom line: if you and your man are both garlic fans, go for it. But don't eat garlic solo and then plant a kiss on your beloved, unless you have mouthwash handy.

Onions

Onions are the oldest of the supposed edible aphrodisiacs. Some say their use as love aids dates back to prehistoric times. Certainly onions were used in ancient Hindu kitchens and appeared in Hindu manuals on lovemaking. During the reign of the Pharaohs in Egypt, priests were not allowed to eat onions because it was thought this would derail their vow of celibacy.

More recently, French newlyweds feasted on onion soup during their honeymoon to restore their energy and rekindle desire after an arduous wedding night. In truth, onions are good for adding flavor to many dishes. It's also possible that they have an antibiotic effect. So there's no harm in doing it French style and feasting together on a steaming bowl of onion soup.

Fruity Fun

For centuries the Chinese have claimed that peaches, so cool and delectable and pleasing to the palate, also spur the sex drive. There's no hard evidence, so to speak, but think how suggestive it could be to hand-feed your lover a slice of ripe, juicy peach.

Bananas also have an aphrodisiac reputation, most likely because of their phallic shape. Still, they're high in potassium and thus, good for you. Besides, imagine the desire you can incite by peeling one slowly and sensually, throwing your head back, and taking it in. With edible aphrodisiacs, presentation can be everything!

Voluptuous Veggies

Asparagus and cucumbers are said to be the vegetables that most inspire ardor. Can you guess why? It's the phallic shape again. Asparagus has certain biological after-effects that might not be so pleasing but the stalks are fun to dip in butter and salt and eat with your fingers.

As for cucumbers, they've been shown to stimulate the sense of smell, especially in women. Since scent plays a role in sex, there just might be something to the cuke's reputation. In any case, having multiple servings of veggies a day is one of the healthiest things you can do for your overall diet.

Pine Nuts

Since Roman times, pine nuts have been thought of as sexual stimulants. No proof exists, although there is plenty of proof that these tiny tree seeds are the key ingredient in a great pesto. Toss some into a food processor with olive oil, basil, and parmesan cheese for a lusty but light pasta topping. Then go ahead and carbo load for love.

Truffles

By truffles I don't mean the candy kind, but rather the rare mushroom-like delicacies so prized by haute cuisine chefs. Both Napoleon and the Marquis de Sade consumed them for their amatory powers, but probably it's their rarity that led to their cachet. Truffles are hard to find, and truffle hunters in Italy and France use pigs and dogs to sniff them out. As a result, these morsels are also very expensive. Black truffles can sell for up to $500 a pound.

Should you feed your lover some rare truffles? He might be flattered that you spent so much on his dinner. But if he's concerned about the household budget, a truffle treat could well dampen his amorous enthusiasm.

Caviar

Like truffles, caviar is costly. Perhaps that's why it's reputed to be a turn-on. But whatever the reason, caviar was prized by expert lovers including Casanova, Dostoevsky, and Rasputin. No harm in spreading a little on a cracker and slipping it between your lover's lips—if he cares for fish eggs, that is.

Chocolate

The Aztec people believed that chocolate had aphrodisiac qualities. When it was first introduced to Europe, it was natural that people continued to associate chocolate with love. In fact, this highly popular substance does have measurable affects on human behavior.

Chocolate contains phenylethylamine and serotonin, both of which are mood-lifting agents that occur naturally in the human brain. The release of these chemicals into the nervous system by the brain causes a rapid mood change, a rise in blood pressure, and an increase in heart rate. In short, chocolate can create a substantial temporary energy boost as well as induce feelings of well-being usually associated with being in love or in lust.

But calling chocolate a bona fide aphrodisiac is stretching the facts. Its effects are extremely short-lived. Alas, when they pass, one's mood can swing the other way. In addition, chocolate seems to have a greater physiological impact on women than on men. Feeding chocolates to your man won't necessarily rev him up. But, hey, if he likes chocolate, he'll be pleased that you shared—and that's as good a start as any toward creating a loving mood.

Teasers & Pleasers

In the 1970s a widespread rumor contended that green M&M candies upped the sex drive. M&M/MARS company, which makes the candy, built a successful ad campaign around the theme, "Is it true what they say about the green ones?" Technically, it's not true, but what the heck. Feed your man a handful and see what happens.

Oysters

Aphrodite was born from the sea, and many types of seafood have reputations as sex aids. Oysters are particularly esteemed in this way. Their genitalia-like appearance is part of the reason. So is the fact that they earned their amorous stripes at a time when their contribution of zinc to the nutritionally deficient diets of the day improved overall health and so lead to a more robust sex drive.

The Placebo Effect

Now here's an interesting proposition. Suppose I were to give you a sip of sugar water and tell you it was a very rare and powerful love potion. Do you think it would get you in the mood for loving? What if you were to do the same to your man? Well, chances are it just might do the trick.

Tantalizing Terms

A **placebo** (Latin for "I shall please") is a medication or treatment believed by the administrator of the treatment to be inert or innocuous. In controlled scientific experiments, placebos are often sugar pills or starch pills.

Remember, the mind is incredibly powerful. As a result, when we believe that some substance induces a particular effect, we may experience that effect profoundly, even if that substance is completely inert. This is known as the *placebo* effect.

Researchers and medical doctors sometimes give placebos to patients who've agreed to take part in placebo-controlled studies. In about a third of such experiments, the patients who get pills with no active ingredient, as opposed to actual medication, find their conditions have improved.

The effect of placebos isn't just on attitude but also on the body itself. When dummy pills are given to subjects who are told the pills are stimulants, the subjects' pulse rates and blood pressures rise, and they show improved reaction speeds. When people are told they've been given a sleep-producing drug, their systems slow.

Placebos can also consist of "fake" treatments. In a study of asthmatics, researchers found that they could produce dilation of the airways by simply telling people they were inhaling a bronchiodilator, even when they weren't. Patients suffering pain after wisdom-tooth extraction got just as much relief from a fake application of ultrasound as from a real one, so long as both patient and therapist thought the machine was on.

The exact interplay of psychological and physiological mechanisms that contribute to the placebo effect is still a mystery. But one thing is clear: the mind is suggestible. That suggestibility can influence both biochemistry and behavior.

The fact that expectation is so powerful goes a long way toward helping us understand why some substances seem to inspire desire. If we anticipate that a certain something will make us feel passionate and create an enhanced sexual reaction, and if we want it to, it very likely will. Once again, it all goes back to the mind. Ultimately, the mind itself is the most potent aphrodisiac.

He Says/She Says

"My girlfriend fed me a bunch of tasty foods she'd heard were aphrodisiacs and wanted to know which of them turned me on. The truth was they all turned me on—but I think that was only because the thought of her investigating aphrodisiacs was so hot!"

—Roger, 29

The Least You Need to Know

◆ The ultimate source of all sexual desire and passion is the mind.

◆ A man loves to plan, hunt, and dream of the future; a woman who empowers him to do so sparks his desire.

◆ A man's lack of faith in himself is the biggest anti-aphrodisiac.

◆ Western science says "real" aphrodisiacs don't exist, but there's no harm—and lots of fun—in trying moderate amounts of healthy foods that are rumored to give love a boost.

◆ Anything can be an aphrodisiac if you think it is—that's how powerful the mind can be.

Chapter 9

Nice to Come Home To

In This Chapter

◆ Creating a welcoming home for your man

◆ Reacting emotionally to light and color

◆ Looking lovely in lingerie

◆ Using scintillating scents and music

◆ Good and not-so-good timing

Home is where the heart is, as the saying goes. A man wants to think of his home as a place of respite from the pressures of the outside world, a place to unwind with those who care about and understand him. But if we're not attentive, our home environment can become just as hectic as anyplace else. The choice is ours.

With a little thought and creativity, any woman can turn her home into her man's oasis—and her own. This chapter is about creating a sensual home environment in which love can thrive.

Honey Do's and Honey Don'ts

Imagine your man has had—as he so often does—a long, hard day in the workplace. Now, finally, he's on his way home. He's looking forward to relaxing, to "cocooning" with you, his woman. But when he walks in you greet him with a "honey-do" list—a detailed enumeration of things that are wrong and need to be fixed right away. Aside from telling him what's wrong, you don't say much. You're in the midst of multitasking yourself. Yes, your day at work and at home was busy, as is evident from piles of unmatched socks on the sofa, unpacked grocery bags on the kitchen counter, and stacks of unopened mail. The TV and a CD player are simultaneously blaring; the kids' stuff is everywhere, and the house smells like yesterday's Chinese food—because that's what you're warming up for dinner in the microwave.

Suddenly his place of work might be looking pretty good by comparison. In fact, he's wondering whether he shouldn't head back there and do a little more work after dinner. Or maybe he'll just do what he usually does—eat on a tray in front of the TV and fall asleep.

> **Uh-Oh's and No-No's**
>
> TV is to a romantic environment as a cold shower is to a hot lover. Sure, TV has its place in a guy's life. But at those moments when you want the focus on the two of you, turn off the talking heads and opt for some music or quiet in the background.

Now imagine this scenario: Your man comes home, and you greet him lovingly at the door with a hug and a soft kiss on the lips. Instead of instructing him to get on with his chores, you tell him to put his feet up. He wonders what you mean. After all, there's usually no room to stretch out because of all the household clutter. But tonight is different. He looks around and notices:

◆ A vase of fresh, colorful flowers on the mantel

◆ A clutter-free dining room table set with two full place settings of the "good" china and silverware

◆ Some new throw pillows on the sofa

◆ A warm, comfy blanket draped across the easy chair

◆ The sound of one of his favorite mellow CDs playing

◆ A few scented votive candles flickering

◆ A few newly framed family photos on the shelves

◆ A few interesting, browse-worthy coffee table books actually on the coffee table

◆ You—looking sultry, smelling great, and smiling

In the bedroom, where he's now following your honey-do suggestion to "slip into something more comfortable," more surprises await him. There's one fragrant rose in a bud vase by his bedside. The bedding has been changed, and a set of fresh, luxurious sheets beckons.

Now his workday seems very far away indeed. He knows for certain that there's no place like home. And he knows you are exactly the woman he wants to come home to.

The difference in these two scenarios doesn't depend on anything expensive or extravagant. With a little forethought (and, for you moms, a tradeoff night with the kids dining at your neighbor's house once in a while) it's possible to create a sensual environment that any man would enjoy coming home to. It will also be the kind of environment that brings out the best in you.

Dim All the Lights

Playing with light and accenting with color is one of the easiest ways to create an environment that is conducive to relaxation and romance. You know by this point that men are, first and foremost, visually-oriented. It stands to reason that anything that appeals to their eyes is a surefire shortcut to pleasing them.

The world-at-large is full of glaring lights, neon signs, and drab office-fixture fluorescence. But it's a dimmer glow that we associate with love. Softer lighting creates a sensual ambience for two reasons. First, it impacts mood. When the lights are low, we tend to speak more quietly and move more slowly. We also tend to stay in closer proximity to those around us. These behaviors on our part create a greater sense of intimacy.

The other reason softer lighting contributes to sensuality is that it makes people look more attractive. When you want to inspect your face for imperfections, you look in a brightly lit make-up mirror. But did you ever catch a glimpse of yourself in a mirrored wall at a softly lit elegant restaurant? If you have, you've probably noticed that wrinkles, puffiness, blemishes, and dark spots are magically minimized.

It's certainly not necessary to swap out all the light fixtures in your house in order to achieve ambience with lighting. With a few simple tricks, you can alter your lighting at any time to achieve a desired effect of calm and romance.

- ◆ If you're lucky enough to have a fireplace, there is nothing like it to fill the room with a dramatic centerpiece of light that will draw you and your man to it like moths to a proverbial flame. Consider laying in a supply of DuraFlame logs so you can start a fire quickly and easily before your man comes home. Also, think about converting a wood-burning fireplace to gas, which allows for an instant gratification fire at the flick of a switch.

♦ Candles are a simple, inexpensive way to alter your lighting—and there's no need to overdo it. A few candles can fill almost any room with an ethereal glow. Because they're not costly, feel free to experiment with different shapes, sizes, and even scents.

Teasers & Pleasers

For an instant makeover, replace the white light bulbs in your bedroom lamps with pink bulbs. Your skin will look smooth and rosy.

♦ Almost any light—including overhead chandeliers and track lighting—can be hooked to a rheostat, which instantly regulates the light's intensity with the mere turn of a dial. Rheostats are easy and inexpensive to install. You can find them at most hardware stores.

Aside from feeling better and looking better in dim light, yet another advantage is that we tend to feel less inhibited whenever the lights are low. If tonight's the night you're thinking of trying something new in bed—a new position or technique or toy, for example—use lighting to help make the leap. Keeping the lights dim can certainly help minimize self-consciousness.

Color Him Pleased

Another way to enhance the sensual aspects of our home is to consciously work with color. I say "consciously" because whether or not we realize it, we are unconsciously reacting to color signals in our environment all of the time. Advertisers and marketing gurus understand this principle well, and use our reactions to color to sell us everything from packaged foods to laundry detergents.

But marketing experts didn't invent the idea of using color to instigate behavior. Mother Nature uses color as part of the intricate process of attraction and mating. The tail of a peacock, the brilliant hue of a flower needing pollination—these are but a few examples. To walk through the woods in springtime is to see nature's brilliant palette in action. Why not follow her lead? After we become aware of some of the emotional responses that different colors stir, we can use color to induce feelings of intrigue, excitement, or calm and contentment.

No one is suggesting that you start repainting rooms and reupholstering furniture. It's preferable to work with color in smaller doses, as accents. You can introduce color into your home with pillows, blankets, quilts, small area rugs, and artwork such as paintings or wall hangings. Using these kinds of colorful objects for color enhancement gives you lots of flexibility. You'll be able to play with color schemes according to what kind of mood you want to create.

Robust Reds and Pleasing Pinks

Of all colors in the visible spectrum, red causes the greatest bodily response. Being in red surroundings can raise the heart rate and pulse. This "warm" color can literally make us feel warm. Red always stirs strong emotions. Historically, red is the color most strongly associated with passion. That's why Valentine's hearts are always red.

Opulent shades of red, such as crimson and scarlet, are particularly associated with eroticism, especially by younger men. Interestingly, however, men with a few more years under their belts are more likely to be sexually stimulated by pink—the pastel that results from adding white to red.

Pink, like red, can be a warm and romantic hue. It's also perceived as soft, delicate, pretty, and feminine. Pink is also associated with health and wellness—feeling "in the pink." When pink moves toward a "hot pink" shade it's, well, very hot.

Reds and pinks can both be used for sensual effect. But don't overdo either color in your environment. Too much red can be over-stimulating and exhausting. Too much pink can make your man feel like he's stepped into Barbie's dream house.

Clues About Blues

Blue is a soothing and reassuring color. Use it when you want your man to be relaxed and calm. Use cobalt blue, so rich and vibrant, to stir erotic interest (it's another "arousal" color for older men). Mix blue with white to prompt an association with heavenly delights.

Beware of overdoing blue on large solid surfaces. Although it calms in smaller doses, it can bring us down if we're exposed to large amounts. That's why we sing "the blues."

Royal Purple

Purple combines the power of red with the class and elegance of blue. Perhaps that's why purple is considered grand, luxurious, and royal. In America, purple also used to be associated with older women, but that has changed of late, and purple has become increasingly popular.

Using deep purple in excess can seem artificial. Best to soften it to lavender if you want to spread it around a bit more. In lavender shades, purple seems far more natural—not to mention more sexy and youthful.

Teasers & Pleasers

If you have a room that doesn't get a great deal of light, bring the sunshine in with lemon yellow or coral touches. Flowers are one way to add these colors to a room without a big investment.

Yellow for Your Fellow

Yellow is the most reflective and bright of all the primary colors. In psychological terms, it signals something new and unanticipated. Yellow has so many wonderful associations: sunshine, fresh lemons, and creamy butter. The color is perceived as cheerful, friendly, and—especially when it veers toward gold tones—glowing.

In its very vibrant shades, yellow is a magnificent accent color. It says: here's something new and different. Surprise!

Going with Green

Green has so many shades and tones it can elicit a lot of different responses. Mixed with a hint of yellow, it connotes freshness, optimism, and renewal. Soft sages and moss greens are restful, as is aqua, which is a blue-green tinted with white. Jewel-tone greens, like emerald and malachite, are seen as luxurious and make your environment seem rich and well appointed.

The Good Earth Tones

We think of brown and its various shades and tones as natural and earthy. Brown is for hearth and home, fresh-baked bread, and hand-woven baskets. Veering toward beige, it is the color of bamboo and sand. Mixed with red, it is the color of autumn leaves. What this all boils down to is that browns and beiges are reassuring. Use beiges along with dark brown accents to say, "All is well in our world."

Simple as Black and White

It seems like a no-brainer to say black is associated with eroticism. It is a highly provocative color, perhaps because it is also a color that implies a hint of danger. We women like to wear black for our men because of these associations and also because we believe black tends to make us look slimmer. It's hard to say anything bad about black as an instigator of sensuality, except that it's a little too easy to get into an all-black rut. Yes, men like black (even black sheets are perceived as especially sexy), but they also respond incredibly well to its opposite.

For a wonderful, surprising change of pace, think about white. White can be extremely suggestive and enticing because it connotes innocence and purity. Try a flowing white nightgown if you want your man to feel likes it's your "first time" all over again.

Lovely Lingerie

We can't leave the topic of pleasing visually without addressing what you might choose to wear for a cozy tête-á-tête at home. After all, there's little sense in making your home look more sensual and appealing if your man is going to find you in a torn pair of jeans and an old sweatshirt. I know that somewhere in your closet or dresser drawers you've got lingerie that you've been saving for a special night for who-knows-how-long. It's time to unearth it and see whether it's still something you feel sexy and glamorous in. If so, great. If not, splurge on something that brings out the real woman in you.

- ◆ Choose an ankle-length gown for an elegant, goddess-like look. If you like, pick one with a slit up the side to give your man a little extra provocation.

- ◆ For a more casual look try a chemise, which resembles a short underdress or slip.

Teasers & Pleasers

If you don't know what style of lingerie suits you best, try a fashion show for your man and let him pick. Or maybe he prefers you best in no lingerie at all.

◆ A teddy is the most daring choice in lingerie. Most of these barely-there, one-piece garments feature a high leg cut. Some have thong backs.

◆ Baby dolls—comprised of bra cups and attached loose skirts that fall about the hips—are a bit more modest than teddies, but totally sexy nonetheless.

◆ Pajamas can be very sexy, after you get away from baggy flannels. Try embroidered silks or sheer knits.

He Says/She Says

"I love it when a woman wears sexy lingerie. But I think lots of women don't know one important thing. Stay away from scratchy laces. It makes it tough to get up close and personal."
—Wayne, 31

Whether you choose a style that reveals a little or a lot, the point is to feel comfortable as well as sensual. Choose something in which you feel unafraid to move about. If you feel a little self-conscious, cover up with a matching robe—all the better to peel off as the evening progresses.

Aroma for the Home

We already know that scent, in the form of biologically produced pheromones, plays a role in sexual attraction and behavior. (See Chapter 2 for more on pheromones.) But all scents are really a kind of chemical communication. They send out signals, and we respond on a visceral level, even if we are not thinking about the aroma or consciously noticing it.

In myths and legends from around the world, aromas have been said to appease spirits and to transform earthly beings into magical creatures. Throughout history, there was also said to be a link between perfumed scents and desire. When Circe set out to seduce Ulysses, she used a powerful aromatic potion. When the Queen of Sheba moved to Jerusalem, she tried to win King Solomon's heart with fragrant spices. Even today, in many traditional societies, the process of seduction routinely begins with women's intensive use of aromatic substances, such as coconut milk and floral oils, which are applied externally and even internally.

You can introduce scent into your environment in many ways. Scented candles, room sprays, and incense are some of the simplest. But what scents appeal to men's sensual sides? Individuals may have very particular favorites, and you should certainly ask your partner—but of the many scents available, the following have wide appeal:

◆ Vanilla. The scent of vanilla is said to produce an increase in sexual arousal almost instantaneously.

- Musk. Musk is believed to closely resemble the smell of testosterone, which is itself a pheromone.

- Sandalwood. An extremely calming and earthy scent, sandalwood can relieve tensions that might interfere with romance.

- Myrrh. Myrrh is a dried sap of the Commiphora myrrha tree. Prized since ancient times, it is said to have healing and rejuvenating properties.

With any scent, the rule is to deploy it with subtlety. Overdo any aroma, and it will seem syrupy and overpowering. Go easy on room sprays and burn incense sparingly. If you're using something in a concentrated essential oil form—as is done in aromatherapy—be sure to water it down. As for wearing the listed scents or any others, be aware that your own body chemistry mixes with each and every scent in a unique way. Go easy—begin with a scented shower gel or bath salt—and test your man's reaction.

Sheet Music to His Ears

Finally we come to the sense of hearing, or—to be more precise—the sense of sensual sound. That means music. Choosing the right music can easily get a man in the mood for love.

Each of us is aware of how powerfully music can alter our emotions. Music can make us laugh; it can make us cry. It can make us feel hot and sexy and uninhibited.

Even better, when we're in the midst of loving, music can give us a second wind. It can heighten our senses, make us more imaginative, and increase our stamina and endurance. If you don't believe it, try running on a treadmill without music and then with it. The former approach is dull and draining; the latter is energizing.

Of course which music you pick is of paramount importance. Although it's a personal choice, some definite rules apply.

- Opt for mellow over manic. Fast, frenetic music, like rap and disco, has its place—but that place is not in your house when you're planning a relaxing feast for the senses.

- Keep lyrics loving and uplifting. Forget whiny or vengeful "you left me" lines.

- Have a variety of music on hand, If you play the same few CDs repeatedly, they will just become boring background noise.

- Avoid anything so unusual or experimental that it might jar your lover. Tribal trance music and atonal jazz may be intellectually interesting, but tonight the intellect is not the point.

- Avoid female vocalists who like to "belt" out a song. Their vocal acrobatics may be astounding, but they can also be distracting.

- Make sure there's enough rhythm to provide a little bit of bounce.

Try to stay away from the cliché. A number of recording artists built their reputations on sounding seductive. Barry White, Marvin Gaye, and Michael Bolton come to mind. Although these talented artists have produced great love songs, we've heard them so often that their very familiarity has rendered them spoofs of seduction. Playing them shows a lack of creativity and of subtlety—two important elements in all seductions.

Instead, entice your man with songs you respond to and that you genuinely believe will strike the right chord with him. Still not sure what to try? Many music stores allow you to preview CDs in the store, and you can listen to tunes on the Internet as well. A few artists you may want to sample:

- Billie Holiday

- John Coltrane

- Eric Clapton

- Frank Sinatra

- John Mayall

- Stevie Wonder

- Natalie Cole

- Bonnie Raitt

- k.d. lang

- Michael McDonald

- Sadé

- Enigma

Feel free to add any artists that are guaranteed to give you and your man goose bumps. Then mix and match by playing six CDs or more on a "random" setting. Or create a personalized playlist on an iPod that you then connect to and play through stereo speakers. Finally, keep the volume at a moderate level. Blaring is hard on the ears and diverts attention from the pleasure of the experience.

Tomorrow's Another Day

Take a look at your home with a fresh eye, and you will notice many opportunities to start using some of the ideas in this chapter right now. A good strategy for beginning is to declutter wherever possible, make certain to have candles on hand, install some rheostats, and begin to add little touches of color throughout your environment. This way, when you are ready to plan a special evening, you won't have as much to do.

Besides, it's best to add your seductive alterations gradually. Although some elements of surprise are sexy, a full-out assault on a man's senses from out of the blue can be disconcerting.

Along those lines, when you do plan a really special evening, try to give your guy a little bit of a "heads up" by sending him a sexy e-mail or leaving him an intriguing phone message during the course of the day. Now he'll have the fun of anticipation— and you run less risk that he'll come home too drained or grumpy to respond as you'd hoped.

Last, if he does ever have "one of those days" just when you've planned "one of those nights," don't take his under-reaction as a personal rejection. These things happen every now and then. Offer him a hug and a rain check. As Scarlet O'Hara said, "Tomorrow's another day."

The Least You Need to Know

- The home should provide a temporary respite from the pressures of the outside world.

- You can alter your man's mood with attention to lighting and color choice—not to mention your choice of wardrobe.

- Scent is a powerful agent of seduction.

- Music can soothe—or stir—the savage beast.

- It's wise to give your man a heads up if you're planning a very special night.

10

Sensual Touch

In This Chapter

- ◆ Man and mankind's love of massage
- ◆ What a sensual massage is, and is not
- ◆ Pleasing massage moves
- ◆ A man's secret turn-on zones
- ◆ Massage oils and lotions

The first loving sensation a man experiences when he enters the world is the welcoming embrace of a woman's arms. From that moment forward, he longs to be caressed by an adoring female. If you want to deepen the connection between you and your partner, one of the best ways to do so is to learn to touch him in ways that stimulate and soothe him. This chapter will teach you about deepening your bond through the magic of touch.

The Bliss of Massage

Question: What is one of the most pleasurable experiences men say they would like to have at the end of a long, difficult day?

Answer: A massage.

Yes, a massage. The idea of literally feeling their cares melt away as they are pampered, relaxed, and reinvigorated by a hands-on experience has immense appeal for modern man. In fact, archeological evidence proves that massage was equally valued by men throughout history.

Artifacts found in China and Mongolia show that stone massage was common. Hieroglyphics that date back to 2500 B.C. show Egyptians receiving reflexology, a massage therapy in which key points on the feet or hands are pressed to bring relief to corresponding parts of the body. Romans loved to be lavished with oils during full-body massage. By around 1400 B.C., the Chinese had developed an intricate system of acupressure meant to balance the flow of life energy, which they call *chi*.

Tantalizing Terms

Chi is the name the Chinese have given to the life force, the vital energy that runs throughout the human body along paths known as meridians. Those who believe in the concept of *Chi* say that an imbalance in this energy can lead to fatigue, listlessness, and even illness. Massage is one of the methods the Chinese have long used to balance *chi*.

In the modern Western world, massage entered the mainstream via Sweden. Around the start of the nineteenth century, professor Peter Ling, a Swedish gymnastics instructor who suffered from rheumatism, read a translation of an ancient Chinese text describing massage techniques. He combined the Chinese methodology with his knowledge of physiology and essentially invented what we know as Swedish massage—a fairly vigorous type of massage used for both relaxation and circulation improvement.

Today, there is a tremendous surge of interest in massage in this country. Its well-publicized benefits include stress reduction, relief from injury or chronic pain, and the healing of both body and mind. But the topic of massage can be a little confusing, since there are almost as many kinds of massage as there are pleasure points in the human body. Here are some of the most widely known forms of massage:

- Sports massage is used to help prevent athletic injury, keep the body flexible, and help the body recover from overexertion or injury.

- Orthopedic massage is the most medicinal form of massage. Performed by healthcare professionals, it combines many techniques including stretching, neuromuscular therapy, and structural balancing.

- Deep tissue massage is a general term for different styles of massage—including Rolfing, Trager, and Feldenkrais—that focus on the body's deeper muscles and connective tissues.

- Reiki aligns body energies by placing the hands above various parts of the body known as "chakras" or energy centers, in a particular sequence.

- Shiatsu incorporates acupressure and other techniques to manipulate the body's vital energies and remove energy blocks by stimulating pressure points.

- Thai massage combines yoga, stretching, twisting, acupressure, and deep massage.

- Stone massage (thermotherapy) combines heat, cold, and pressure, in the form of smooth hot and cold stones, which are applied to and removed from various body parts in a sequence.

Still, despite many massage options, and despite the fact that we all relish the *idea* of sinking into a blissful state of repose while being lavishly stroked and rigorously rubbed, many of us—especially men—consider massage a great luxury. It's something a guy might do in a rush if he happens to be lucky enough to have an extra 15 minutes at an airport that features chair massages along its concourse. It's something he might indulge in at the gym, once in a blue moon, if he's feeling especially sore.

But massage doesn't have to be a rare event for your man. And it certainly need not be given by a stranger. That's because there's a type of massage that is slightly different from any of the listed categories—and you can do it yourself.

Staging a Sensual Massage

When you think of the term "sensual massage" you may think that is simply a euphemism for sexual stimulation, but that is not the case. Certainly, sensual experiences can create an erotic mood and might be natural lead-ins to lovemaking—but sensual massage is, first and foremost, given for its own sake. Its purpose is twofold: to lavish your partner with delicious tactile sensations and to bring the two of you closer together.

Sensual massage takes place in an environment that feels private, quiet, cozy, and comfortably lit (in short, the kind of environment you learned to create in Chapter 9). It generally takes place between sexual partners. But sensual massage makes no demands on the person being massaged except that he relax and enjoy. It takes the emphasis off any kind of "performance."

Uh-Oh's and No-No's

Be clear about your expectations. If you're motivated to offer a massage because you definitely want sex, don't fool yourself—or try to fool your man. Communicate your desires beforehand. Be aware. a skillful massage may even make your man fall asleep. Don't be upset if he does. Take it as a compliment.

As lovely as all this may sound in theory, and as much as men long to be touched in this way, it can sometimes be a bit awkward to figure out how to offer your man a sensual massage experience. Men are sometimes uncomfortable about being passive recipients of pleasure. They may feel guilty about not having to do any work, or shy about "letting go." If this is the case with your guy, simply suggest a "back rub." Who can say no to that?

Now that the question of how to begin touching him is solved, you can get your partner loosened up by stroking his shoulders, neck, and back while he's clothed. After a while, you can suggest removing some clothes, lying down, and taking the massage to the next level.

It's Nice to Be Kneaded

If you're a beginner at giving massages, you're no doubt wondering exactly what it is you should be doing. You might feel like you're all thumbs or that you might risk hurting your partner. A good strategy to begin with is to start massaging with long, slow gliding stokes along the entire back side of your man's body. You can alternate these "glides" from featherweight pressure to a heavier touch, and then back again. Now you can expand into some other techniques commonly used by masseurs and masseuses:

◆ Knead your man by gently grasping an area—such as a calf, thigh, or fleshy area over the hip—and working your hands as if you were kneading dough.

- ◆ Cup your hands and, with palms facing downward, gently thump up and down the body.

- ◆ Press areas that feel tight or knotted with the heels of your hands or with your thumbs.

- ◆ Give little finger kisses by touching your partner as if you were playing a fast-paced tune on the piano.

- ◆ Softly glide the palm of one hand over his entire body, barley grazing the skin.

- ◆ Try some rapid, rubbing strokes that warm the skin with friction.

Different nerves respond to different kinds of touch: feather-light, pressure, texture, and so on. Always be responsive to your partner. Ask him what feels good. Be aware of how his body is communicating his likes and dislikes and "not-so-sures" to you. If he's pulling away or tensing up, change what you're doing. If he's groaning with delight, do more of the same.

Over time you will learn what strokes, rhythms, intensities, and special tricks really turn your man to putty in your hands. But remember to keep an open mind. Vary your touch according to mood and keep trying a few new moves now and then to keep things interesting.

His Pleasure Points

You're probably also wondering what parts of your man's body to focus on the most. Of course, any part of the male body can tingle with delight during a sensual massage. Certain pleasure zones—his groin, his nipples, his ears and lips—will react with particular intensity. But what you might not know is that men have many less well-known spots on their bodies that can radiate with pleasurable sensations when touched and teased. If you want to send a chill down—and back up—his spine:

- ◆ Caress his jaw line by gently rubbing your fingers from the bottom of his ears to the tip of his chin.

- ◆ Trace the outline of his lips with the tip of your index finger.

- ◆ Press your thumbs into the neck tendons that stretch from the bottom of his ear to the top of his shoulders.

- ◆ Make gentle circling motions on the nerve-ending rich areolas that surround his nipples.

- Stroke the muscle that begins at the outer edge of his armpit and runs down the side of his body.

- Offer a feathery touch to the tiny hairs above his tailbone and soft pressure with your palm at the base of his spine.

- Spread your palm just above his genital area; then pull your fingers inward, grazing this very sensitive skin ever so lightly with your fingernails.

- Stroke the insides of his thighs with your palms and then lean forward and let your hair fall softly across the same area.

Keep in mind, too, that most individuals have erogenous spots that are unique to them. No matter how unusual you think a turn-on spot may be, if your man says it feels good, stroke it. On the other hand, if he asks you to avoid a spot that you think ought to give him pleasure, back off. He is the expert on what his body is experiencing.

In addition, although there's no harm in a tiny tickle in the course of a sensual massage, a full-out tickle attack will surely break the mood. Tickling can easily go from fun to irritating, and men don't like to feel that out-of-control sense that a tickle victim can experience.

The Notion of Lotion

Using a lotion or oil for your massage adds yet another sensual dimension. Massage oils and lotions reduce friction, keeping the body silky, slippery, and slick. These substances make it easier for the stoker to stroke and for the recipient to languish in the experience. Many of them also smell wonderful.

Keep in mind, however, that men are not as familiar or comfortable as women with the notion of lotion applied to their entire body. Where we get out of the shower and typically apply a full-body moisturizer, they generally get out of the shower, towel off, and jump into their boxer shorts. Be respectful of any reluctance on your partner's part. Rub a little bit of whatever you'll be using on the back of his hand to get him used to the texture and scent. Hold and rub the lotion in your hands first to warm it. Never pour the oil directly on your man's body—it feels cold and creepy. After your man gets comfortable with the oil or lotion, feel free to rub the substance into his back, arms, legs, buttocks, chest, shoulders, and neck. Use the palm-warming technique each time you apply more.

For an even warmer experience, you can try specially formulated warming oils that will slowly heat as your massage progresses. Although not the best option for full-body massages, warming oils are great for massaging small, concentrated areas, such as breasts, buttocks, thighs, arms, and—here's a favorite—the insides of the knees.

When choosing an oil or lotion, it's best to use one specifically developed for massage. It will leave less of a sticky residue than, for example, a hand lotion. Also keep in mind that lighter is better. A lighter substance will be easier to work with. In addition, its subtle scent will be more pleasant than a heavy, overwhelming aroma. With scent, it is quite possible to have too much of a good thing.

Another thing to keep in mind about massage oils is that many of them create stains that are difficult to remove. Either use sheets you're willing to get rid of, or buy a special sheet to put on your bed, floor, or whatever surface you are using for your massage.

> **Teasers & Pleasers**
>
> Here's a recipe to make your own minty fresh massage oil. Mix together 10 tsp. grape seed oil, 3 drops eucalyptus oil, 4 drops rosemary oil, and 2 drops peppermint oil. Mint is a natural scent that men respond to very positively. Blend ingredients well, pour into a small bottle, and seal thoroughly.

Another option is to visit a fabric store and buy a large swath of fabric in a soothing color (see Chapter 9 on color signals). Be sure it's made of silk, pure cotton, or other natural material that will feel good against the skin.

A nice aspect of having a dedicated sheet or fabric swath is that whenever your man sees it, it will call up an association of pleasure. He will know that it's time to enjoy a sensual massage.

Seal It with a Kiss

Another important kind of sensual touch—one too often underutilized—is the kiss. Women who are married or who are in long-term relationships often complain that their men simply don't kiss them enough. Sure, they may exchange a kiss with their partners once a day or so, without much thinking about it. But there's a general feeling that kissing has lost its special quality.

At its finest a kiss is an intimate bridge to another soul. It is a mingling of the breath and the heart. Traditionally, a marriage is sealed with a kiss to symbolize the unity of a couple. In fact, it seems we are pre-wired for kissing. Our brains are said to have special neurons that help us locate each other's lips in the dark. (Try it and see!)

The first time you and your man kissed, you probably felt a tingle throughout your bodies and a flip-flopping feeling in your stomachs. Even your pulses sped up. Should every kiss be on that level? Well, no. You wouldn't get much done if your good-bye kiss each morning was such a heart-stopper. Nevertheless, some expert kissing interludes now and again can truly rekindle a couple's sparks. And the best way to get kissed more—and to get kissed better—is to start kissing more, and to pay attention to how you do so.

Artful Kissing

Sure, a kiss might seem like a simple thing—the simplest way, in fact, to express love and affection. But like many activities that appear innately simple, kissing can be an art form in itself. The best way to master the many subtle elements of a truly artful kiss is to break it down.

- ◆ The eyes. It's a personal preference whether you kiss with the eyes open or shut, but always look your partner lovingly in the eyes before and after.

- ◆ The lips. Part the lips ever so slightly as you approach your "target." Lips should never be tensely locked or dangling ajar. Kiss with a light but firm pressure combined with a delightful sense of yielding.

- ◆ The tongue. The tongue is a flexible muscle capable of many kinds of movement. Vary those movements throughout the course of a kiss. You can graze your tongue teasingly across your partner's lips to start. Then slowly begin to caress his tongue with your own. The tongue can roll, lick, flick, and encircle. Don't be afraid to explore. But never try to thrust your tongue so far into your lover's mouth that he feels like he's about to get dental x-rays.

- ◆ Saliva. An artful kiss should be moist, but not so wet as to remind us of those slobbery middle school kisses when we had to wipe our chins afterward. It's possible to unobtrusively swallow as you kiss. Try to swallow after each breath.

- ◆ The head. Don't be a statue. Let your head swivel slowly and naturally from side to side as you kiss. If your head's movements and your partner's don't seem to be in tune, try running your fingers through his hair and softly massaging his scalp so you can subtly adjust his movements.

- ◆ The embrace. Never forget the importance of the kiss's complementary caress. Nothing feels more comforting than being in the arms of the one you love. Kisses and hugs go together naturally, of course. Hugs are embellished when you run your hands up and down your partner's back or move the hands in circular motion along his spine. No need to stop there, either. Run your fingers through your man's hair, caress his face, rub his shoulders, and pull him close to you.

- Rhythm and pace. Kisses can be fast and furious, long and lingering, delicate and tender, quick and playful. In many cases, kisses start with a slow, languid tempo that gathers speed and intensity as they turn more passionate. Varying the rhythm of your kisses is a wonderful way to give kissing your man some new dimensions. Explore changing the tempo and speed of your kissing as you go along. Segue from intense, passionate kisses back to lighter, teasing ones. Try kissing *around* his lips for a little while and then returning to his mouth. Your man will be surprised and excited and intrigued as you move from a boil to a simmer and then back again.

If you're unsure about your kissing technique, revisit the advice your girlfriends probably gave you in adolescence. Practice on your hand! You'll only feel silly for a moment—I promise. Soon you'll be convinced that this simple self-assessment method really works.

Specialty Kisses

With all art forms, after you've mastered the basics it's possible to adopt more intricate methods and maneuvers. Kissing is no exception. For a really pleasing pucker, experiment with some of these specialty kisses:

- Key Lime Kiss: Suck on a lime or lemon before kissing to add some citrus-y zing.

- Soda Straw Kiss: For a quick and sexy sensation, gently but suddenly suck the air from your partner's mouth

- Ice Queen Kiss: Give your guy chills—literally—by putting an ice cube or some crushed ice in your mouth right before you smooch.

◆ Hands-Off Kiss: For a pleasing tease, deliberately refrain from making any contact except pure lip-to-lip.

◆ Anti-Gravity Kiss: Smooch him Spiderman style. You don't have to hang upside-down; just find a way to approach him from an angle that aligns your top lip with his bottom one and his bottom lip with your top one.

◆ I.O.U. Kiss: Give your man a quick but "I mean business" kind of smooch when you know you or he has to go somewhere soon. It will leave him with that stoked-up "I can't wait to get home" feeling.

Teasers & Pleasers

Do the math! The average person will spend about 20,160 minutes kissing in a lifetime. In addition, kissing for one minute can burn 26 calories.

Finally, keep in mind that some of the most thrilling kisses are kisses that are unanticipated. The next time you're just sitting around watching TV or walking around at the mall, try reaching out for your guy and planting a hot one right on his kisser. You'll both be amazed at how satisfying and stimulating a surprise kiss can be.

The Least You Need to Know

◆ Sensual massage can be an end unto itself, or lead to even more intimate things.

◆ Some men are shy about accepting massage pleasure, but most can be easily convinced.

◆ Be open to exploring little known pleasure zones that can set a man to tingling with delight.

◆ Massage oils and lotions can make a great experience even better.

◆ Kissing can recapture the chemistry in a relationship, reminding you of why you both got together in the first place.

Part 4

Be a Spice Girl

One surefire way to please a man in bed is to add variety to what goes on there—and not by buying new sheets. Revitalizing your lovemaking will give your man more energy and more self-confidence—not to mention heightening his interest in becoming a better lover himself.

This section of the book will help you to expand your lovemaking repertoire by adding some new activities and tweaking familiar ones with a few interesting twists.

Chapter 11

Taking a Position

In This Chapter

- The position rut
- Pleasing positions
- About anal sex
- The joys of Tantric sex
- Exercises for sexual fitness
- Enhancing pleasure with lubricants

Do you have a favorite position for sleeping? Of course you do. That's a habit you're not likely to break. What about a favorite position for passion? It's great if you and your man have a tried and true method for lovemaking that you both thoroughly enjoy. But guess what? This is one habit you should try to make a bit less habitual. Experimenting with some new positions will please your man by adding new sizzle to your sex life. This chapter tells you how.

Variety Is the Spice of Life

I'm sure that if you've ever looked at any book on the topic of lovemaking you've come across the topic of positions for intercourse. Sometimes this topic can be very daunting and intimidating. So right off the bat, let me say that there's nothing wrong with you or your love life just because you and your partner might not have tried a hundred different positions for sex, let alone twisted yourself into pretzels trying to achieve some of the more exotic variations.

Many couples experiment with different positions at the beginning of their relationship, but then settle into one or two favorites that reliably bring each partner satisfaction. They either alternate them during different lovemaking sessions or segue from one to the other during a single session. These positions become a kind of default setting for love. If you and your partner fit this pattern, it's quite possible that your man has never complained about it. After all, men love it when their women invite them into their bodies under just about any circumstances. The act of entering and penetrating the woman they love is, in and of itself, incredibly pleasurable both physically and emotionally. But think of it this way. The act of eating a nice dinner is also pleasurable, but doesn't your man enjoy it when you serve up a wonderful new dish now and then and start to incorporate it into your dining repertoire?

Embellishing your bedroom repertoire with some new positions is like adding delectable icing to a cake. It can rekindle a kind of enthusiasm you may have forgotten was possible. Don't believe it? There's even scientific proof. In a research experiment, a group of male and female college students were shown the same sexually explicit video once a day for four days. Most of them showed diminished excitement by the third day. By the fourth day, some of them were bored. On the fifth day, the researchers showed a new video with the same actors but a new sexual position. Viewer arousal rocketed to nearly the same level as the first day.

Teasers & Pleasers

If your man is into history, plan a nice break from the History Channel. You and he can investigate some ancient sex guides that precede even *The Kama Sutra*. The Chinese had sex manuals 500 years before the Hindu classic appeared. The Greeks had Ovid's *Ars Amatoria*, a handbook for courtesans.

Now, don't get nervous. I'm not suggesting that every woman reading this book make it her goal to become a sexual contortionist. If really exotic positions are of interest to you, you can certainly explore some texts like *The Kama Sutra*. In Hindu, the word kama refers to sexual pleasure, which the ancients believed was one of life's three main purposes (the others are spiritual piety and worldly success). Sutra means a text. Kamasutra literally means "treatise on sexual pleasure." This guidebook to leading an eroticized life is best known for its detailed cataloguing of sexual positions—some of which look as if they might require even a yoga master to make several trips to the chiropractor after the loving is over.

In all seriousness, *The Kama Sutra* is a wonderful resource. It's inspirational to view the incredible diversity of sexual positions. Besides, the book is also notably concerned with the pleasure of both women and men, and that, of course, makes it a win/win for you. But those of you who want to start a little more gradually and stay a bit more mainstream, fear not. Plenty of positions are possible for people with virtually every level of flexibility, strength, and stamina. To start, set a modest goal of adding one or two new positions to your tried and true ones. You'll find that each new position brings with it new sensations and affords you new ways of expressing your love. Sharing a few new positioning pleasures with your man may encourage you to try even one or two more. And then, who knows?

Before we move on to some actual positions, I'll tell you a secret. Although virtually hundreds of positions have been drawn, photographed, and written about, they are all variations on a few basic themes: man on top, woman on top, man entering from behind, side-by-side, standing, and sitting or kneeling.

> **Teasers & Pleasers**
>
> Talk about input! *Men's Health* magazine runs a website called PositionMaster that suggests positions based on five different variables that users select. The variables include flexibility, rigor, and ejaculatory control.

Man on Top

Also known as the missionary position, this is the most common position for lovemaking. The missionary position allegedly got its name from Christian missionaries in the South Pacific and Africa. The missionaries maintained that based on their interpretation of Genesis, in which man is said to be the superior gender, this was the ordained way to make love.

Neither its prevalence nor its historical context makes the missionary position dull or unsatisfying. Men like it because it puts them in control in terms of how deeply and how quickly they thrust. Many women and men also consider it the most romantic position because it allows lovers to gaze at one another's faces and easily lends itself to kissing and hugging before, during, and after intercourse.

You might think you know all there is to know about this position: The woman lies on her back, and the man mounts her. You might also think this is the one in which the man does all the work. But hold on a second. You can actively do many things to increase your man's pleasure, and your own, while doing it missionary style:

- Maneuver your hands between his legs and stroke or tenderly squeeze his testicles as he thrusts.

- Massage or insert your finger into his anus (considered a favorite move by many men).

- Wrap your legs around his hips, increasing your pelvic tilt.

- Place your knees on his shoulders to increase penetration.

You can also try any number of variations on the missionary theme. The man-on-top position allows for lots of creativity. Feel free to improvise, or try these known pleasers:

- The Squeezer Pleaser. While in the missionary position, drape your legs over your partner's shoulders. Then bring them down toward your breasts. Now cross your calves. This compresses the lips of your vagina, which increases the sensation of friction for both of you.

- The Crisscross. Place your knees on your man's shoulders, cross your ankles, and place your feet on your partner's chest. This is said to stimulate the loving energy in his heart. It also stimulates your G-spot because it allows the penis to put pressure on the inner, upper wall of the vagina.

- The Pearl Necklace. Sandwich his penis in between your breasts; then lift the breasts upward and toward each other. Now you've created a tunnel similar to that of the vagina. Your partner can climax by thrusting between your breasts, and you can then see how this technique got its name.

CAUTION

Uh-Oh's and No-No's

Women whose partners have large penises sometimes avoid the man-on-top position for fear penetration will be too deep. You can control this by lying with your legs flat against the bed. By the way, the average size of an erect member is 5¾ inches. The largest erect penis reported is 14 inches. In general, more than 7 inches is considered large.

Woman-on-Top

In the woman-on-top position, the woman straddles the man and either lies or sits astride him. In this position, the woman does the thrusting. Yes, it is more work for the woman, which is an aspect of this position that many a man enjoys. Now he can lie back and enjoy as well as be pleased by a wonderful view of his partner in all her naked glory. Remember, a man is a visual creature. As such he truly appreciates the sight of his lover with her breasts bouncing up and down and her hair cascading over her face as she moves up and down.

Some women feel self-conscious in the woman-on-top position. This is usually true if they are insecure about the look of their body. But, trust me, men are hardly apt to be critical of your shape in a situation like this. In fact, playing with the woman-on-top position can be a way for a woman to become more secure about her body.

> **He Says/She Says**
>
> "My fiancé told me he loves it when I'm on top because he can see how much I am enjoying myself during sex. He says that's the ultimate turn-on for him."
> —Susan, 30

Some women also resist this position because they assume their man will resent them taking more control of intercourse and being the "dominant" one. Yet, many men find this an extremely exciting proposition. If you've never tried being on top, you might also discover that having more control over the angle and depth of penetration makes it easier for you to have an orgasm.

There are a number of things you can do to increase pleasure in the woman-on-top mode:

- ◆ Encourage your lover to caress, lick, pinch, or suck your breasts, which are within easy reach of his hands and mouth.

- ◆ Have him stimulate your clitoris manually, or do so yourself while he watches and enjoys.

- ◆ Kiss or softly pinch your man's nipples.

- ◆ Lean slightly backwards, reach behind you, and stroke his testicles.

As with all of the position categories, woman-on-top allows for many spicy variations. Try squatting over your man for even deeper penetration. Try facing backward to alter the angle of penetration.

The man-from-behind position is commonly known as doing it **doggie style** because rear entry is how dogs mate—as do most mammals. Some people don't like this terminology because of its animalistic connotations. But that's just what others love about the term. The idea of being "an animal" during sex can be quite stimulating.

Man Entering from Behind

In this position, also known as *doggie style*, the woman supports herself on her hands and knees while the man enters her vagina from behind. For variation, the woman might support herself on her elbows, or even lie completely flat.

Many couples swear that doing it doggie style makes for some of their most erotically charged lovemaking. Some women say they adore the feeling of being "taken" this way, and their men love to do the taking. Men are also visually stimulated in this position by the sight of their partner's rear end. An added feature of this style of lovemaking is that penetration can be very deep.

It's true that the rear-entry position does not allow for eye contact. But there's an easy solution for this: Try doing it doggie style in front of a mirror. Among the other things you can do to vary and enhance this position:

◆ Have your man stimulate you with his hands as he penetrates you.

◆ Reach around and fondle his testicles.

◆ Let him fondle your breasts from underneath.

◆ Start out doggie style, then push your rear back so he is sitting on his heels as you rock to and fro.

Side-by-Side

A lot of couples might not have experienced the joys of sex side-by-side. Side-by-side positioning can make for gentle, slow, relaxing sex, because in this position, the man can typically thrust for a long time before reaching an orgasm. If you and your man ever enjoy snuggling in the "spoons' position while you doze off, you don't have far to go before turning this into a lovely lovemaking session. Afterward, you can drift off in one another's embrace.

In side-by-side sex, both partners lie on their sides with their legs apart. If they like, one partner's leg can rest over the other. If the woman lifts her knees up a bit, she may find it allows for easier penetration.

To enhance side-by-side sex, try these embellishments:

◆ Have him caress your breasts as he thrusts.

◆ Let him stroke your clitoris while he is inside you.

◆ Draw your knees all the way up into the fetal position for greater tightness.

◆ Lay side by side facing toward him and wrap your legs around him.

One popular variation on side-by-side sex is the scissors position. The woman lies on her back and the man lies beside her on his side. She raises her leg and he passes his leg between hers making a scissors affect with his legs and entering her from the side. Both partners can move around freely without tiring. Couples that like making love when they first awaken say this is an excellent morning position.

Standing

Why stand when you can take a load off your feet, your man might want to know? The answer, say lovers who like to do it in a vertical position, is that having sex standing up seems erotic, urgent, and somewhat risky. Risky because it's the kind of thing you can do—or fantasize about doing—in an elevator or a closet.

Because it's a position that can be achieved without the removal of much clothing, standing is also considered the ideal way to have a quickie. If quickies themselves are not in your repertoire, think about sprinkling a few in among your longer lovemaking sessions. Men usually love that "gotta have you now" dynamic that underscores fast, spontaneous sex.

One caveat, however: standing sex requires some degree of balance and flexibility. Usually one partner is shorter than the other, but both have to find a way to align themselves for intercourse. What often works best is for the woman to wrap her legs around the man's waist. Unless the man is particularly strong, it helps to have the woman supported by a wall behind her.

You can spice up a standing position with these techniques:

◆ Wear really high heels so that you can align your genitals with your man's while you both keep your feet on the floor.

- Keep as much clothing as possible on and suggest your man do the same.

- Try merging a standing position with rear entry—you stand on tiptoes and he bends his knees to achieve a good angle.

Standing is one of those positions that you most likely won't use a majority of the time. That's what so much fun about it. It's a great way to add variety to your love-making.

> **CAUTION**
>
> **Uh-Oh's and No-No's** _____
>
> Ever consider having sex on the stairs? Don't take it lying down (like you've seen in *The Thomas Crown Affair* and *Risky Business*). Ouch. Instead, stand one step above your man then place the leg nearest the railing over it. Put the hand nearest the railing just above that leg and use your other hand to hold onto your man's shoulder for balance. He can hold on to the railing with one hand and put his other hand on your hip.

Sitting or Kneeling

Sitting and kneeling positions also allow for a break in your lovemaking routine. These positions can enhance a woman's tightness and provide a sharper angle for entry. They also allow for good eye contact and kissing, although they don't allow for a lot of movement by either partner.

Try these variations:

- Straddle your man, facing toward him or away, while you are seated in his lap.

- Have your man kneel between your legs and enter you.

- Initiate a quickie in a nice, comfortable, easy chair.

Another nice thing about sitting or kneeling positions is that they are easy to transition into from other positions. For example, if you are in the woman-on-top position, you can just pull your legs forward and your man can sit up. If you are in the man-on-top position, he can do likewise.

Knocking at Your Back Door

Now we come to what some of you might consider a sore subject: anal sex. Although anal sex is enjoyed by many heterosexual couples, some people—especially some women—find the idea repugnant. On the other hand, you would be surprised how many men may be intrigued by the concept, even if they have never expressed it aloud.

Men who have tried anal penetration contend that the anus provides a very tight fit. A good amount of pressure is applied to their penis by the anal muscles. Many also admit to enjoying the psychological rush that comes from entering "the forbidden land."

As for women, you might be surprised how many have tried this style of lovemaking. According to the Kinsey Institute, 43 percent of married women have done so. Of those, about 40 percent say they found the experience a positive one. In fact, a woman's anus contains many nerve endings that, when stimulated, can generate many pleasurable sensations.

If your man wants to try anal sex and you are agreeable, start very slowly. Your sphincter muscle, the muscle at the entry of the anus, will need to be relaxed to prevent discomfort. Your partner can start to explore this part of your anatomy with a finger, with his tongue, or with a vibrator or dildo. (See Chapter 14 for more on sex toys and their uses.) If gentle thrusting of a finger or two fingers feels good, you might be ready to try intercourse. Always use plenty of lubricant on the penis as well as the anus.

If it turns out this style of lovemaking is not for you, so be it. There are so many delicious ways to make love, you needn't feel that any one of them is the be-all and end-all. No form of lovemaking will ultimately be pleasurable unless both parties are enjoying it.

> **CAUTION**
>
> **Uh-Oh's and No-No's**
>
> If your man is going to penetrate you anally, keep good hygiene in mind. Have him wear a condom or wash off his penis before reentering the vagina.

Tantric Tantalizing

A wonderful way to continue to explore the pleasures of lovemaking is to learn a bit about what is called the Tantra. Rooted in Eastern spiritual philosophy, Tantra, derived from a Sanskrit word meaning "woven together" incorporates many practices aimed at making lovers feel more connected to one another and also connected to a higher plane of consciousness through sexuality.

One of the key principles of Tantra is that the journey takes precedence over the destination. Lovers who adapt Tantric lovemaking techniques may devote hours to a sexual interlude, while delaying climax as long as possible. When orgasm does occur, it is said to be a transcendent, rapturous experience. Often it can even be a *full body orgasm* (FBO).

Tantalizing Terms

A full body orgasm (FBO) is the sensation that every part of your body—not just your genital area—is vibrating when you climax. FBOs are said to be attainable by a path that includes prolonging foreplay, controlling the breath, and becoming more aware of your partner's energy and of all your bodily sensations.

Aside from leading to more intense orgasms, a foray into Tantric sex can improve your love life by helping you to really take advantage of all the physical and emotional pleasures of lovemaking by remaining focused on the moment. No more of your mind wandering off to work and household chores smack in the midst of sex! Importantly, Tantra also helps lovers deepen their respect for, and even awe of, one another.

As for sexual positions, the Tantra contains a myriad of them. So many, in fact, that if you are interested, you should consider picking up one of the many books devoted solely to Tantra, which are readily available in bookstores and New Age shops. Some positions, you'll find, require a good degree of flexibility, but many are achievable by "amateurs." The goal of Tantric positions is not to put lovers in traction, but to enhance intimacy. Thus, many of the positions allow for eye contact and full-body closeness. In the Lotus position, for example, the woman wraps her legs round her partner's waist as both partners sit facing one another.

Possibly your man has never heard of Tantric sex. Perhaps he's not especially likely to be receptive to anything based on Eastern spiritual thought. But that doesn't mean you should rule out exploring this avenue to pleasure and then incorporating some of its knowledge with your own. It's up to you whether or not you want to share details about where you're finding such wonderful inspiration. A simple, "Oh, I read it somewhere" might suffice. He'll probably be too ecstatic to press for specifics.

Teasers & Pleasers

A Tantric technique said to intensify orgasm involves a kind of cresting and falling foreplay known as "riding the wave." First, the man inserts his penis in the vagina and rests it there. He then withdraws it and uses it to massage the clitoris and vaginal opening before sliding back in. The cycle is repeated several times, with both parties feeling as though they are a hair's breadth away from orgasm. When climax does occur, it's especially intense.

Sexercises

One way to shore up your foray into sexual variety is to get in better shape for sex. That's right, I'm talking about exercise again. Sex is a physical act, and you will feel more open to trying new things when you are secure in your body's capabilities. Several sexercises can make your sex life better and better and your man happier and happier.

Come On and Kegel

Quite possibly you've heard of Kegel exercises. Perhaps your gynecologist or obstetrician has encouraged you to do them. But have you? It's never too late to start.

Kegel exercises tone the PC (pubococcygeal) muscles, which run from the back to the front of the pubic bone and encircle the vaginal area. By learning to tighten and release these muscles, you will make your vagina tighter.

The best way to locate your PC muscles is to sit on the toilet with your legs wide apart and urinate. Consciously stop the flow of urine in midstream. The muscles you use to do that are your PCs.

After you know where they are, you can give the PC muscles a workout at any time. Simply tighten and release them—at least 50 times a day. After you become adept at this, you can vary the exercise holding each tightening stance for a longer period, or by tightening and releasing in small, slow increments.

You can flex your Kegels anytime, anywhere. No one will see you doing this very private exercise. Your partner, however, will definitely know something is different.

Put More Elvis in Your Pelvis

Moving your pelvis while you make love allows for increased contact and friction, heightening pleasurable sensations for you both. To tone the pelvic area, lie on your back with your arms stretched out to your sides, knees bent, feet shoulder width apart, and heels on the floor. With your shoulders back, squeeze your buttocks, raising your pelvis but keeping your lower back on the floor. Hold for one count, then lower. Do 25 to 30 repetitions once every day.

Now practice rotating your pelvis. Stand with your feet apart, knees slightly tucked. Slowly tilt your pelvis forward. Then shift it to the right, putting most of your weight on the right foot. Then shift your weight to the back, lifting your behind. Then rotate left with most of the weight on your left foot. Do 25 to 30 repetitions once every day.

> **Teasers & Pleasers**
>
> Belly dancing is a very enjoyable way to give your pelvis a workout. Classes in the art are easy to find and might even be at your local YWCA or community college. They're great fun and have the added benefit of teaching you to move in a seductive, serpentine way.

No More Absent Abs

Toning your abdominal muscles will strengthen both your back and your pelvis. Ab work will give you more stamina for sex. A tighter tummy may also help you feel better about your appearance.

Many exercises will tone and flatten your tummy, but it's hard to think of any that beat basic crunches. Crunches can be divided into upper tummy and lower tummy crunches. For the upper, lie flat on the floor and bend your knees. Place your hands behind your head and lift your upper torso facing upward and then lower yourself. For the lower tummy, do the reverse crunch. Raise your legs slowly and lower them. Repeat each crunch for 3 or 4 cycles of 20. Do these cycles daily.

The entire routine should take only about 10 minutes. You will be surprised how quickly you will see results if you stick with it. Within no time, you'll have an enviable, well-toned stomach.

Better Quads for Better Bods

Quadriceps are the exterior muscles in the front of the thighs. They are called "quads," because they are divided into four parts. Strengthening your quads will enable you to try new positions, especially some of the more intricate woman-on-top ones.

Ballet pliés, which you may well recall from a childhood dance class, are wonderful quad builders. Stand beside a waist-high chair and hold onto it with one hand. Stand with your feet a bit more than shoulder-width apart. Point your toes outward toward the walls. With your back and head straight, bend from the knees as far as you can without compromising your straight back. Hold for a few seconds. Repeat 20 to 25 times daily.

A Tube of Lube

Want to know a slippery secret about making sex more pleasurable for your man and for you? In a word, lubricants. You might think you don't "need" a lubricant if you don't have a problem with vaginal dryness. The truth, however, is that lubricants can benefit everyone. Lubricants enhance the ease of penetration. They also help promote longer sexual encounters by eliminating soreness.

If you've never tried a lubricant, you're not alone. Sex surveys show that relatively few lovers lube up. They may feel it's "unnatural" or "messy." But those who use lubricants swear by them. Even if you self-lubricate very well, I promise you that if you begin using a commercial lubricant, your man will thank you.

He Says/She Says

"At my bridal shower, one of my girlfriends gave me a basket of sex aids. In it was a popular strawberry-scented lubricant. I brought it on my honeymoon as a kind of a lark, but my husband and I were both amazed at how much it added to our sex life. It was a real revelation. Now he tells me, 'Don't leave home without it.'"
—Sandy, 23

Some tips for using and enjoying lubricants:

◆ Put it where it counts. The best places to use a lube are on anything that will be inserted or penetrated, as well as any area that will be ribbed or stroked.

◆ Choose a lube that doesn't remind you of your gynecologist's office. Many women have a negative association with the kind of lubricant jelly applied to speculums in gynecological exams. Let's face it: internal exams are not sensually pleasant experiences. Stay away form anything that smells medicinal.

◆ Incorporate lube application into your foreplay. Some lovers view lubes as an interruption. Yes, it takes a moment to squeeze some lubricant onto your hand and then apply it, but you and your partner can do this to one another, or your man can watch with anticipation as you apply lube to yourself. When you reach for the lube tube, he knows something very pleasurable is about to take place. That should get him even hotter.

♦ Try a tasting session. Lubes can work very well for oral sex, but many people think they taste bad. To the contrary, a delightful range of flavored lubricants are available, including cherry, strawberry, vanilla, piña colada, mint, banana, peach, bubblegum, chocolate raspberry, caramel cream, and—of course— passion fruit.

CAUTION

Uh-Oh's and No-No's

When shopping for a lubricant, always read the entire label. An oil lube will break down the latex in condoms; water-based lubes won't. A spermicidal ingredient called Nonoxynol-9 can be irritating to both men and women with skin sensitivities. It also tastes bad and numbs the mouth, so it's a poor choice for oral sex.

♦ Don't go overboard. If you apply too much lube, you will know it, because your sensations will diminish. This is easy enough to remedy, however, especially with a water-based lube. Just wipe some off with a towel or some tissues.

Don't feel for a moment that by using a lube you are doing anything to undermine Mother Nature. Yes, it's wonderful that she thought up self-lubrication. But added lubricants are just as natural as any other lovemaking enhancer: seductive lingerie, mood music, dim lighting, or a steamy video. (By the way, you'll find more about such videos in Chapter 14.)

The Least You Need to Know

♦ Varying sexual positions will increase your man's arousal.

♦ You don't need to be a yoga master or gymnast to try new lovemaking positions.

♦ All sexual positions, no matter how esoteric, fall into one of six simple categories: man-on-top, woman-on-top, man-from-behind, side-by-side, standing, and sitting/kneeling.

♦ Anal sex might be unappealing to some, but many heterosexual couples enjoy it.

♦ Tantric sex is about intimacy and connection as well as techniques that lead to intense orgasms.

♦ You don't need to have a "problem" to use a lubricant; lubes enhance the pleasure of any sexual encounter.

Chapter 12

Blow Him Away

In This Chapter

- ◆ What men love about oral sex
- ◆ Raising the subject of oral sex
- ◆ Great reasons to please your man orally
- ◆ Getting beyond your reservations
- ◆ Basic techniques and positions
- ◆ Oral tricks to rock his world

If this book were to contain only one chapter on pleasing a man sexually, there's an excellent chance this might be it. Men absolutely adore receiving oral sex and appreciate a woman who can perform it skillfully and enthusiastically.

Many women don't feel confident about their own expertise in this area. Small wonder. After all, it's not the sort of thing you take a course in or learn from your mom or grandma. Very often, women say that oral sex is something they would like to get better at. It's a sure bet that your man would be grateful if you took this opportunity for self-improvement.

Why He Really, Really Likes Oral Sex

Just what is it about *oral sex* that pleases men so much? There are reasons of sheer physical gratification, to be sure, but man does not live by the physical alone. Among the many different ways oral sex provides pleasure to a man …

♦ It offers direct, focused stimulation where they feel it most.

♦ Soft lips and a wet, warm, flexible tongue can provide the kind of sensation nothing else can.

♦ It signals that the woman performing it wants to give him pleasure.

> **Tantalizing Terms**
>
> **Oral sex** is an act which uses the mouth and tongue to stimulate a partner's genitals. This act, when performed on a man, is technically called *fellatio*, a term derived from the Latin *fellare*, which means "to suck".

♦ A man finds it incredibly sexy to watch a woman taking him in her mouth.

♦ Oral sex can be mentally stimulating, too, making him feel "worshipped" or "powerful."

♦ If it culminates in orgasm, that orgasm is especially intense.

♦ If it's done as a means of foreplay, it will make him rock hard.

♦ He can just lie (or sit or stand) back and enjoy it.

Oral sex makes men happy for so many reasons that every woman determined to please her man ought to consider giving it a try.

Raising the Subject

Maybe your man has never expressed a desire for oral sex out loud. But don't confuse his not asking for it with his not wanting it, or at least being intrigued by the idea of it. If you're not sure whether he really, really wants it, you can find out in two ways. One is to just surprise him in bed and go for it. If you're feeling bold, and if your man is the type who likes surprises, there's nothing wrong with this direct approach. However, if you are uncomfortable with this type of spontaneity or think it would be awkward to dive right in, so to speak, then talk about it first. Pick a time when your partner is relaxed and open and when the two of you are feeling close. Timing can be everything:

- Don't bring the subject up while he's watching a play-off game.

- Don't ask him when he's busy grilling steaks (you might find your dinner dropped on the ground or burned to a crisp).

- Don't ask him when he's driving (not if you want the car to stay on the road).

Be tactful. Don't just blurt out, "Honey, do you want me to go down on you later tonight?" If oral sex hasn't been part of your intimate repertoire, tell him you've been thinking about it, are curious, and that you're interested in seeing what it's like to please him in this new way.

Be sensitive. If your man seems reluctant, don't take it as a rejection. Maybe he's a little shy. This can be especially true if he's somewhat self-conscious about his body. Give him a little time to think it over. As he does, he'll soon summon up a staggering amount of zeal.

Ten Great Reasons to Get Good at Oral Sex

If you're going to pleasure a man by giving him oral sex, it's only fair that there's something in it for everyone. Luckily, there's a lot in it for you.

Many women have never stopped to contemplate the many advantages of becoming skilled at oral sex. There are many to consider. Here are the Top Ten:

10. No muss, no fuss. Having a good hair day and want to keep it that way? With oral pleasuring, you don't have to worry about "pillow head" or disheveled clothing.

9. Portable is pleasurable. Oral sex is perfect for experiencing intimate encounters in a variety of different locations. Because you can wear more clothing during pleasure, you can even do it outdoors in most types of weather.

8. No birth control necessary. Because you don't need to stop for condoms or spermicides, it's much easier to give oral pleasure in the heat of the moment.

> **Teasers & Pleasers**
>
> Oral sex is a great way to keep your man sexually fixated on you and only you. According to *The Journal of Sex Research*, oral sex is an important reason why male clients seek female prostitutes.

7. You have your period. If it's your time of the month and you don't care to have intercourse, you can still pleasure your man. Now you can have great sex 365 days a year.

6. It's a great appetizer for him. Performing oral sex on a man without inducing orgasm can make him extremely hard and be a great lead-up to dynamite intercourse.

5. It's great foreplay for you. Being so outrageously up close and personal with a man's genitalia can be enthralling to a woman. The stimulation of performing oral sex can get you well lubricated.

4. It makes for a great "quickie." If time is short, oral sex culminating in orgasm can make for great speed sex.

3. It's gratifying for you. It is sexy and very satisfying to see your man squirm and moan while under your control. The more you practice, the more intense his reaction will get.

2. It's a way to show love. By pleasuring with your mouth, lips, and tongue, you are saying that your man is the most important thing right at the moment, and you are going to concentrate completely on him. He will be bowled over by the fact that you have made him the center of attention.

1. He'll be inclined to reciprocate. After oral sex is part of your sexual repertoire, your man might well be tempted to abide by the Golden rules of "do onto others as they do unto you."

All in all, learning to be good at something so good is a win/win scenario.

Overcoming Your Inhibitions

Despite its many pleasures and benefits, some women feel squeamish about performing oral sex. Even if part of them really wants to, another part seems to pull back. But, ladies, it's time to get over those inhibitions in the name of some serious man-pleasing.

Every common objection can be met with strategies for getting over those particular reservations. All you really need is an open mind and a "can do" attitude.

"I'm Afraid I'll Gag"

This is one of the two most common objections to oral sex, and it's not an unreasonable one. Mother Nature gave all of us a gag reflex in order to protect us from harming our throats with dangerous objects. One way to help overcome the reflex is to remember to breathe through your nose as you take your lover in your mouth. Another is to switch back and forth from oral to manual stimulation, giving yourself regular breaks. If you don't want to take him out of your mouth, simply shift the angle of the penis periodically so that it rubs up against the inside of your cheek instead of the back of your throat.

The gag reflex can also be part psychological, so use the power of suggestion. Before beginning, tap yourself on the temple and repeat silently in our mind, "I will not gag." In addition, remind yourself that the power of your own arousal will likely be so strong that gagging won't occur.

"I Don't Want to Swallow"

This is the second of the top two objections. Many women object to the taste or texture of semen. But whether or not you want to swallow is your choice. The truth is that many men are turned on by the idea of a woman swallowing their semen. It can make them feel worshipped and adored. But guess what? Only 20 percent of women say they swallow at the culmination of oral sex, and most men are not bothered by this fact. They can reach as intense a climax whether their partner swallows or not.

You have many good alternatives to swallowing semen. One is to let your partner's semen dribble out of the side of your mouth. Another is to let him climax against your closed lips or against the smooth warmth of your cheek. Another is to switch from stimulating with your mouth to stimulating with your hand just before he orgasms. The he can ejaculate into or onto other sexy places, like your chest or neck.

The one thing you don't want to do is to make a big to-do out of spitting his semen out and indicating that it is in some way unpleasant. Remember, tact and etiquette play a constant role in all good relationships, even in bed.

> **Teasers & Pleasers**
>
> Semen generally tastes a little salty. If you want your man's semen to taste sweet, feed him a sweet dessert. It needn't be fattening either. Fruits such as honeydew, cantaloupe, kiwi, and strawberries will do the trick. Pineapple is reputed to be especially effective.

"Oral Sex Is Hard Work"

Oooh! Aren't we prima donnas? Where is it written that men should do the majority of work during sex? Of course oral sex takes some effort, but if you are really feeling exhausted, you probably just need to make a slight change in technique. Don't feel as though you have to fling your whole upper body around. Stay localized and concentrate on what matters: the movement of your mouth and tongue.

Also, oral sex shouldn't be a pain in the neck, literally or figuratively. You should control the position and the pace. Your man will be only too happy to let you take the lead while he relaxes and savors the experience.

"I'm Sensitive to Smell"

Many women feel squeamish about the smell of a man's genitals. Unless he's just come in from, say, a long day of bareback horse riding, your man will just smell natural—a bit masculine and musky. Aesthetically, that's not a bad thing. If you're really concerned about smell, however, suggest a joint shower before sex. In fact, you can even try performing oral sex in the shower.

"Nice Girls Don't Do That"

Oral sex is more and more widely accepted in our culture as a natural, normal part of the sexual experience. Many couples incorporate it into their lovemaking repertoire either as foreplay or an end unto itself. If you ask your girlfriends, I bet lots of them will tell you they do it. In any case, there is nothing "dirty" about a woman performing oral sex on her man. The taboo against it comes from outdated stereotypes and from not understanding what it's all about.

"I Might Hurt Him"

The trick to not hurting your partner is simply not to use your teeth. During oral sex, the mouth should be made to simulate the feeling of a vagina. It's easy to pull your lips back over your teeth. After you master this simple rule of thumb, you should be in no danger of doing harm or causing pain. But rest assured that if you were doing anything to cause him discomfort, he would tell you. No man will grin and bear it when it comes to this sensitive area of the body. If there's a problem, just correct it, and don't make a big deal out of it.

"I'll Never Get Good at It"

The first secret to getting good at oral sex is the same secret to getting good at anything: practice, practice, practice. The second is responsiveness to your partner's desires. Read on to discover basic and advanced techniques, but bear in mind that when it comes to oral sex, your partner can be your best guide. Encourage him to tell you what feels best and what he would like you to do more or less of.

He Says/She Says

"Before I tried performing oral sex on my husband, I practiced my technique on a cucumber. I admit to feeling a little silly at the time, but I was more confident when faced with the real situation."
—Jeannine, 27

The Basics

Every man has particular preferences when it comes to having oral sex performed on him, but it never hurts in any endeavor to have a basic roadmap to follow. Then, as things move along, it's fun to experiment with detours. There are no hard and fast rules when it comes to giving your lover the gift of great oral sex (and no, there will not be an oral exam). The following steps, however, form a general map upon which you can later refine and improvise.

◆ **Work your way up—and down.** As with all sex acts, much of the pleasure of oral sex lies in buildup and anticipation. Never treat oral sex as something you want to hurry up with and get accomplished. Instead, work your way up to the overall thrill of the experience by kissing, nibbling, and stroking your man all over. Employ a few erotic massage techniques in his genital area, beginning while his underwear is still on. Then slowly peel off his boxers or his tighty whities.

◆ **Think about ice cream.** Yes, that's right, ice cream. At this point you're ready for direct oral foreplay—licking. So imagine you've been handed a scrumptious sugar cream cone topped with two scoops of your favorite flavor. The only thing is, it's a hot summer day, and you need to keep the ice cream from melting. Do what you would normally do in this situation, lick from the bottom to the top of the "cone" (his shaft). Then lick in slow, sensuous circles and swirls. Then flick your tongue quickly across the top of the cone (the head of the penis). You can alternate all of these licking techniques.

◆ **Take him in gently.** With your lips relaxed, as though you are ready to savor a tiny dollop of ice cream from atop the cone, take only the top of the head of his penis (the glans) into your mouth. You can apply a bit of subtle suction at this point, but don't overdo it. You're not trying to be a shop vac here. Simply having the head of his member in your mouth provides a great deal of stimulation and pleasure for your man.

Uh-Oh's and No-No's

Don't be so quick to turn out the lights. There is a strong visual component to pleasuring a man with oral sex. Men are very visually oriented, and they love the sight of their penis being taken into your mouth. If direct lighting makes you self-conscious, try candlelight or leave the blinds open and let the moon shine in.

He Says/She Says

"My girlfriend was really good at oral sex, and I always enjoyed her skill and enthusiasm. But until recently one thing she never did was involve my testicles. One day I just guided her free hand in their direction and moved it across 'the boys.' She got the hint and has incorporated that move into her routine."
—Rob, 31

- Slide slowly. Inch your mouth down the shaft of the penis. Use your saliva to keep him well lubricated. From time to time, move your mouth back up the shaft. You can even tease him—and take a momentary breather—by taking your mouth off altogether for an instant. Then dive back in, going a little lower than where you left off.

- Establish a rhythm. When you've reached the base of his penis with your mouth, firmly—but gently, and without touching your teeth to him—enfold his penis with your lips and tongue and speed up your up-and-down motion. As you sense your man's pleasure building, narrow your focus to one specific stroke and establish a rhythm—a predictable and consistent beat. (Men differ in their rhythm preferences, but soon enough you'll know whether your guy likes a slightly slower of faster tempo.)

- Involve your hands. Hands can be great helpers in performing oral sex. While you are moving your mouth and tongue up and down, try using a hand in conjunction with those movements. Wrap that hand around the base of the penis and stroke in the same direction in which your mouth is moving. Notice that you'll still have one hand free. Many men love it if that idle hand is put into service by caressing their testicles.

- Communicate. As you work your way through all of these basics, take a moment here and there to check in with your partner about his likes and dislikes. This is especially important as you are beginning to get used to pleasuring him with oral sex and might not yet know his preferences or be completely attuned to his sexual body language. Ask questions like …

Do you like it (touched, stroked, licked) like this?

Should I touch you here?

Harder? Softer?

Faster? Slower?

What else would you like?

It's not necessary, or desirable, to initiate a lengthy conversation here. And this is certainly one instance where a happy groan or grunt as a response from your man is a perfectly acceptable form of dialogue.

♦ Use sound effects. Speaking of groaning and grunting, your man will feel enormously thrilled if he hears you emitting sounds of pleasure as you perform oral sex on him. Better yet, a nice "mmmmmm, mmmmmm" on your part will feel wonderful as your lips vibrate against him.

♦ Linger. When your man is bucking and grinding, you'll know his orgasm is near. But that doesn't mean your job is done. Men love it when their partner prolongs the afterglow by allowing their member to remain at rest in the safe cocoon of their mouth. If they drift off to sleep while encased in this way, they will doubtless have sweet dreams of you.

Teasers & Pleasers

To prolong his orgasm, gently squeeze the glans of his penis with your lips every few seconds while he is ejaculating.

After you've mastered a technique that your man appreciates, feel free to stay the course for as long as you like. Oral sex never seems to get boring for him, even if approached the same way most of the time. But keep your mind open to new possibilities in this exciting realm of man pleasing. Before long, you might just want to get a little more frisky and fancy.

Positions for Oral Sex

One way to vary the oral sex experience is to alter the positions that you use. As with any type of sex, variety adds a special spark. And playing with positions can mean opening the gateway to new sensations, for you and for your partner.

Man on His Back

Having your man lie flat with a pillow beneath his head provides easy access to his genitals. It also allows you the freedom to move about and alleviate any strain on your neck or back. Within this position are many variations:

◆ You can be on your stomach between his legs, propping yourself up with your elbows.

◆ You can have him put one or both legs over your shoulders.

◆ You can kneel or crouch between his legs, leaving your hands free to roam.

◆ You can wrap your arms under his thighs.

◆ You can sit on his legs and force them flat. (Some men find this sensation of immobility very exciting.)

◆ You can sit on his chest, facing away from him.

In any of these variations, the man gets the lovely feeling of relaxing and reclining during sex.

Woman on Her Knees

This is the image that comes to mind when many people think of fellatio. Kneeling in front of your man, whether he is standing or seated, is a great choice for spontaneous oral sex, for "quickies," and for sex in different locales like the shower or outdoors. It also offers an advantage in that it allows you to grab your man's buttocks and guide his genitals toward you. Although the kneeling position isn't for anyone who has knee problems, crouching or squatting can be good alternatives.

Is being on your knees demeaning? Certainly not—it's exciting, especially if you approach it in the right spirit. Take charge of the situation. Push your man up against the wall and have your way with him. He'll beg you for more, and you can think of what you're doing as a generous gift you are giving him.

Man Hovering Above

Here the man puts his knees on either side of your upper torso and hovers above your face. From this vantage point the man can thrust or stay still while you move your head. This position allows you maximum access for licking or sucking his testicles, which many men thoroughly enjoy.

Woman on Her Back

If you lie on your back, with your head tilted off the edge of a bed or sofa, your throat will automatically open wide—much more widely than in any other position. The man is standing and doing the thrusting. This makes for good *deep throating* (swallowing the entire length of the penis into the throat at once) while reducing the gag factor.

> **Tantalizing Terms**
>
> **Deep throating** has evolved into a verb. The term comes from the title of the randy 1972 film, *Deep Throat*, in which adult film star Linda Lovelace played a woman who discovers that her clitoris is located in the back of her throat.

Simultaneous Mutual Oral Sex (69)

Commonly known as *sixty-nine position*, simultaneous mutual oral sex is something couples tend to either really enjoy or would rather forego. The advantage is instant reciprocity and the opportunity to climax together. But some feel that it is too distracting to be the simultaneous giver and receiver of such pleasure. The only way to know whether this pleases you and your partner is to give it a try.

> **Tantalizing Terms**
>
> The **sixty-nine position** gets its name from lovers who position themselves with one partner upright and one inverted, thus upside down relative to one another—like the numbers "6" and "9." This position is also known by its French numerical moniker, *soixante-neuf*.

You have a couple of options for the sixty-nine technique. Your man can be on his hands and knees over you, or you can reverse that position with you on top. Many consider side by side, head to toe, the most comfortable approach and the easiest to sustain.

Variations on a Theme

Are you ready to add some variety and whimsy to your oral sex adventures? If so, you can do many things to add to or vary the sensation of taking your man in your mouth. Try a few of the following tricks to arouse and amuse:

- The Mint Trick. Suck on a strongly flavored breath mint or cough drop. Wait until it begins to dissolve, tuck it in the side of your cheek, and then take the penis into your mouth. The tingling sensation it gives your man can be quite enjoyable.

- The Ice Man. Some men prefer a chilly sensation. Try moving a few pieces of crushed ice around in your mouth and then lick.

- The Fireman. Offer a warming sensation by performing oral sex between sips of tea or coffee.

CAUTION

Uh-Oh's and No-No's

The back of your throat is slippery and pliant, unless you are dehydrated. A lot of alcohol or salty foods doesn't mix well with oral sex. Keep a glass of water handy, just in case.

- The Humdinger. Sound vibrations add to his pleasure. Pick a tune you know—it could be anything from a classical piece to Happy Birthday to a marching band song—and hum it while you please him.

- The Mars Butterfly. Flick your tongue back and forth over the slit in his glans. He'll really go crazy if you accentuate this by prying the slit open just a bit with your fingers.

- The Outback. Run your tongue lengthwise across his perineum—the space behind his scrotum but in front of his anus. This area is thick with nerves and extremely sensitive to touch.

- The Tea Bag. Have your man get on all fours above you. Scoot down slowly, grazing his chest and belly with a path of kisses as you go. Then take his testicles in your mouth and suck.

These techniques are playfully erotic. They're great little surprises, like sending an unexpected candy gram. Use them to liven up your love life when things have been getting a bit too predictable, or just save them as a special treat for when you really want to blow him away.

It's All Good

Not every woman will feel comfortable with all of these advanced techniques. There's certainly no need to pressure yourself into undertaking them if you're scared or self-conscious. They're just fun options to keep in mind. Your man will be happy if you get creative and show your adventurous side, but he'll also be content if you simply get good at the meat-and-potatoes of fellatio. As one man put it: "There's simply no such thing as bad oral sex."

The Least You Need to Know

◆ Men appreciate oral sex because of the unique sensual pleasures it offers.

◆ Even if your man has never requested that you try performing oral sex, that doesn't mean he wouldn't be very receptive to your suggestion.

◆ Oral sex offers so many advantages to women that it's worth reconsidering any objections you might have.

◆ Like any sexual technique, oral sex takes practice, but practice makes perfect.

◆ Fancy tricks offer a nice change of pace, but most men will be thrilled with a woman who is enthusiastic and determined to master the basics.

Chapter 13

Spice Talk

In This Chapter

- ◆ Why love and language naturally go together
- ◆ How sounds enhance the sensory pleasure of sex
- ◆ Overcome spice talk shyness
- ◆ Telephone trysts
- ◆ E-mail teasers
- ◆ Redeemable pleasure coupons

Now that we've discussed oral pleasuring, it's time to learn about aural pleasuring—that is, the sounds that can spice up your love life. Just like the birds and the bees, humans are capable of conveying countless mating-related nuances with sounds. Unlike other species, however, we can also weave words into the mix.

The possibilities for enhancing passion and sexual pleasure with words and sounds are limitless—because they involve our endlessly creative brains and imaginations. All you need to do is stop being shy and loosen your tongue. If you can talk, you can talk spicy.

The Language of Love ... and Sex

Can you imagine falling in love and not saying the words, "I love you"? Can you imagine being enamored with a man without singing his praises? Of course not. It's impossible to separate love from its verbal expression, because our brains are wired to express powerful emotions through language. As the Italian sociologist Francesco Alberoni points out, even "when the most simple and unaware person falls in love, he (or she) is forced to use the language of poetry."

But even if we're really verbose when it comes to talking of love, many of us quiet down considerably when it comes to the act of lovemaking. Even in the throes of passion, we might censor our instinctive urge to cry out or speak up. Even if our thoughts are X-rated, we might behave as though we are in a silent movie.

But, when it comes to making love, silence is not golden. In fact, it's boring. Spicy words and sounds can heat up any sexual encounter.

Does your man want to hear from you during sex? Yes, yes, yes! No, he doesn't want you to give him marching orders (remember the sexual etiquette covered in Chapter 7). He wants you to encourage him, to spur him onward and upward.

Men absolutely love the reinforcement they get when the woman that they are making love to tells them she adores and appreciates what they're doing. They love it when she gets so carried away she simply can't hold back her moans and groans. Many even love it when her language veers toward racy.

But, hold on. You might be shy. In fact let's see whether you are. Find a quiet spot where you know you won't be overheard by anyone; then try saying these things out loud:

- Penis
- Testicles
- Vagina
- Clitoris
- Breasts

Now, try them in their slang forms:

- Cock
- Balls

- Pussy
- Clit
- Tits

Ah ha! If you're already blushing or giggling at such mainstream body part terminology, you're hardly going to evolve from silent loving to shouting, "Give it to me harder, big boy." Well, not in one fell swoop. In fact, you might be nowhere near experimenting with full-fledged "talking dirty." That's okay. Let's start slowly and see how far you want to go. You might surprise yourself—and your man.

Spicy Sounds

"Sounds thicken the sensory stew of our lives," wrote poet Diane Ackerman in *A Natural History of the Senses.* When people make love, all of their senses are in a highly receptive and responsive state. A man is enjoying what he sees, touches, tastes, and smells. He would certainly like to hear something enjoyable as well.

Even if you're not up to talking during sex, rest assured that a woman's sighs, moans, groans, and growls are highly stimulating to a man in the midst of lovemaking. They add flavor to the fare. They tell him that his partner is enjoying the sensations she is feeling and that she approves of what he is doing and how he is doing it. They can also imply—and this is a real turn-on—that she is so caught up in the moment she is not entirely aware, on a conscious level, of what sounds she is making.

If you are really allowing yourself to let go and enjoy sex without stifling the sounds of instinctual gratification, your lovemaking "vocabulary" might well include:

- "Mmmmmmmm"
- "Oooooooh"
- "Uuuuuhhh"

And as the French say, "Ooh la la."

> **CAUTION**
>
> **Uh-Oh's and No-No's**
>
> Afraid the kids might overhear some steamy sounds? Little ones do seem to have acute hearing abilities. Turn on some mood music for a muffling effect.

Sound involves the whole body and can expand and intensify orgasm. But what if you are (perhaps literally) biting your tongue because you are self-conscious about making noise? You might need to relearn this basic instinct. Don't worry; it is completely within your capabilities.

Take a Deep Breath

When we have sex, our breathing becomes deeper and more resonant—in part because the tissue in the nose becomes engorged and restricts the flow of air—hence the term "heavy breathing." In many cases we are not conscious of breathing this way. Becoming conscious of the breath, however, can be the first step toward producing spicy sounds. Here's how you can practice:

1. Find a private place to lie down, or sink into a warm bath.

2. Picture yourself in the throes of passion. Allow yourself to envision exactly what you're doing and what's being done to you.

3. Notice how the rhythm of your breath has changed.

4. Focus on your deep inhalation. Feel air entering your nostrils and filling your diaphragm.

5. Focus on your long exhalation. Feel the rib cage dropping and the breath being pushed up and out.

6. Now add a sound that can ride the wave of your breath. Start with a simple hum. Let the sound originate in your diaphragm, come up the back of the throat, and escape slowly through closed lips.

7. Now repeat the last step with a new sound. Try "Ohhhh."

Before long you will experience a relaxed, autohypnotic pleasure. If fact, this should be so much fun you won't need much persuasion to try this exercise again and again. Before long, your brain will begin to make the connection between sexual breathing and sexual sounds of pleasure, and you will produce these sounds more spontaneously during lovemaking.

Spicy Sound Tape Exercise

Now you're ready to hear your sexy, stimulating sounds just the way your man will hear them. Use a tiny microcassette recorder (they are inexpensive and lightweight) to capture your sound effects. Play them back (go ahead, be brave!) and see what a turn-on they truly are.

Consider this exercise your dress rehearsal. Now you're ready for opening night. No doubt you will encounter a very appreciative audience.

The Big "O"

No discussion of stimulating sounds is complete without a mention of orgasm. When we climax, we are truly in an altered, transcendent state. An orgasm is the peak of sexual arousal when all the muscles that were tightened during stimulation suddenly relax. During orgasm, a woman's heart rate skyrockets. Breathing quickens and blood pressure rates increase; muscles throughout the body spasm, especially those in the vagina, uterus, anus, and pelvic floor.

Orgasms generate immense physical pleasure. During orgasm, chemicals called endorphins are released into the bloodstream, causing enjoyable sensations to ripple through the body.

Many women emit spontaneous, unexpurgated sounds of pleasure during orgasm. They might cry out loudly or yell passionate words with enormous enthusiasm. But other women seem intent on keeping their orgasms as quiet as possible.

Don't keep your climax a secret! Your man will be thrilled to know he is providing you with such immeasurable satisfaction. When you are in the throes of orgasm, don't devote one scintilla of energy to holding back your sounds of ecstasy.

He Says/She Says

"Listening to my wife have an orgasm is just about the best part of sex for me. It thrills me to know I can do this to her, give this sensation to her. It drives me wild."
—Ken, 45

Asking and Telling

The easiest way to begin using words to accompany sex is to follow a simple formula of asking and telling. While you're making love, ask what your man likes, and tell him what you like.

Ask him:

◆ Do you like it when I touch you here?

◆ Does this feel good?

◆ Do you want more of this?

Tell him:

- That feels so good.

- I love it when you do that.

- More, more, more!

Asking and telling are not only erotically charged, but also incredibly useful. They allow you to get and give gentle guidance and make subtle course corrections if need be. Perhaps the best thing about asking and telling, however, is that you can take it as far as you like in terms of the exact words you choose. You can speak in general terms, as in the previous examples, or you can be as graphic as you wish. For example: "I love it when you (fill in the blank) me, baby."

Spice Talk Writing Exercise

If you're ready to think about elaborating on your descriptive abilities for spice talk, try putting some of those passionate thoughts down on paper as a first step. After we see something in writing, it is easier to imagine saying it out loud.

All you need is a sheet of paper, a timer (use a simple kitchen timer or set your microwave), and a pen. Don't use a pencil. Erasures imply second thoughts and self-censorship. The point is to tap into your erotic unconscious.

Now, picture yourself in a sexual scenario that really gets your juices flowing. Let your imagination run free. Think of exotic locales in which you've always longed to make love. Picture your lover (this could be your current partner or someone you dream up just for this exercise) looking super hot. See exactly what you're doing in detail. Don't feel you have to limit yourself to things you've already done. Ask yourself, what have I really always wondered about doing?

When you're well-steeped in your fantasy, set your timer and give yourself a total of two minutes to finish the following sentences. Fill in the blanks as though you are speaking to your partner in this steamy scenario you've created. After you've started to write, do not stop to revise. Just keep going. Don't worry; spelling and grammar don't count.

Lover, here's exactly what you're doing to me …

_____

_____

_____

Lover, here's exactly what I am doing to you …

_____

_____

_____

Lover, here are the exact sensations I am feeling in my body right now …

_____

_____

_____

If you truly do this without stopping to censor, this exercise should help you overcome many of your inhibitions. It's extremely liberating to use the power of the written word in this way. If you've ever read a romance novel, you know exactly what I mean. Why do you think so many of them sell millions and millions of copies?

Spice Talk Mirror Exercise

Okay, are you ready? Because now it's time to articulate. Come on, you can do it. Follow these steps:

1. Take what you've written and go stand in front of a full-length mirror.

2. Read your steamy passages aloud—but do so in a whisper. Whispering is not only a sexy and seductive way to communicate, but also a way to feel less self-conscious about what you say.

3. As you whisper your words, watch yourself. Notice whether your body language negates your words. Are you crossing your arms and legs or holding your hand in front of your mouth? Those are tip offs.

4. If you see any body language blockages, work on relaxing and releasing them. Repeat in your mind, "I release this block to intimacy." Then inhale and exhale deeply as you alter your posture.

5. Now reread your passages aloud.

The point of this exercise is not that you memorize these exact words, nor that you recite these passages aloud to your partner. Anything but! Spice talk should be spontaneous and in the moment. But now that you've talked spicy face-to-face with your mirror, it should be easier for you to talk spicy face-to-face with your man. Stick your toe in the water and test a few words out on your man. Observe his reaction, and feel free to ask him what he likes.

Telephone Trysts

Telephone sex is a multimillion dollar industry. Have you ever wondered what its appeal is to men? As many guys have pointed out, the thrill of hearing hot, sexy talk from a disembodied voice—while the imagination fills in the gaps—comes through loud and clear.

Phone sex with your partner might not be something you've ever considered. But it can be a potent vehicle for building erotic anticipation and for adding fuel to the fires of fantasy. It can help keep romance and intimacy alive if you have a long distance relationship or if one or both of you travels a lot. But even if you are rarely more than a mile apart, phone sex can be a terrific supplement to the rest of your sex life.

Happily, cell phones have added a whole new dimension to phone sex. Now you and your man can send chills down one another's spines while you're walking down the street, shopping at the supermarket, or sitting in the waiting room at the dentist's office.

He Says/She Says

"Sometimes I call my boyfriend when he is on the train on the way to work and I just go to it. He says he loves to just sit there with a silly grin on his face. One day a man who is often on the same train said to him, 'You must really love your job. You always look so happy when you're on your way in.'"
—Michele, 25

What should you say during telephone trysts? Whatever you like! You certainly don't even have to use four-letter words if that makes you uncomfortable. In fact, nuance can be much more exciting.

Try starting with some of these openers:

♦ I had a dream about you last night ... do you want to know what we were doing?

♦ I thought of you this morning when I was in the shower. Let me tell you about it.

♦ Let's get together this weekend and do something we've never done before. I have an idea ....

♦ When you get home I'm going to have you right on the living room rug. I'll be thinking about it all day.

♦ I'm going shopping for lingerie later. Let me tell you what I'm going to try on ....

♦ Do you know what I'd be doing to you if you were here with me right now?

Are telephone trysts as satisfying as the "real thing?" Many men are completely enthralled with them. Both women and men say that this type of contact can be so intense, it can easily lead to orgasm. Try it yourself and find out.

E-gads! E-mails

Internet sex is known as online sex, cybersex, or virtual sex. Some of its devotees refer to actual "in the flesh sex" by the somewhat pejorative term, offline sex. In his book, *Love Online: Emotions on the Internet* (Cambridge University Press, 2004), Israeli philosophy professor Aaron Ben-Ze'ev says people claim they experience the wildest sex through the Internet. Why? "You feel very safe. And if you are safe, you can speak more about yourself. And build intimacy."

If you haven't tried sex via the Internet, the millions who have might well ask what you're waiting for. Now, I'm not talking about doing it with virtual strangers; I'm talking about doing it with your partner. It's just as easy as e-mailing your man to "please bring home a quart of milk." But asking him instead to "please bring home your hot buns ASAP" is a lot more fun. Think how ecstatic he will be to find a little spicy jewel of an e-mail buried among his work memos and sales spam.

Naturally you want to be discreet if your e-mail will be filtered through your man's company server. But that's no problem. E-mail users are usually familiar with numerous acronyms used to abbreviate common phrases. Some oft-used ones include BTW (by the way) LOL (laughing out loud), IMHO (in my humble opinion), and BFN (bye for now).

Teasers & Pleasers

Want to try online spice talk with an increased level of instant gratification? Get you and your man logged on to an instant messaging program and chat away.

Why don't you and your man invent a shortcut online vocabulary of your own? You can be endlessly creative. To start you off, here are some suggestions:

- IWYN I Want You Now
- LMT Love Me Tonight
- YTMO You Turn Me On
- IH4Y I'm Hot for You
- IMYBB I Miss You Big Boy

Well, you get the idea. Your personalized love acronyms can provide a quick, enjoyable way to punctuate the day and ignite the spark of love. And, of course, like all other kinds of spice talk, you can take this medium as far as you wish, and as far as you dare. Way to go (or, WTG)!

Make Your Own Pleasure Coupons

All this high-tech spice talk is very nice indeed. We're lucky to live in an era when it's so easy to send a sexy message careening through cyberspace at the press of a few buttons. Nevertheless, low-tech techniques will also be much appreciated by your man.

For some instant spice, try gifting your man with some redeemable pleasure coupons. Hide them where they will surprise and delight him. Imagine how thrilled he will be to open his briefcase, his shaving kit, or his gym bag and find a lovely little handwritten note that contains a promise like one of the following:

- This coupon entitles you to one full-body, head-to-toe massage. All body parts included.
- This coupon entitles you to one nude hot tub session with one hot nude.

- This coupon entitles you to view one hot striptease performance. (Refer to the special striptease lesson in Chapter 14.)

- This coupon entitles you to a session of oral sex.

- This coupon entitles you to share a sexual fantasy with me.

- This coupon entitles you to breakfast in bed: a glass of champagne, a bowl of strawberries, and me.

- This coupon entitles you to dress me up in anything you like and then undress me.

- This coupon entitles you to one steamy night at a motel with me and without the kids or the dog! You may redeem this coupon at _____ on _____.

Talk about making someone's day a little bit brighter. By the way, be sure whatever you write on your coupon is a promise you are willing to keep. You can certainly set a mutually agreeable time for your man to collect what's owed him—but no take-backs are allowed. Be a good sport and enjoy some good, hot spice.

The Least You Need to Know

- Words and sounds do much to enhance the pleasures of sex.

- Men are gratified and encouraged by hearing their women's pleasure during lovemaking and orgasm.

- With practice, anyone can get over their shyness and find a level of spicy sounds or spice talk with which they're comfortable.

- With cell phones and e-mail, technology can be an aid to spice talk—but low-tech talk is great, too.

- Use love coupons to brighten your man's day with the promise of a wonderful night.

Part 5

Mixing It Up

Men crave adventure. It's in their genes. Maybe day-to-day life doesn't offer them as much opportunity for adventure as it did when they had to go out and take down a woolly mammoth for dinner. That's all the more reason why their night-to-night life should offer opportunities for exciting forays.

This part of the book will help you satisfy your man's thirst for exciting escapades by adding a note of adventure to your sex life. It also includes detailed advice on encouraging him to experience the thrill of pleasing you like you've never been pleased before.

Chapter 14

Fantasy Island

In This Chapter

- ◆ Men's top fantasies
- ◆ Fantasies turn into reality
- ◆ Favorite fantasy roles
- ◆ Erotica is better together
- ◆ Love toys for you and your boy
- ◆ The art of the striptease

Do you ever wonder what your man is thinking about when he stares off into space and lets the hint of a smile play around his lips? Did you ever consider why he might flush and sweat slightly when he looks at, say, the annual swimsuit edition of his sports magazine? Did you ever dare let yourself think about what he might be thinking about when he masturbates or sometimes even when the two of you make love? If he's perfectly normal—and I'll bet he is—he spends some part of his waking hours indulging in imaginary sexual adventures. I say, good for him!

Imagination and sexuality go together so naturally that you can't have one without the other. Most people want to keep some aspects of sexual reveries private. But what if some aspects could move from the realm of the imagination into the realm of reality? There's nothing wrong with committed lovers introducing a note of adventure into their sex lives now and then.

Perhaps you think of your sex life with your man as having boundaries around it. You've been afraid to cross some lines, even if you've been curious—even if you've been very tempted from time to time. But self-imposed boundaries can be pushed back if you and your man mutually decide it's okay. That's the subject matter of this chapter. For now, don't rule anything out. Just let yourself imagine "what if …"

Men's Favorite Fantasies

Virtually every study on sexuality shows that the overwhelming majority of us have sexual fantasies at various times and in various situations. Ninety-five percent of men say they have them when they pleasure themselves. More than 50 percent say they fantasize while having sex with a partner. There's no shame or blame in that, and it doesn't mean they love their partner any less. It's simply the mind's way of enlivening an activity. Fantasizing during sex is so common that Johnny Carson once quipped that when turkeys mate, they think of swans.

Have you ever stopped to wonder what, exactly, guys like to imagine when it comes to sex? According to a compendium of surveys, the following rank high on the average man's list of steamy sexual scenarios:

- Making love with someone new
- Making love with a forbidden partner (like his best friend's girl)
- Making love with two or more people
- Making love in an exotic location
- Making love with a stranger, on the spur of the moment
- Making love under force
- Making love in forbidden spots where you could easily be discovered
- Making love with someone of the same gender
- Watching his partner make love to someone else
- Making love with a celebrity

You may well be wondering whether having a sexual fantasy means that the person having it actually wants to do the thing that he is imagining. In many cases, the answer is no. The genesis of sexual fantasies is complex. They may evolve out of deep-seated psychological preoccupations, some of which go all the way back to childhood. You can't assume that because someone has a thought about, say, being tied up during sex or engaging in group or same-gender sex that this in any way fits in with their image of themselves in the real world.

On the other hand, some people may have always toyed with the idea of acting on some of their sexual fantasies. All they've been waiting for is the right moment and the right person with whom to try it. Could it be you?

Bringing Fantasy to Life

As a way of adding some adventure to your sex life, you might want to think about exploring with your man some of those fantasies that he might wish to bring to life. With fantasy, the two of you can transport yourself to anywhere at any time and make love in any personae. Using your imaginations in tandem can not only be erotically stimulating but also bring a deeper level of intimacy to your relationship.

Sharing and acting out fantasies, however, can be a tricky business. Doing so requires a clear consensus and a significant emotional comfort level on both your parts. Since the two of you are in a long-term, committed relationship, you probably already have a solid amount of mutual trust. But here are some special things you can do beforehand to make the fantasy-to-reality transition an emotionally safe and sexually satisfying experience:

- Talk about the details of the fantasy and see whether the scenario is something each of you can actually picture trying.

- Discuss possible positive consequences that might result from trying the fantasy. (Would it be fun? Would it turn you both on?)

- Discuss possible negative consequences that might result (such as embarrassment or jealousy).

> **CAUTION**
>
> **Uh-Oh's and No-No's**
>
> It's not cool to continue in fantasy mode if one partner is uncomfortable—but it can be hard to tell whether protests are real or part of the play. Agree ahead of time on a "safe word," a red flag that will alert your lover that you want to stop and return to reality.

- Rough out a kind of storybook script for the fantasy (with a plot and characters).

- Have an agreement about limits and boundaries, veto power, and how you'll signal each other to stop or negotiate next steps.

- Agree that either one of you can stop the fantasy play at any time.

- Consider watching an adult film together that incorporates this type of fantasy (more about this shortly).

- Dabble in the fantasy before trying it out in a full-fledged way by improvising a few lines from your script the next time you make love.

- If you're comfortable with your appetizer, go for the whole enchilada!

Naturally, if you act out a fantasy and don't care for it or don't find it gratifying, you don't have to do it again. But that doesn't mean you can't try another. Like many couples, you and your man might find that fantasy adds a thrilling new dimension to loving. It offers a break from everyday life and an opportunity to expand the range of your sexual bond.

Award-Winning Roles

One of the things lovers most enjoy about fantasy play is acting out different roles. In our day-to-day existence, we are constrained in terms of how people perceive us and how we're allowed to behave. We women may be wives or girlfriends, mothers, working women, PTA volunteers, and the like. But what if we could, just for an hour, be an exotic dancer, a Victorian queen, or an impeccably trained geisha? Our men might be husbands or boyfriends, dads, employees or bosses, and fixer-uppers around the house. But what if, for a little while, they could be cowboys or kings, ringmasters or rogues?

Many people say it's amazing how liberating and exciting it can be to assume a temporary role in the course of lovemaking. Some also say they feel that role-playing has enabled them to unearth lots of hidden talent in the acting realm. Although they might not win an Academy Award for their performances, their partners' enthusiasm is often reward enough for their efforts.

Needless to say, what role you play is limited only by your powers of imagination. If you would like a few starter ideas, however, some roles are perennially popular. Considering some of these may help you plant some seeds for your own fantasy garden.

Schoolmaster and Naughty Schoolgirl

What a naughty girl! The schoolmaster caught you giggling and passing notes, or— worse yet—skipping class. Now it's time for your detention and punishment. Under your short, pleated skirt (a perfect match for your ankle socks and patent leather Mary Janes) you're sporting waist-high cotton briefs. But now the schoolmaster instructs you to take them off! After a few light spanks on your bottom, you decide to take your revenge. You turn over and slowly, tauntingly unbutton your crisply starched white blouse. Who's in trouble now?

Note: For a variation on this fantasy, try role switching. Let your man be the naughty schoolboy who's forgotten his homework—again. You be the very, very strict schoolmistress and teach him a lesson.

Sultan and Slave

Like the veiled temptress, Salome, you can make your man's every wish your command. All he has to do is snap his fingers or clap his hands—whatever signal you decide on can signal his whim. But don't give in too quickly. You can captivate him by draping a veil across your body and performing a slow, undulating dance. Perhaps he'll later use those same scarves to gently bind you while he takes his pleasure.

Setting the scene goes a long way toward creating the right mood for this exotic fantasy. You can scatter throw pillows and rugs on your bedroom floor, hang drapes from the ceiling to make a tent, and massage your sultan with scented oil. Visit some belly dance supply shops or websites for Middle Eastern music CDs, veils of delicate gauze, and sequined skirts, or hip belts adorned with jangling *faux* coins.

For variation, try a different royal treatment—perhaps one where you are queen and he a humble page obliged to service you in any way you desire.

Geisha and Patron

Transport yourself and your man to the land of Nippon. Don an elegant kimono and graciously serve him tea. Japanese *geisha*—who played a very different role from that of the sober wife in traditional Japanese society—were trained

Tantalizing Terms

The word **geisha** literally means "art person" or "artisan." Geisha were very common in the eighteenth and nineteenth centuries and are still in existence today, although their numbers are dwindling. The geisha tradition evolved from the Japanese equivalent of court jesters, hence the emphasis on wit and entertainment.

from childhood to entertain men in various artistic fashions, including dance, song, and witty conversation. So let your creative, esoteric side shine through as you cater to every one of your man's senses before relinquishing yourself to his embrace.

Perfect Strangers

You and he notice one another across a crowded room. You make eye contact and begin to move toward one another as if magnetized. Without exchanging a single word, you know what will happen between you. Your actions are inevitable, and the force driving you is irresistible. Trying not to draw attention to yourselves, you slip outside to a terrace or off to an unoccupied bedroom—perhaps even a tiny powder room. Unable to control your passions a moment longer, you tear at each other's clothing and quickly couple—all the while aware that your ardor might be discovered at any moment.

Cowboy and Saloon Hostess

"It gets mighty lonesome out there on the trail, ma'am," he says. He looks so rugged in his Stetson, jeans, and boots that you can't resist making him glad he came to town. After bringing him a drink and massaging his aching body, so tense from riding all day, you invite him back in the saddle. But be careful, a cowboy is always reluctant to take off his boots, no matter what the occasion.

Like a Virgin

No matter how long you've been together, make tonight your wedding night. Dress the part by wearing white silk and adorning your hair with flowers. Provide him with an elegant smoking jacket and silk boxer shorts. Undress each other slowly, as if you are discovering one another's bodies for the very first time. Then, since you are an innocent neophyte, let him show you exactly what to do to make him happy ever after.

Movie or Literary Characters

The sky's the limit when you take on the personae of sexy characters in books or films that have struck a chord with you. You can be the shy governess with a burning passion, the plain Jane secretary who blossoms when she lets down her hair, the wealthy ice queen who melts in the arms of a poor boy. He can be a debonair playboy, a gladiator, a smooth-talking con man, a bank robber, or a bullfighter. You can even be Shakespeare's Romeo and Juliet (before the final act, please), Jane's Austen's Elizabeth Bennett and Mr. Darcy (you'll unleash the lusty devil beneath the upper-class veneer), or Margaret Mitchell's Scarlet O'Hara and Rhett Butler (you know you can make him give a damn).

A Lotta Erotica

Speaking of film and fantasy, one way to garner ideas and inspiration for your fantasies, and to stoke your appetite for loving, is to partake of some adult entertainment with your man. It's quite likely this may be something you've never even considered, in fact, perhaps you're thinking: "Ugh, porn is a guy thing."

Certainly we've been led to believe that sexually explicit films arouse men because men get excited by the mere image of sex, whereas we women need a storyline involving an emotional bond—a relationship—in order to feel engaged. That's why we appreciate erotic scenes within the context of romance novels or within feature films that have a plot involving romance and passion.

Teasers & Pleasers

For a change from standard adult films, the *Shane's World* series—produced and directed by women—brings a half dozen real people and adult video stars together at various locations for a few days. Because nonscripted human connections are being made, the sex scenes can be far more appealing to us relationship-oriented types.

But scientific evidence shows that you might be surprised how aroused you can get if you are willing to give some XXX-rated entertainment a try. In a Northwestern University study, more than 90 gay and straight men, women, and male-to-female transsexuals were shown erotic film scenes with a probe attached to their genitals to indicate when they were aroused. The men and the transsexual subjects were aroused only by scenes that featured members of their preferred-partner gender. Women, however, were aroused by all of the material—whether it featured lesbian scenes, gay male scenes, or mixed-gender scenes. Although this might seem counterintuitive, there are two possible explanations. One is that women—without being gay themselves—still find other women's bodies erotic because our society so eroticizes the female form. Another is that women, in general, have had relatively little exposure to pornography. Where a man might be bored or jaded, a woman will still be intrigued. Whatever the reason, the bottom line is that while men are upfront about their enthusiasm for this kind of fare, women may be secretly hungering for more.

CAUTION

Uh-Oh's and No-No's

What kind of erotica you ultimately view—if any—is up to you. Different people have different feelings about this kind of material and how it makes them feel. When does erotica cross the line into obscenity? The call is subjective, but as Supreme Court Justice Potter Stewart famously said of obscenity, "I know it when I see it."

Here's yet another reason to think about exploring this avenue of potential pleasure if your man is open to the idea. Think of all the times you've dragged him to "chick flicks." Did he complain when you made him sit through *You've Got Mail* and *Sleepless in Seattle*? Well, maybe he did, but at least he was good sport enough to tag along with you, eat some popcorn, and behave himself. Now it's your turn to rent or download, say, *College Frolics* or *Happy Hookers*, dim the lights, lock the door, and see what happens.

You might never be a huge fan—but then again you just might. Meanwhile, it's very likely your man will be aroused just by your presence and your willingness to give this intimate activity a shot.

Erotic Mainstream Films

Of course you might discover that XXX- or even X-rated films are not your thing. If that's the case, you might want to consider some hot but mainstream R-rated movies. These well-known films, available at any video store, contain scenes that are steamy, but not explicitly graphic.

- *No Way Out*, with Kevin Costner and Sean Young (check out the limo scene)
- *Body Heat*, starring William Hurt and Kathleen Turner (watch him shatter glass just to get to her)
- *The Thomas Crown Affair*, with Pierce Brosnan (check out the stairway scene)
- *Risky Business*, starring Tom Cruise and Rebecca DeMornay (ride the choo-choo)
- *The Postman Always Rings Twice*, starring Jack Nicholson and Jessica Lange (what a way to clear the table)

- *Bull Durham*, with Kevin Costner, Susan Sarandon, and Tim Robbins (a triple play for the baseball fan)
- *Basic Instinct*, with Michael Douglas and Sharon Stone (well, you know …)

If your guy has never seen these movies, assure him that he won't be sorry. Even if he has seen them, they'll be cast in a whole new light when you watch them together, in private, each knowing what the other is thinking about.

An Audio Alternative

If film is not your thing—or if it is, but you would like to try expanding into new media—you should know that a new interesting alternative has come on the scene in the form of audio erotica.

A variety of adult audio CDs are available in which women tell erotic stories. The theory behind this new medium is that listeners will have an enjoyable, interactive experience because they will instinctively visualize the intimate situations to which they're listening. An added bonus: erotic CDs are ultra-portable. You and your guy can listen to women sharing their sexy stories and enticing fantasies as easily as you can listen to music. These audio erotica tapes might be just the thing for your listening pleasure during your next long road trip together.

For those with a literary bent, there's also an audio book route to pleasure. Try the audio versions of the Sleeping Beauty Erotica Series. They're by A.N. Roquelaure, a pseudonym for Anne Rice, author of the famous *Interview with a Vampire*. You might also consider a series called Women Write Erotica. It's written by women for women, but it might be something your man would enjoy having read aloud to him.

DIY Erotica

Since your spirit of creativity is such an essential part of pleasing your man, you might also want to consider making your own erotic home movies—or audiotapes or still photographs, for that matter. Today's digital technology is ready-made for such adventures, because nothing has to be sent outside the home to be processed. If the spirit moves you, give that camcorder a respite from chronicling the kids' soccer games and birthday parties while you and your guy have a party of your own. Whether you work from a script of simply improvise as you go, starring in your own erotica can be a heavy-duty turn-on. You can release your "inner adult star," and your guy will be thrilled with the technical "do it yourself" aspect of such projects.

Love Props for Pleasing

Whether you're up for a sexual adventure on or off-camera, lovemaking can also be greatly varied and enhanced by using sex toys. Sex toys have become more and more mainstream in recent years. They're regularly reviewed in magazines. They're sold on websites and at a growing number of specialty shops. A number of books have been devoted exclusively to the topic.

Maybe you've even got a few girlfriends who've sneaked off to some of those popular shop-at-home sex toy parties while their men think they're off burping Tupperware.

On the other hand, maybe you're like millions of women who, although curious, have never touched a sex toy; maybe you aren't even sure what sex toys are. Perhaps your man is the same way. So, this, too, might be something new and adventurous that you and he can try together.

Sex toys are any items that can be used to make sex more enjoyable. They are, however, different from sensual aids—satin sheets, scented candles, and mirrors—in that sex toys are directly involved in sexual activities. You might protest that you and your man need no accoutrements to make passionate love, that your bodies alone are more than enough. No doubt they are, but keep in mind that novelty usually infuses love-making with a jolt of new energy. Besides, everyone likes to accessorize.

Vibrating Together

Vibrators are among the most common sex toys. You can now purchase vibrators at your local adult store or online (check out Appendix A) if you are shy. Even if you get a basic model that doesn't appear in any way sexual, it can do very pleasant things when applied to the genitals. Vibrators meant to be specifically sexual, however, are much more aesthetically desirable. They come in more shapes, sizes, and colors than you can imagine. They range from traditional eight-inch phallus-dimensioned contraptions to sleek, finger-fitted devices. They can be loud or soft in sound, strong or gentle in touch, fast-paced or deliciously slow. In fact, there are so many ways to vibrate that some women joke these types of toys can render men superfluous. But that really is just a joke, of course.

You can use your vibrator to get you in the mood or to keep happy when your man is otherwise engaged. But you can also integrate it into your lovemaking by having your man watch you use it or help you use it. In addition to being used on the vulva, vibrators can be placed between a man and woman during intercourse, producing extra sensations for both of you.

Ring-A-Ding-Ding

Penile rings are a win/win accessory. They provide adornment, and some men find they can slightly add to the size and firmness of an erection. In addition, the type of penile rings that have a knob or other extension can stimulate a woman's clitoris or labia during intercourse. There are a wide variety of rings—actually leather, rubber, or metal bands—designed to be worn at the base of an erect penis, where they encourage blood flow to remain in the male organ.

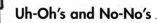

Uh-Oh's and No-No's

Never have your man use a ring that is too tight or that causes discomfort. It can cut off blood flow to the penis and be very dangerous. Never leave a ring on his penis for more than half an hour. Jelly rings are safest because they're stretchable and can be easily removed when needed.

Pleasing Plastic

Dildos are penis-shaped plastic, latex, or silicon items intended to be inserted into the vagina or the rectum. Unlike vibrators, they don't move unless you move them.

Dildos come in many styles. Some very much resemble actual penises—although dildos are stiffer than a lot of penises and stay that way indefinitely. For this reason, many couples use dildos to prolong their sexual encounters.

Teasers & Pleasers

Don't be sexist. Dildos are equal opportunity pleasure devices. Ask your man if he'd like you to use a dildo on him. You can use it to stimulate him anally, which many guys find very erotic.

A dildo can be used by a man on a woman, or the woman can use it on herself as her partner watches. A dildo may be especially useful when used in addition to oral or manual stimulation of the vulva.

Ties That Bind

Some couples like to reinforce their fantasy scenarios by using a variety of restraints for bondage. Some lovers feel freer to express themselves when restrained, and others enjoy being "forced" to relax and just receive pleasure. A wide variety of restraints are available in every material from silk and velvet scarves and ropes to leather buckling bonds, which allow you to clamp your lover's wrists or ankles together in a single, swift motion, and metal handcuffs.

Blindfolds are also related to the bondage dynamic. For some individuals, not being able to see what their partner is doing can add significantly to their arousal and enjoyment. Homemade blindfolds tend to slip off or feel uncomfortable, but a sleep mask (the kind you might use to catch a nap on an airplane) can fill the bill nicely if you want to give it a try.

He Says/She Says

"When my wife read about a new sex toy shop that opened in a nearby town she suggested a 'field trip.' We didn't buy a thing, but we certainly had an enjoyable time imagining what people did with all this paraphernalia. It gave us a lot of food for thought, you might say."
—Eric, 52

For Swingers Only

Sex swings and slings are specially designed for holding a man or woman in a semi-reclining position with the legs open. The swing hangs from an eyebolt or a special stand and allows for all kind of positions that would be difficult or impossible without the swing. These items are expensive, and there's usually a body weight limit for them, but if you and your man are up for a trip to a sex store, they're at least worth some window-shopping fun.

Skin Deep

Body play can utilize oils, balms, and other liquids. But for a novel change of pace, try erotic body dusts—a light powder that you sprinkle on and then rub into your lover's skin. Body dusts are infused with sensual scents like honey or berry, and although they don't generate slippery friction, they'll leave your lover's body extremely smooth for a unique feel during lovemaking. For added fun and spice, most body dusts come with a feather tickler to use when applying the dust to your partner's skin.

Another unique skin-deep option is body rock candy. Remember rock candy? It reacts with saliva to fizz and sizzle on your tongue. In this case, you spread it on your lover's limbs, torso, back, or behind and enjoy a sizzling sensation on your tongue as you lick it off. (There's an old urban legend about rock candy and soda causing people to explode. Fear not. It doesn't.)

Pleasing Strip Teasing

Many women feel shy about initiating fantasy-related activities with their men. But of the many, many possibilities, there is one that nearly every woman I've ever talked with has thought about. Many have even tried it to some degree—much to their men's delight. That activity is the good old-fashioned striptease.

A striptease is a great way to show your man how sexy you think you are—and without a doubt he will agree.

Certainly, even the most spontaneous, casual striptease-type removal of a few items of your clothing will make your man's eyes pop and jaw drop. But for those times when you really want to give him a special pleasing treat, you can take things to the next level. Gypsy Rose Lee will have nothing over you if you follow this step-by-step guide to putting on a strip show:

1. Prepare what you wear underneath. Let the grand finale include some sexy underwear, like a matching lacey bra and panties set.

2. Accessorize, accessorize. Whatever you wear on top, make sure your outfit includes lots of items you can teasingly take off one by one. Some items you may want to include are long evening gloves, a scarf or feather boa, and a dangling necklace. Button-down blouses are far preferable to tops you pull off over your head. High heels are a must.

3. Select your music. You'll want something with a good beat to encourage a little hip swiveling, bumping, and grinding. But don't choose music with too fast a tempo. It's best to take your time. A personal favorite: Chaka Khan singing *Hey, Big Spender*.

4. Remember the "tease" part. As far as men are concerned, a striptease performance is more about the teasing than the stripping. Tantalize your audience of one by dancing suggestively, tossing your hair, and brushing up against him and then pulling away. (Don't let him touch or grab you, however. That's for later.)

5. Fling. As you take off an article of clothing, toss it in your lover's direction. (Remember fling, don't wing. Hitting your guy in the eye with a garter belt spoils the mood.)

6. Keep eye contact. It sends your man the message that you're doing this for him, and only him.

7. Draw out your ending. After you've removed everything but your dainties, slow down and tease even more. Allow your lover to really enjoy himself as you pull your panties or G-string down over your hip and then cover up again.

8. When you're finally *sans* clothing of any kind, touch yourself provocatively. Then let it be his turn.

If you're shy about stripping for your man, practice in a mirror. Think of it as a dress rehearsal—or, rather, an *undress* rehearsal. You'll probably have so much fun solo that you'll be eager for opening night.

The Least You Need to Know

◆ Sexual fantasies are extremely common, but simply having one doesn't mean a person wants to act it out.

◆ Couples can safely explore sexual fantasy material when both agree on the rules of play.

◆ Fantasy roles are limited only by your imagination.

◆ Adult films can offer new ideas and inspiration—and many women are more turned on by them than they think they will be.

◆ Sex toys can add extra excitement to your lovemaking because they add novelty.

◆ Stripteasing is a surefire pleaser because men thrive on the feeling of anticipation it gives them.

Chapter 15

Letting Him Please You

In This Chapter

- ◆ Why any man can be a better lover
- ◆ Teaching him about foreplay
- ◆ Guiding him to your erogenous zones
- ◆ Self-pleasuring with and without him
- ◆ Initiating sex without feeling silly

Would you be pleased if your man was more skillful in bed? More sensitive to your sexual needs? More enthusiastic about lovemaking? Those are rhetorical questions, of course. What woman wouldn't?

Well, this may come as a surprise to you, but your man would very much enjoy giving you more pleasure. Almost nothing makes a man feel more self-confident, more virile, more alive, and more proud (justifiably so!) than really satisfying a woman sexually. You might not realize it, but you have the power to help your man evolve into the kind of lover he's always wanted to be. This chapter will tell you how to achieve this ultimate win/win.

Slowing Him Down

In sex surveys that ask women their number one grievance about lovemaking, the answer is usually "not enough foreplay." Many women contend that their men rush toward intercourse and orgasm without giving them enough time to warm up. This, in turn, interferes with the women's ability to have an orgasm.

But if your man is not spending enough time on preliminaries it's likely not because he's uncaring or indifferent. It's because his sexual response mechanisms are simply different from yours. A man's sexual response is like a light bulb that gets turned on and goes from cold to hot in a flash. As a woman, your sexual response is more like what happens when you plug in a curling iron. You have to wait while it gradually warms up. But when it's ready, it's good and hot.

When women are asked how long they would like their men to engage in foreplay, their answers average out to 17 minutes. (Remember that's an average number, which means most women answering are probably mentioning a round number like 15 or 20 minutes). But putting pressure on your man by naming any specific amount of time would be counterproductive. If you want your man to slow down and devote more time to warming you up, you can try many positive methods.

- In a flirtatious tone, tell him before you start making love that you're really in the mood for a nice appetizer before the meal.

- Whisper in his ear, "You know what would really turn me on?"

- Encourage him to linger and explore by doing unto him the kinds of things you would like done unto you.

- When he's doing something you like, give him positive feedback such as, "Yes, yes, take your time, lover."

- If he's missing the mark, gently guide his hand and then reinforce him with more positive words that encourage lingering.

If your lovemaking preliminaries are routinely taking only a few minutes, your man might be a bit startled at first when you alter the pattern and change the rhythm. But he'll respond well if he gets the idea that you want to prolong lovemaking because you like it so much. It's unlikely you'll go from 2 or 3 minutes to 17 minutes overnight, but if you continue to reinforce him even each time he slows down and dallies, he may soon be a master chef in the appetizer department.

Introduce Him to Your Hot Spots

As part of sex and sex play, a woman wants her man to touch her where it feels good—really, really good. The areas that feel best when sexually stimulated are known as erogenous zones. Informally, they're known as hot spots. When a woman's hot spots are touched ever so lightly, a delicious tingle can reverberate throughout her whole body. When the right amount of pressure is applied, they can send her careening toward the heights of orgasm.

You might think that your man should instinctively know about which of your spots are hot and which of your spots are not. But the truth is that even you might not know all there is to know about your hot spots. There may be some wonderfully sensitive areas that neither of you has ever tried stimulating.

If you want to let your man please you, you owe it to yourself to unlock the hidden potential of all your hot spots. The more you know, the more he can know. That's what it's all about.

The Clitoris

The *clitoris*, a small pink knob of flesh, is sometimes known as a "magic button." That's because it can generate some intensely pleasurable sensations. In fact, it seems to have been made for pleasure alone, because the clitoris is the only sex organ with no known reproductive function. Many women say that oral or manual stimulation of the clitoris is the best way for them to achieve orgasm.

Your man is much more likely to locate your clitoris with ease if you know precisely where it is. Do you?

Above your vagina is a smaller opening called the urethra, where urine comes out. Above the urethra is the clitoral hood, which may be camouflaged by pubic hair. A good way for your man to find the clitoris is by touch. During sexual arousal, the hood becomes puffier and puffier, but the clitoris remains inside it. If he puts his finger on the hood and presses down gently he'll discover a shaft of rigid tissue, anatomically equivalent to the head (glans) of the penis.

Tantalizing Terms

The word **clitoris** from a Greek word meaning "little hill." But it's been recently discovered that the clitoris is much bigger than previously thought. It extends in two "arms" about nine centimeters back into the body and high into the groin.

Women are very particular about how they like their clitoris stimulated. You might be one of those for whom a gentle, teasing caress sends you hurtling into ecstasy. Or you might like firmer pressure. You might enjoy the same kind of stroke over and over, or you might find that repetitiveness makes your clitoris feel numb. If you want to have your man experiment with touching your clitoris, ask him to trace the alphabet on it with his finger or tongue. You'll most likely find a winning touch before you can say "ABC." Whatever your pleasure, be sure to let your man know when he is doing a good job of pressing that magic button.

Also, don't let your man become confused. The clitoris seems to shrink out of sight in the instance just before a woman climaxes. This is a sign of turn-on, not turn-off. It happens because the hood of the clitoris is becoming engorged with blood.

The Labia Minor

These are the inner lips of a woman's genitals, and they are very hot spots. Ninety-eight percent of women in the famous Kinsey studies of sexuality reported being able to feel a touch on the inner or outer side of these lips. The fleshy outer lips of the vagina—the labia majora—are considered far less sensitive.

The Vaginal Vestibule

The funnel shaped area just above the inner lips of the vagina, as well as the first inch and a half of its interior is a surefire pleasure zone. Mother Nature has generously supplied it with nerve endings. By comparison, the deep inner walls of the vagina have far fewer nerve endings to stimulate. The fact that the entrance to the vagina is so sensitive is one of the reasons that a man's penis size is not of paramount importance to a woman's enjoyment of intercourse.

The G-Spot

The G-Spot was named for Dr. Ernst Grafenburg, a German gynecologist who discovered this erogenous zone on the inner, upper wall of the vagina. Some women don't believe they have a G-spot. But this is just a somewhat technical term for a bean-sized area of tissue that hardens when a woman is aroused (making it easier to find at that time). The fact is that every woman has one. The question is whether you are one of the women who finds that pressure applied to this spot makes for some very fine whoopee.

If you'd like to have your man help you find out, lie down on your back and have him insert one or to fingers into your vagina with his palm facing the ceiling. If he bends his fingers slightly and feels along the vaginal walls he will find a roundish, sensitive area somewhere between your bladder and your pelvis. If he keeps rubbing it, you may like it. But if you don't find the sensation enjoyable, don't fret. Just move on to a known hot spot and enjoy.

He Says/She Says

"I always thought the G-spot thing was a myth. But one day I was very relaxed, and my husband was exploring around with his fingers. I had a strange sensation. For a moment it just felt like pressure on my bladder, but when that passed I had an incredible orgasm. My husband was so proud of himself I thought he would burst. Since then, he loves to try to 'score the touchdown' as he calls it."
—Lisa, 36

The Perineum

The perineum is the area between the vagina and the anus. It's made of tissue similar to that of the vaginal lips and so contains many nerve endings. Although it is very sensitive for a lot of women, it often goes unexplored.

Because this is a part of the body that's not normally exposed, your man may feel like you are giving him special privileges by letting him explore it. This can be very exciting for you both.

This area is extremely sensitive and fragile, so encourage your man to stick to a light touch at first. If you find yourself aroused by this for some time, he can apply a bit more pressure.

The Breasts and Nipples

Men love breasts. In fact, it would be nice if we women liked our breasts half as much as our men do. Sex surveys show that although 90 percent of women say their partners like to kiss or stroke their breasts during sex, only 50 percent of the women actually enjoy it.

The breasts are, in fact, rich in nerve endings and ripe with pleasurable possibilities. All breasts respond sooner or later to sensual touch. Possibly, we would enjoy breast play more if we could encourage our men not to pay them too much attention too soon. Men are so enthusiastic about breasts they tend to overstimulate them too quickly.

If this sounds like an issue you have, let your man know you want him to start softly and teasingly—for example by touching a breast softly, then lifting his hand away for a moment before continuing. When the nipples become hard, that's a sign of arousal and indicates that you could well be ready for more intense stimulation. Your lover's best bet is to watch your reactions as he licks, kisses, sucks, strokes, or squeezes. You can also indicate your wishes by gently guiding his mouth or hands.

The Buttocks

Many women enjoy having their buttocks attended to and with more vigor than most men might imagine. Because the rear end isn't sensitive in the way a nipple or a clitoris is, more pressure can be applied. You and your man might both really enjoy him kneading and squeezing your buttocks. It's true that many women are self-conscious about their behinds, but having your man spend time in this area might give you a whole new appreciation and even make you more comfortable with your backside.

The Neck

The poor underrated neck! It is actually one of the hottest spots on the female body. Maybe we were turned off to necks in high school when guys thought we actually enjoyed getting hickies (most of us don't). Still, if your man covers your neck with tender kisses, it's likely you'll soon be feeling pretty fired up. (Where do you think the word necking came from?) Try to find a way to let him know that this technique can turn a goodnight kiss into much, much more.

The Ears

Bundles of nerve endings in and around the ears render them supersensitive to touch. You can find out for yourself by using the pads of your index finger and thumb to massage the outer ears with slow, firm movements. If you do this in your man's view and indicate how good it feels he may just want to try doing it to you.

Another thing you might appreciate is the sensation of gentle blowing in your ear. But this is a highly individual preference—so much so that some women enjoy such a sensation in one ear but not the other. As for a tongue in the ear, many women find that "wet Willie" sensation less than pleasant. But, whatever turns you on ....

The Toes

Yes, the toes. Not every woman likes to have her toes played with, but those who like it, really, really like it. Having your toes nibbled, kissed, or gently sucked can send chills up your spine. You can offer your man easy mouth-to-toe-access in many man-on-top positions when you simply lift your legs. Remember to get a lovely, softening pedicure and painted toenails for additional inspiration!

Letting Him Watch

A wonderful way to teach your man how to please you is to let him watch while you pleasure yourself. Remember, men are visual. They are great at executing the "watch and learn" model.

I know the idea of touching yourself while someone watches might be a little unnerving at first. But think of the advantages of giving your man this kind of lesson. For one thing, you will be offering him precise, detailed instructions. For another, watching you turn yourself on will be a surefire turn-on for him.

Let's not put the cart ahead of the horse, however. You can't show your man how to satisfy you if you don't know how to satisfy yourself. If you've always been reluctant to experience the joys of masturbation, now is the time to overcome your resistance. Masturbation is not only good; it's very good for you.

Me Masturbate?

Many women think masturbation is just for men. Happily, it is an equal opportunity sexual endeavor. It's also one you can enjoy at your convenience if, say, your man is out of town. Mother Nature must have meant for women to masturbate because there are some very specific female health benefits that result from the practice. Masturbation can relieve menstrual cramps, strengthen the pelvic muscles, and even fight yeast infections by increasing blood flow to the pelvis. It's certainly also great for alleviating stress.

Besides all of this, masturbators make better lovers. Masturbation provides an excellent opportunity to get better acquainted with yourself sexually. By experimenting with different rhythms and techniques, you get more in tune with your sexual responses. After you discover what works for you, you can show and tell your partner what turns you on, and your confidence as a sexual partner will increase.

Finally, if you're experiencing a bout of diminished sexual desire, as most women do at some point, masturbation provides a private, low-key way to reignite your pilot light.

Ten Steps to Doing It Yourself

If you think that women or men masturbate the same way, you're way off. Although each individual has his or her own style of masturbating, women in general take a more slow and languorous approach. Masturbation and the buildup to it can be extremely gratifying experience.

Because many women are taught little or nothing about their genitals, we sometimes need a little guidance, information, and affirmation in order to discover the wonders of masturbation. If you're a novice, this 10-step plan should be a great start. If it's been too long since you've pleasured yourself, this should inspire you to seize the day.

1. Make some private time. Clear at least half an hour, preferably an hour. Ensure your privacy by locking the door. Turn the phone ringer off and the answering machine on.

2. Remove most or all of your clothing.

3. Relax. Take a warm bath or have a glass of wine if wine calms you.

4. Find a comfortable position. Most women start out lying on their backs, legs bent, and spread apart.

5. Fantasize. Recall an exciting sexual encounter or embellish a favorite sexual fantasy. If you need a jumpstart, thumb through a sexy magazine, read an erotic story, or watch an adult video.

6. Discover. Run your hands over your body, lingering on the most sensitive areas. If you like, you can look at your genitals in a hand mirror (especially if you're unfamiliar with them) and explore the different parts to see what feels nice. Find and touch your inner and outer labia, your clitoris, your vagina, and your perineum.

7. Get wet. Apply a little lube or simply wet your index and/or middle finger with saliva.

8. Stroke. Using one or two fingers, rhythmically stroke your vulva, paying special attention to your clitoris and inner labia. Experiment with different tempos, pressures, and motions. Try placing a finger on either side of the clitoris and stroking up and down, or rubbing the clitoral hood with a circular motion. Pay attention to how your body responds and build the excitement. Keep experimenting until you find a motion that feels as if it will lead to climax.

9. Breathe and swivel. Breathe deeply; don't hold your breath. Rock your pelvis as you would during intercourse.

10. Go for it. If you're on the verge of orgasm, but can't quite get over the hump, focus on a really hot fantasy. Add stimulation by caressing your nipples, or try thrusting another finger in and out of your vagina. Continue the stimulation through the orgasm; then lighten up.

Because most women orgasm from stimulation of the clitoris, and since clitoral masturbation is easy to do, that's the example I've given here. But you can, of course, also masturbate using vaginal penetration or G-spot stimulation (a vibrator or dildo can be used as an aid). There is simply no wrong way to masturbate.

Starting Him Up

Myth: Women don't initiate sex because they don't have to.

Reality: Women don't initiate sex because they feel shy, silly, and self-conscious. Sometimes they're afraid of rejection; sometimes they are scared they will be thought of as sexually demanding.

One of men's chief desires when it comes to women and sex is that they would like their partners to make the first move—at least now and again. They say nothing would make them feel more desired. They have an excellent point. Most women simply don't do this often enough, if at all. But men misunderstand why women are so reluctant to initiate sex. It's not because we've just gotten complacent about being the pursued ones instead of the pursuers. It's that we're embarrassed and afraid. These feelings tend to be the result of social conditioning.

Many of us have been taught that it is not our place to be the initiator. Our society taught us that girls needed to wait for boys to ask them to dance, to ask them on a date, to ask them to go steady, or to propose marriage. Naturally, it was up to the man to indicate when he wanted to have sex. If we were sexually forward, we were led to believe that it would be considered very unappealing.

True, in the very early stages of a relationship a woman might scare a man off by being too forward. But no one ever bothered to tell us how men in long-term relationships really feel. They find it extremely appealing when their wives or girlfriends want to get the ball rolling. They consider this a wonderful affirmation of their attractiveness and validation of their virility. They're flattered as all get-out. After all, everyone wants to be wanted.

The bottom line: It's time to get over it. If you want more sex, you need to take some responsibility for starting things up more often. I know you might feel a bit silly at first, but you will put that behind you as you learn to express your love and desire in this way more often.

Choosing to initiate sex can be done in any number of styles, from subtle to fabulously outrageous. You can surely find one that suits your personality and your relationship. Here are just a few examples:

♦ Collaborate with your man to develop a special "sign" that indicates your interest, like leaving a rose on his dresser or putting on a special CD.

He Says/She Says

"I told my wife I wish she would jump me every once in a while. I couldn't understand why she didn't let me know when she was in the mood. I'd probably be happy to comply. Now she does tell me, and it has made a wonderful improvement in our sex life."

—Shane, 44

♦ Put a post-it note on his pillow that says, "How about it, Handsome?"

♦ Use your redeemable pleasure coupons (see Chapter 13).

♦ Before you get into bed, make eye contact with your man and take off whatever you're wearing—every stitch.

♦ Be brazen: Plop yourself in his lap, wrap your arms around him, and say out loud, "I want you now."

If you're not sure exactly how your man would like you to go about initiating sex, ask him. He'll be only too glad to instruct you.

As with all matters in the romance department, of course, be sensitive to timing. Just as there are times when you're not in the mood for lovemaking—no matter how much you love your man—there are times when he feels the same. Don't take it the wrong way if physical exhaustion or mental distractions leave him wanting nothing more than a hug on any particular night. Respond with understanding, as you would want him to do for you.

Helping Him Last

Many women wish that after their man got started up he would last longer as a lover. It might surprise you to know that many men are concerned about the same thing. It's been estimated that about one third of all men are concerned that they ejaculate too rapidly.

Exactly what is "normal" is hard to say. It has been estimated that the average young male will ejaculate after 3 or 4 minutes of continual thrusting. Some good news: Men do tend to slow down a bit as they age. But just about any man at any age can last longer if he and his partner make that a goal.

Together, you can try a number of methods to prolong his pleasure, and yours. Be careful to phrase any suggestion along these lines in a positive manner. Rather than complaining that your man comes too soon, tell him you would like to discover ways that both of you can stretch out and savor your lovemaking. Then you can …

♦ Get your man nice and relaxed before sex with a sensual massage.

♦ Try one of the many side-by-side positions, which tend to foster a more leisurely approach to intercourse.

♦ Experiment with woman-on-top positions, in which many men take longer to ejaculate.

♦ Explore Tantric techniques, such as "riding the wave," which are designed to make love last longer as well as increase its physical and emotional pleasures. (See Chapter 11 for more on positions and Tantric sex.)

> **CAUTION**
>
> ### Uh-Oh's and No-No's
>
> Having an alcoholic beverage or two can cause a man to take longer to ejaculate. But be careful. A bit too much, and he may find that he is unable to ejaculate at all. In addition, excessive use of alcohol diminishes libido and decreases a man's ability to have a full, firm erection.

The Start/Stop Technique

As a couple, you can also learn a start/stop technique recommended by many sex therapists as a way of training a man to delay ejaculation. The technique involves an exercise solely focused on the man's pleasure—but with a big payoff for the woman down the road.

You get undressed and get into bed, creating an atmosphere free of distraction. You kiss and caress until your partner is aroused. Then you stroke his penis until he is very close to climaxing. Now you stop, wait 10 or 20 seconds, and start again. Repeat this process three or four times. Do this "drill" for several sessions.

For the next few sessions, the woman's hand is lubricated so that it more closely resembles the feel of a vagina. After that drill has been mastered, the man actually enters the woman's vagina while she is on top, he stops moving when he is near ejaculation, until he can last up to five minutes or so.

In the final phase, instead of stopping still at the point of near-ejaculation, the man simply slows down. Or he may rock his hips from side to side so that his motion is circular instead of thrusting. This helps to sustain the length of pleasure for both partners, who may ultimately even climax together.

The Squeeze Technique

If your man wants to go ahead and practice ejaculatory control on his own (the dear overachiever!), tell him about the squeeze technique. In this technique, the man masturbates to the brink of climaxing, then keeps a still hand firmly squeezed on his erect penis. He then repeats the process.

Some men who have mastered the squeeze technique say it has enabled them to actually have multiple orgasms. Needless to say, if your man can double or triple his pleasure, that means more pleasure potential for you as well.

The Least You Need to Know

- Men heat up quickly, women slowly—but with attention to foreplay, you can meet in the middle.

- Women need to be familiar with their erogenous zones so they can provide their men with a good roadmap.

- Masturbation is not just for men: It has health benefits for women and can make you a better lover.

- Men want their women to initiate sex more often, and you can do so in a style that works for your personality.

- Many men say they want to last longer during intercourse; their women can help.

Part 6

Emotions in Motion

Question: When does a man feel the most loving? *Answer:* When he feels most loved. Underneath their bravado, men are highly sensitive creatures who need—and deserve—emotional TLC.

This part of the book will help you please your man on an emotional level by offering him the things he most longs for in this realm: acceptance and understanding. Because life has its rough spots for everyone, it also helps you help your man through inevitable disappointments and even through the male midlife challenge. If you bolster his ego when it needs some extra support, he'll never let you down.

Chapter 16

You Can't Change Him: Don't Try

In This Chapter

◆ Letting go of unproductive expectations

◆ Understanding his beliefs about masculinity

◆ Learning to overlook minor matters

◆ Dealing with your man's bad moods

◆ Dealing with passive-aggressive behavior

◆ The antidote to power struggles

In the preceding parts of this book, you learned a lot about pleasing a man sexually. For women, sexual and emotional relationships are usually inseparable, but you may wonder whether the same thing is true of men. In long-term relationships, *it is*. Sure, men might place a higher value than women on physical arousal and satisfaction itself. The underlying truth, however, is that over time a man is unlikely to gain much pleasure in making love to a woman whom he feels does not value him for who he is.

Loving Him, Warts and All

This book's very first chapter reminded you that, first and foremost, a man needs acceptance from his woman. That acceptance should be unconditional—that is, with no strings attached. But many of us do enter long-term relationships with all kinds of "strings." We fall in love with a man's potential instead of with the man himself. We harbor all sorts of expectations that *he will change* and only then will he be the true man of our dreams.

Sometimes we are honest with ourselves about our expectations. We have a *conscious expectation* when we are aware of how actively we are wishing and hoping for a change—for example, acknowledging that we want our guy to shift career paths and make more money. We might openly talk about our conscious expectations, although we are sometimes more likely to do so with other people than with our partner himself. An example would be if you married a man and confided in your mother that "he will be a great provider once I can get him to stop dreaming of opening a restaurant and get him to go to law school."

Sometimes our expectations are not so straightforward. We might be keeping them below our level of awareness. These kinds of expectations are *unconscious expectations*. They are even more dangerous to a relationship because they are unspoken and un-examined. Unconscious expectations can become burdens; for example, you might expect your man to automatically stop hanging out with his friends after marriage or evolve from a messy type into a neatnik as soon as he cohabits with you. The expectations are like baggage that seems to grow heavier and heavier as we carry it along. Each day, as your man proves that your assumptions about his miraculous behavioral over-haul are incorrect, you become a bit less enchanted with him. Neither one of you is even quite sure why this disenchantment is taking place, but it is. Suddenly you both feel as though there is an elephant in the living room, and you're not supposed to say anything about it.

He Says/She Says

"I'm a bit of a slob. I admit it. When we were dating my girl-friend never commented on the fact that I don't always hang up my clothes when I take them off. As soon as we got married, she seemed to take this as a per-sonal insult. Isn't that changing the rules in the middle of the game?"
—Hugh, 28

Having expectations of your man that you do not share with him is setting him up to fail. If your agreement to be with a man for the long haul is con-tingent upon him altering something about himself or his goals, you owe it to him and to yourself to be honest. If he is agreeable, fine. If he's not, you need to sit down and have a long talk with yourself. Remember, a long-term commitment means "for richer, for poorer, for neater, for sloppier," and so on. No one ever took a vow that said, "for so long as you do everything I want."

Guys Will Be Guys

Many of women's expectations for eventual change in their partners are based on the mistaken assumption that men and women are exactly alike deep down. This might seem like a very modern way to look at things, but it is flat-out silly. Why have two different genders if they were going to be exactly alike?

Men and women are different. They see the world and their roles in it in different ways. You can respect this truth or not, but ignoring it would be ignoring a fundamental law of the universe—like gravity.

Boys and girls are wired differently, in terms of hormones and brain chemistry. But the way they learn to be boys and girls also depends on a tremendous amount of social conditioning. It takes about 18 months of life for a child to identify themselves as a boy or a girl. Yet from the day they are born—and often before if parents are aware of their unborn child's gender—boys and girls are regarded differently by their parents. Girls get the pink nursery; boys get the blue nursery. Boys get more rough-house play than girls. Girls are encouraged to share their emotions more than boys. Without realizing it, boys and girls adapt their behavior to conform to these kinds of cues. As children grow into adolescents and adults, they continue to use gender differentiation to make sense of the world, to interpret other people's behavior, and to modify their own actions and reactions.

Along the way, boys develop *masculinity ideologies*. They learn and embrace certain socially acceptable standards concerning what it means to be a man. These ideologies are sacred to men. As women, we need to understand how important they are. We need to restrain ourselves when we find that we are trying to get our guy to give up these guy-like ways of thinking.

Tantalizing Terms

Masculinity ideologies are ideas and concepts that individual men hold about what it means to be a man.

Men and Self-Reliance

One of men's key masculinity ideologies concerns self-reliance. Even in the face of hardship, men do not believe it is manly to seek help from others. Sometimes this can truly confound and even anger women. It makes no sense to us why our guy would rather:

◆ Waste time driving around attempting to find an elusive destination rather than simply pulling into a gas station and asking for directions.

◆ Stand knee-deep in water while foraging in a toolbox rather than calling a plumber to fix a leak.

◆ Insist on shoveling his own driveway after a snowstorm even if he's not in great shape and ends up huffing and puffing.

We simply don't understand why men behave in such a "pig-headed" fashion because our gender, unlike theirs, is conditioned to seek support. We don't see any disgrace in saying "Hey, I'm in over my head here." Doing so does not threaten our female identity. It doesn't mean diverging from our female script. Men, on the other hand, see reliance on others—especially other men, or on strangers—as an admission that they are less masculine than they ought to be. They hate to admit ignorance, and they resent appearing to be dependent.

You may not like it when your man behaves in such "irrational" ways. But, remember, taking an independent stance is not irrational to him. If you attempt to badger your guy into seeking help when he feels he is up to a task, your insistence might have exactly the opposite effect from that which you desire. He will resist seeking support with *even more determination* because now he suspects that you doubt him. Now he has to prove his manliness to you as well as to himself. Let him be. He probably will figure out what he needs to do, even if he doesn't do so on your timetable. If not, he may well figure out a way to "trade" some expertise that he has with a resource who has the information he requires.

Men and Competitiveness

Men are especially reluctant to ask for help when they feel they cannot reciprocate. They might ask a buddy for a favor if they can quickly do a favor for that same buddy in turn. But one thing men never want to do is appear to be in a "one down" position. They don't want to appear as though they are in second place. That's because they embrace the masculinity ideology of competitiveness.

Some men's competitiveness often shows itself in ways that look silly or "childish" to us women. They want to demonstrate dominance and power over other men in social interactions and in physical contests. We've probably all watched our guys knock themselves out trying to outdo someone else, even when we see the contest as not a fair match. Men hate to lose at any sports match, for example. Even the most "informal" of contests takes on significance for them. Some may drive themselves to the brink of collapse during a game of tennis or racquetball even if their opponent is 10 years younger and practices three hours a day. We look at this behavior and think of the dangers. But if we point the danger out—especially in front of the other guy—we'll only serve in egging our man on. Once again, restraint is advised; your guy is trying hard to act like a guy.

He Says/She Says

"My husband insists in paying the check when we go out with an old friend of his who makes a lot more money. For a long time it disturbed me, but I know now that if I complain about it makes him feel self-conscious about the difference in their incomes. I think it is money well spent if it allows him to feel proud that he can afford to treat his well-off buddy to dinner once in a while."
—Christine, 42

Men and Emotional Self-Control

An especially significant masculinity ideology has to do with emotional self-control. Men believe they should keep most of their emotions to themselves and that they should never appear to be unnerved even when they are under stress. Because it is considered masculine for men to display aggression, they might admit to being angry. However, men think that to express feelings such as fear or sadness is to appear "girlish."

Mothers work harder to manage excitable and emotional male infants than they do their female infants. From a boy's toddler years on, both parents participate in gender-differentiated development of language associated with emotions. Peer groups complete the job. Young girls typically play with one or two other girls in activities that foster learning emotional skills of empathy, emotional self-awareness, and emotional expressiveness. Boys, on the other hand, play in larger groups in structured games in which traits such as risk-tolerance, stoicism, and toughness are learned.

Women, accustomed to sharing their emotional life with other women, often find it hard to accept that expressing vulnerable emotions can be anything but beneficial. We understand the value of "a good cry." We subscribe to a feminine ideology that encourages us to let things out. Why is our guy keeping things in, we wonder? Isn't that unhealthy?

Although there is some proven benefit to expressing one's entire range of emotions *under certain circumstances*, you must keep in mind that men will opt not to appear vulnerable in any situation that can be considered public. Learning to communicate with your man and help him communicate is important (more on this in Chapter 17). However, expecting your guy to communicate in the way that *you* do will lead only to your disappointment, and his silence.

Change Your Response, Not Your Man

Do individuals change over time? Sure. Can you count on them changing the way you want them to? No! Can you make them change because you wish they would? No! And do you really want your man to change in ways that undermine his true nature. No!

Still, even knowing all you now know about men and about the importance of accepting them, I bet you still have a list of things you really would like to alter about your man. Examine that list carefully. Now, brace yourself: The only way you can hope to address these matters in a way that is constructive to your relationship is to *change your response to them.*

Even if nagging or whining results in a temporary "success" in getting your man to give up a behavior you find irksome, there will be a backlash. This is because of something known as reactance theory. Reactance theory suggests that when people perceive that their autonomy or self-control has been threatened, they will take steps to restore it. There's little point in getting your guy to exchange one behavior for another that you find equally annoying. That sort of thing could go on forever, and who in the world would take pleasure in that?

A better strategy is to do something completely new and different. If you've been complaining, take another tack. If you've been moping, lighten up. Only then will there be any possibility of something new happening.

Any two people form what is known as a relationship "system." Systems are made of dynamic, interconnected parts that form a whole. When one part of a system alters, other parts *naturally* compensate in order to keep things in balance. When you change your response to your man, you can initiate a subtle change in your relationship system without forcing anything and without making your man feel like less of a man.

The Art of Overlooking

One way to alter your relationship system is to simply learn to let certain things go. Ladies, life is short. It's also blissfully imperfect. Not everything is worth making a fuss over.

Go on and make a list of all the "annoying" things your man does. Now, look it over carefully and objectively. Mark the items that, in the long run, really don't matter so much. They are the things that you feel downright silly citing as the causes of a lost relationship. Imagine what others would say, for instance, if you explained that you left your fundamentally wonderful guy because he never picked up his socks.

Many of the chief annoyances we women say we have with our men are little more than inconveniences. They are behaviors that cause no harm—unless you count offending our sense that we want to control everything as harm. A sample list of such annoying but fundamentally unimportant things that your man does might look something like this:

- He refuses to throw out stuff I know he'll never use.
- He has a favorite chair/desk that doesn't fit the rest of the furniture.
- If he falls asleep with the TV on, he wakes and complains if I change the channel.
- He insists on talking to me when I'm reading.
- He aims for the dirty clothes hamper—but misses.
- He takes items out of the dishwasher without unloading the whole thing.
- Ditto for the clothes dryer.
- He hasn't thrown out a newspaper since the fall of the Berlin Wall.
- He hasn't made the bed since then either.
- He never brings in the mail.
- He hoards the Sunday paper.
- He pokes fun at my favorite television shows.
- He hangs the toilet paper roll "over" instead of "under."

What would happen if you were to turn a blind eye and let such relatively minor wrongdoings slide? Try it and see. Perhaps you've become used to compensating for your man when he doesn't do something on your timetable. If so, he has gotten used to the fact that you will "fix" the things you don't like. Perhaps you've gotten used to sighing and moaning when he violates your sense of order and decorum. If so, he has either learned to tune you out or to make temporary amends and then do the same thing all over again.

When you overlook a behavior for a certain amount of time, it will begin to dawn on him that something has changed. In fact, the more inflexible you have become over time, the more noticeable the change in your responses will be. You are no longer following your man around cleaning up messes. You are not nagging. You may both be surprised at what happens.

When a woman I'll call Tracy finally decided to overlook a habit she found irritating, here's what happened:

"My husband and I had agreed to take turns doing the dishes. When it was my turn I'd do them right after dinner, but whenever it was his turn, he would leave them until 'later.' Usually, I would be so bothered looking at a sink full of dishes that I would take care of them myself and then be resentful. Finally, I decided to let it go. I deliberately didn't even look at the kitchen sink. I distracted myself. I went to bed with the dishes undone. But when I got up in the morning, they had been done! After that, I noticed that my husband liked to do the dishes late at night. He never did them on my schedule, but he did do them. In fact, he said that for him, this was a relaxing transitional activity before winding down and going to sleep. Now I'm perfectly okay with our arrangement."

Tracy allowed herself and her man a little leeway. She changed her response to him and became more flexible, He, in turn, discovered a way to do his agreed-upon chore that actually gave him satisfaction. It was a win/win scenario.

People are different, of course, and the way in which your relationship system will shift when you learn to overlook the little things can't be predicted with complete accuracy. But things *will* change—even if only in the sense that you become more relaxed, and the general mood of your household improves. After all, in the grand scheme of things, stressing out over things—like which way the toilet paper roll goes—takes away from your ability to enjoy yourself and your relationship.

Teasers & Pleasers

Learning to let go of little things will change your relationship for the better. It will change you, too—into a calmer, more easygoing soul.

Doing a 180-Degree Turn

Another way you can alter your response to your man is to do a complete turnaround involving one of your usual reactions or routines. Learning to see the other side of an issue will help you be more understanding and may well nudge your man into doing the same. Let me show you what I mean:

Stacey was annoyed that her husband always seemed to get caught up in arguments that took place between his brother and sister at holiday time. These arguments involved everything from whose house people should gather at to what the three siblings should get their parents as a gift. Since Stacey's husband, Tom, always took his brother's side, Stacey took his sister's side. She wasn't even exactly sure why she did this, except for some vague idea that women ought to stick together. In truth, Stacey thought both brother and sister were right in some ways and wrong in others. The next time this ritual argument occurred, Stacey decided to point out that Tom's brother had some valid points. Her husband, now freed of his reflexive need to defend his brother, suddenly realized that his sister had some valid points as well. The usual differences were resolved more quickly—and *without* Tom and Stacey fighting about the issues between themselves.

Doing a 180 is extremely liberating. It lets you try a new role on for size. It also liberates your man to stop reacting as if on "automatic pilot." When you see the other side of any story, he may well do the same. Then it's easier to meet in the middle.

Acting "As If"

In many instances, misunderstandings occur in a relationship strictly out of a sense of anticipation that something might go wrong. Yet the self-fulfilling prophecy principle tells us that the more we expect the worst, the more likely we are to get it. Another way of altering your behavior is to go from expecting the worst to expecting the best. Here's an example:

Whenever Mimi and her husband, Bruce, were flying off to a vacation she stressed out because she knew he would procrastinate and leave his packing until the last minute. Then he would leave late for the airport and get them there with little time to spare before their flight. Because of Bruce's past flirtations with lateness, Mimi would assume each time a trip came up that this would continue to happen. She "helpfully" began to pack Bruce's things the night before (only to find he didn't like the things she packed and decided to change the contents of his suitcase at the last minute). She harangued him all the way to the airport that maybe they should change lanes or try another route to save time (only to find that he silently refused to follow her suggestions). Then Mimi decided to try a new approach. The night before their next trip she calmed herself down and acted as if she expected everything to go smoothly. She didn't pack her husband's bags. In fact, when he asked her advice on what to bring, she said, "Oh, you always know to bring exactly the right things." She did not suggest a midcourse correction *en route* to the airport either. In fact, when Bruce looked nervous about the time Mimi assured him everything would be fine.

Uh-Oh's and No-No's

Don't confuse acting *as if* with being deceitful. Remember, you always have a choice to see a glass half empty or half full. Making the positive choice should come from your heart.

With each successive trip to the airport, Bruce arrived a little bit earlier. Mimi may not ever have gotten there as early as she would have liked, but she learned that by acting *as if* she was certain her husband would not fail her, he never did.

Acting as if you expect the best is always a great gift to give your man. Your faith in him will boost his self-esteem. This, in turn, will provide him with a reservoir of energy and enthusiasm for everything he does.

Men and Their Moods

Another thing that many women would like to change about their men is their moods. In fact, we women seem to take our men's moods more personally then our men take ours. Most men take it as a given that women will be susceptible to different emotional "weather fronts" at different times. They may not love this about us, but they accept it. If only we were so accommodating.

Men are as prone to emotional ups and downs as we are. It's unfair of us to assume that they will be stalwart and steady from day to day, hour to hour in the privacy of their own homes *especially because they so often have to keep up a front in public*. We need to allow our men their moods. The important thing to remember about moods is that, like the weather, they pass—that is, unless our own reactions serve to worsen them and set them in stone.

Grumpy, Sleepy, and Dopey

Every woman who wants to please her man ought to be emotionally generous enough to allow him a transition time from work to home life—just the way you would like him to do for you. The fast pace of the workplace, its continual demands, and its emotional pressures are difficult to shake off instantaneously. A long or crowded commute home usually doesn't help with decompression. So give a guy a break:

- ◆ Don't overpersonalize his moods.

- ◆ Don't overreact to a less-than-cheery attitude.

- ◆ Don't try to out-mood his mood with your own negative demeanor.

If he's grumpy, sleepy, or dull and dopey when he walks in the door, give him a smile and a hug and act *as if* his need to imitate one of the crankier Seven Dwarves will soon pass. Your understanding and willingness to give him some breathing room will turn him into another character altogether: Happy.

The "Yes, Dear" Mode

Many women complain about a male mood they refer to as the "yes, dear" mood. This is such a familiar default position for many men that it is the subject of endless sitcoms and comic strips. Typically, men are shown hiding behind the sports page of the newspaper, replying "Yes, dear" to whatever their partner says without paying any attention whatsoever. You can be sure that whatever they're agreeing to will never be attended to. This type of behavior is known as passive aggression.

Passive-aggressive behavior is not so much a mood as a mode. It involves outwardly complying with someone's wishes, only to thwart them—as if by accident. The end result is that the person on the receiving end of the "yes, dears" feels frustrated, dismissed, and ignored. It's crazy-making to have someone say, "yes," when they don't mean it. Why would a man do that? If he keeps it up over a certain length of time, you're bound to *explode*, right?

Well, hopefully not. If your man is prone to the "yes, dear" syndrome, an explosive response has never gotten you anything in the past except a vicious cycle of finger-pointing, blame, and more passive aggression. Continuing to erupt is never going to get you anything else.

It's far better if you understand the cause of passive aggression—fear of conflict. Although men are conditioned to be competitive and aggressive, most are reluctant to be overly

He Says/She Says

"My wife complained that I just 'yessed her along' to keep her quiet. I finally told her she was right. If I said 'no' she hollered at me. I think she didn't realize the role she was playing in my behavior. Now, we have an agreement that I can say no without getting yelled at."
—Joe, 50

aggressive where their romantic partners are concerned. The more your partner is reluctant to express his own feelings of frustration to you, and the more he dreads your angry response, the more he'll tend to take the cautious "yes dear" approach. You, in turn, feel increasingly irritated. You act in ways that your man perceives as increasingly angry. And so the cycle goes on and on.

Perhaps it has never occurred to you that your big, strong man is actually afraid of *your* anger and will do nearly anything to deter it. But this may well be the case. Work toward a climate of safe and open communication within your relationship. Make it okay for your man to say he is upset with you. After all, it's not the end of the world if he is. People in long-tem relationships are bound to be mad at each other once in a while. Your acceptance of all your man's feelings—including any occasional anger he has toward you—can go a long way toward changing the pattern of passive aggression. There's nothing wrong with saying, "Honey, I know you're mad at me, and it's okay. People who love each other can be mad at one another. In fact, it would be weird if that wasn't the case."

Avoiding Power Struggles

For all of women's complaints, most of us say we really would rather not waste time and emotional energy in power struggles with our partners. If you're stuck in a power struggle or conflict with your partner, the best thing you can do is to be *empathetic* toward him.

> **Tantalizing Terms**
>
> **Empathy** means understanding and entering into another's feelings. It allows us a window into someone else's point of view.

Put your need to be right on the shelf for a bit. Instead, put yourself in your partner's shoes to understand his perspective. Really try to imagine the situation—whatever it is—as though you were he. You may have quite a revelation. Suddenly a point of view that seemed ridiculous to you a minute ago may start to have a kind of logic.

Being understanding and validating your partner's feelings does not mean you have to agree with him. Nor does it mean you have to give up on getting your own needs met. It's okay to focus on what you would like from your partner as long as you simultaneously remember what it is he needs from you. Being empathic is an extremely valuable thing to do because it broadens your own view of the world and because simply feeling understood can often mean more to your man than his winning any particular battle.

The Least You Need to Know

♦ Expectations that a guy will change when he's with us are counterproductive—especially if he doesn't even know about them.

♦ Your man's beliefs about masculinity are part of lifelong scripts that you shouldn't try to edit.

♦ Rather than trying to change your man, change your response to his behavior; your relationship system will alter in a natural way.

♦ Men are entitled to their moods, and bad ones will pass more quickly when they're allowed to run their course without blame.

♦ The best antidote to passive-aggressive behavior is creating a safe emotional climate in which a man can communicate—let him know all his feelings are okay to express in words.

♦ The best antidote to power struggles is empathy—putting yourself in your man's shoes can give you an enlightening new perspective.

Chapter 17

Guy Talk

In This Chapter

- ◆ Why and when men need silence and space
- ◆ Why men resist advice
- ◆ When complaining equals blaming
- ◆ Direct requests versus manipulation
- ◆ Taking an interest in his topics
- ◆ Reading your man's body language

You may think you and your man speak the same language. In the strictest sense, you do. After all, you both share a common vocabulary and the same rules of grammar. When you say, "Please pass the salt, honey?" he knows what you mean. Or does he?

The truth is there can be a world of difference between what a woman says and what a man hears. It's not uncommon for the true intent of a woman's speech to get lost in translation, so to speak. Unbeknownst to you, you could be upsetting your man not so much with what you say, but how and when you say it.

Communication is another one of those areas where women expect men to think and behave like women, but they don't. By continuing to recognize and explore the differences between you and your man, you can improve your relationship, build trust and cooperation, and make him more content overall.

When Guys Talk—and Don't

TRUE or FALSE: When a man withdraws into silence, it means he doesn't love you.

Answer: FALSE.

We women are big talkers. When we are under stress, we talk even more than we normally do. For us, speaking openly about whatever is bothering us is a way of alleviating anxiety. This is usually not the case with men.

When a man is facing an immediate problem, he's most likely to retreat from conversation so he can try to work out a solution in his own mind. As long as the problem remains unsolved, he will remain quiet and preoccupied. He may take a break from attempting to solve a large problem by engaging in solitary pastimes like watching baseball, browsing the newspaper, going for a solo drive, or playing a video game. But even so, part of his mind is still working on the problem.

At times like these, a man is uninterested in and unavailable for heart-to-heart talks with you, his partner. He is not apt to pay you as much—if any—quality attention. But this does not mean he doesn't care about you. If anything, the opposite is true. Chances are that solving whatever problems he is coping with (for example a problem with work, or a problem with finances) will benefit you both.

The best thing to do when a man is in retreat mode is to respect his space and his quietude. Yes, you love your partner and want to help him. But *this is really the best way* to do so. Insisting he "open up" at this point is not helpful.

Uh-Oh's and No-No's

If you suspect your guy is upset, let him be. If he says "It's nothing," or "It's no big deal," stop asking questions. These are his cues to you that he needs time and space to work it out.

Unfortunately, many of us just can't give up the urge to pursue a man when he is in retreat mode. In fact, often the more he retreats, the more we go after him. We ask him all kinds of questions about what's on his mind. We assure him that we know when something is bothering him. We assure him that we are there to help him. But none of this is what he needs right now. In fact, the more you try to draw him out, the more time he will spend being withdrawn.

Most of us find it very difficult to endure the fact that our man is distant from us as he tackles whatever issue needs tackling. It helps to remember that *this is not about you*. It's when you let your self-esteem get damaged by his reclusiveness that you get yourself into trouble. You pursue him too aggressively and have exactly the opposite effect you want to have. To prevent this from happening, make sure you have fallback activities and companions available to you when your man is in retreat. For example:

- Call a girlfriend and chat.

- Go out for a brisk invigorating walk or bike ride.

- Pick up an un-put-downable book.

- Work in the garden.

- Put on a headset and play your favorite music.

- Do a crossword or jigsaw puzzle.

- Give yourself a facial.

Any of these activities will not only distract you from trying to draw out your space-requiring guy but will also raise your spirits and make you feel better about yourself. As for your man, he will feel proud of *himself* when he is able to come up with a strategy for handling whatever is on his mind.

Teasers & Pleasers

Always have engaging activities or willing friends available to you for those instances when your guy needs alone time. You'll both feel better sooner when you're not anxiously waiting for him or blatantly worrying about him.

Advice Is Nice ... Or Is It?

TRUE or FALSE: It can never hurt to offer a sound piece of advice to a man.

Answer: FALSE.

Many of us also feel that it is part of our jobs as wives or girlfriends to give our man good advice. After all, they like to give *us* advice all the time. This is another fundamental communication difference between men and women. While it's okay to ask "Do you want my take on this?" men definitely do not want any *unsolicited* advice from us. To them, it's just a sign that we want to control them.

Mastery and competency are extremely important to men. They want to appear fully capable. Even if we don't mean to imply that they're *in*capable when we offer unwanted advice, that is what they infer. We may think we are simply helping, but they may think we are correcting and criticizing.

On occasion, a man might erupt in angry defensiveness when we offer a minor unsolicited suggestion on even a tiny matter, like how to fold up a baby stroller or how to solve a small software glitch on the family computer. It's tempting to think him immature and overly sensitive at such moments. But small matters are not always insignificant to him. For one thing, your man may feel that if he can't solve the little things, you'll never trust him with the big ones. For another, he may experience your suggestion as an echo of past criticisms, especially if he felt overly criticized by either of his parents or if he has been recently second-guessed at his job. In such cases, his negative reaction may be quite intense. If his response seems irrational and out of proportion, you'll know you hit a nerve.

He Says/She Says

"When my husband is in a rush he can make careless mistakes. Once we were on our way out the door when my son asked if he could fix the remote controller for his video game. My husband put in new batteries and it still didn't work. I just knew he put the batteries in backwards. But did I say anything? No. I let him discover it for himself. Even though it took an extra minute or two to figure it out, he felt okay about making a mistake and then correcting it himself. If I had pointed it out to him he would have felt foolish. That's just the way it is, and I know it by now."
—Sophie, 41

No matter how fundamentally good or "right" you think your advice is, keep it to yourself unless you are asked for it. If you are asked for it, that's great. I know a man who would never dream of sending out an important business letter or report without his wife, a professional writer and editor, proofreading it for him. I know another who always asks his wife's advice on what to wear to an important meeting because, as he laughingly puts it, he "has the fashion sense of a color-blind circus clown." And certainly, plenty of men ask for their wives' or girlfriends' input when an important decision is on the line, so long as they feel that advice will be given in a calm and compassionate manner.

Uh-Oh's and No-No's

If you're asked for advice, stick to the subject. Don't try to force improvements in areas that your man thinks are going fine. In guy terms: *If it ain't broke, don't try to fix it.*

But if you are asked for advice, give it graciously. Never gloat about having an area of expertise that your partner does not possess or about having an insight that eluded him. At least, not if you want to continue to be given the chance to assist him in the future. Finally, stick to the subject at hand. Being asked for one piece of advice does not give you *carte blanche* to begin a major overhaul of your partner.

Avoiding Blame Games

TRUE or FALSE: A man often feels a woman is blaming him when she talks about her problems.

Answer: TRUE.

We women are very good at complaining. Sometimes it feels good just to have a nice gripe session. We get to blow off steam. And somehow, that makes the problem, whatever it is, seem less bothersome for a while.

Although there's nothing wrong with a good old-fashioned rant session, you need to be careful about doing so in front of your man, unless you take certain precautions. Men are so hypersensitive to criticism and blame that they hear some even where none is intended. Here are some examples:

She Says	What He Might Hear
I hate my job.	If only you earned more I could quit work.
The kids are driving me crazy.	You are an ineffective parent.
This house is a mess.	You're a slob.
I hate my hair.	You never tell me I'm pretty.
I don't feel sexy.	We don't have enough sex.
My car is making that weird noise again.	Why can't you fix my car?
I need a vacation.	You never take me anywhere.
I'm exhausted.	You don't do enough around here.
I'm sick of this wallpaper.	Why don't you paint?

Do any of these male interpretations seem familiar? Even if you didn't mean a single one of these types of complaints to be interpreted as your man understood them, you can inadvertently cause a rift in your relationship by engaging in lots of generalized complaining without observing and being sensitive to his reactions. If you're just in a mood or want to get things off your chest, say so. Thank him for listening and for being there for you. Tell him it feels good for you to vent once in awhile and that you appreciate his listening.

Another thing to watch out for is that your husband may interpret even some of your casual gossip as a veiled disapproval of him. If you go on and on about a friend's husband and his fabulous new job, for example, your man may hear you saying, *"Why don't you get a great new job?"* If you tell him your sister got a beautiful diamond necklace for her anniversary, he may hear, *"So don't even think of getting me another scarf."* Choose your gossip-mates wisely. Another woman is almost always eager to indulge in this kind of girl talk.

But what if you are really envious of a friend whose man did something admirable? What if, in some way, you do hold your man partially responsible for one of your problems? It's unreasonable to imagine that two people in long-term relationships will never have complaints about one another. Still, presenting them in an accusatory fashion will never be productive. Your man will simply feel hurt and rejected. Wait until you are feeling calm enough to ask for his support in a levelheaded manner.

The Art of Directness

TRUE or FALSE: The best way to ask your man for something is to be indirect.

Answer: FALSE.

The best way to get a guy to do something is to simply and straightforwardly ask him to do it. Men don't like the feeling that they are being trapped, tricked, or manipulated into doing anything. They also don't appreciate lengthy or whiney requests. And they certainly don't respond positively to requests that contain a veiled accusation. They prefer short, direct questions to which they can answer yes or no.

Productive Requests	Unproductive Requests
Would you let me know your travel schedule?	I have no idea when you're coming and going. I can't make plans. Can't you tell me your schedule?
Would you mow the lawn this weekend?	My mother is coming and the yard looks like Animal Kingdom. Could you at least mow the lawn?

Productive Requests	Unproductive Requests
Would you please get this plate off the top shelf?	I can't reach this plate. I've been trying for 10 minutes. Can't you do it?
Would you go with me to the parent-teacher conference?	I dread going to these parent-teacher conferences. Can't you at least go with me one time?
Would you invite your folks for Thanksgiving?	Your folks don't like me. Can you ask them to come for Thanksgiving? Or else they won't.
Would you please feed the dog?	Am I the only one in this house capable of feeding the dog?
Would you put gas in the car?	Do you know how close I came to running out of gas? Can't you just take care of it?

The requests in the right-hand column all have components that men find irritating, maybe even infuriating. They are snappish. Some are quite harsh. They're also too long and too tentative. Men don't want to be asked whether they *can* do something; they want to be asked whether they *will* do something.

The Art of Asking Questions

TRUE or FALSE: A man never appreciates it when you ask him lots of questions.

Answer: FALSE.

Men don't like a woman to subject them to lots of questions when they are in retreat mode. They also don't like to have their decisions questioned. What does give a man pleasure, however, is when a woman exhibits her interest in a topic he likes to talk about by *keeping* him talking. And the best way to keep him talking is to ask questions.

In study after study, people rank as the best conversationalists those who listen well and who engage them into talking more about their own areas of expertise. So, if you really want to score points with your guy, take a genuine interest in something he knows a lot about. This could be cars, politics, sports, history, or what have you. Just give him a chance to show his stuff.

◆ Any Civil War buff will be only too pleased to give you his opinion on the turning points of key battles between North and South.

- Any political junkie will be happy to give you a blow-by-blow analysis of a debate he saw on C-Span in the wee hours.

- And any baseball stats aficionado will always be happy to tell you more anecdotes about World Series errors in play than you ever dreamed existed.

Don't feign your interest, though. Find something to enjoy about your man's breadth and depth of knowledge, something you genuinely respect and admire. In fact, whenever you can, arrange for an opportunity where he can show his knowledge off in front of others who will be suitably impressed. Now you'll really get him talking.

Male Body Language

TRUE or FALSE: Men never give external hints about what they are feeling inside.

Answer: FALSE.

Communication, of course, is not only about what is spoken, but also about what is unspoken. Learning to interpret your guy's physical stances and gestures will help you immensely with knowing how to time your more important conversations with him. Reading body cues will be especially useful in terms of knowing when he is in an open, expansive frame of mind or temporarily closed off. It will also help you notice when he is feeling insecure or more confident about himself.

The following table will clue you in to some key body language shorthand:

When He Does This	His Message Is
Smoothes his collar or hair	Notice that I'm attractive.
Brushes imaginary dust from his shoulder	Notice that I'm attractive.
Hooks his thumbs in his belt (when facing you)	I'm virile.
Hooks his thumbs in his belt (when facing other men)	I'm unafraid, and this is my turf.
Places hands on hips	I'm big and strong.
Buttons and unbuttons jacket	I'm slightly nervous.
Touches fingertips, forming a steeple shape	I'm very confident.

When He Does This	His Message Is
Points one or both feet at you	I'm interested in what you're saying.
Leans in toward you	I'm interested in what you're saying.
Holds your gaze, pupils dilated	I find you sexy.
Flushes in the cheeks	I find you sexy.
Clasps hands behind his back while walking	I'm self assured, a bit superior.
Crosses arms in front of chest	I'm defensive.
Leans backward as you speak to him	I'm unreceptive to you.

After you learn to read these signs without having to think about them too much, you will intuitively be able to use them to better the communication between you and your partner. One final thing you need to understand is that many things can affect a person's body language in the moment. Experiment and see. You can actually change your man's body language—and underlying mood—simply by warming up to him, smiling, and engaging him in a topic of interest to him.

Uh-Oh's and No-No's

Keep your body language interpretation skills to yourself. Never tell a man, "Aha, I see how you're feeling by the way you're standing." You might just make him self-conscious about his body and how he expresses himself.

The Least You Need to Know

- ◆ Men and women may speak the same language—but their communication styles and needs are quite different.

- ◆ Men require silent space to work out problems in their heads.

- ◆ When a woman complains, a man hears blame—let him know "it's not his fault."

- ◆ If you want something from your man, it's best to be direct about it.

- ◆ When your man is talking about a topic that interests him, flatter him by asking questions.

- ◆ A man's body language can tell you whether he is open or closed to communication from you at any given time.

18

Midlife and Other Crises

In This Chapter

- ◆ The fragile male ego
- ◆ When life lets him down
- ◆ Your man at midlife
- ◆ Fighting fair
- ◆ The joy of making up

Having you by his side is a buffer against many of life's day-to-day dilemmas for your man. However, regardless of how content you make him, you can't protect him from some of life's major challenges. You wouldn't want to even if you could, because it is when life tests us that we grow. Nevertheless, dealing with a man in the grips of disappointments can be a challenge in itself. This chapter will help you help him through some of the tougher times.

Anatomy of the Male Ego

Some people say that women are actually tougher than men when the chips are down. There is some truth to this. Men are brought up to act as though they are thick-skinned. So, when life throws them a curve, they are at somewhat of a disadvantage. They are not allowed to curl up and have a good cry or stamp their feet in the throes of a good, old-fashioned tirade. Unlike the fairer sex, they're not even allowed to feel sorry for themselves while they curl up, eat too much rum raisin ice cream and watch reruns of *The Bachelor*.

These temporary meltdowns can actually serve as coping mechanisms that help a person gather their strength and rally to meet a crisis head-on. Because men can't resort to these types of meltdowns without our culture disapproving, they keep much of their hurt and dismay inside. Internalized despair can sap their energy and drain their enthusiasm for even the parts of their lives that remain whole and worthwhile.

By now you know that men's egos are fragile things—more like eggshells than those supposedly thick skins. But when your man is in the midst of a struggle, *you can't let on that you know how vulnerable he is*. A man's dignity is especially important to him at times when he is beset with troubles. What he needs now more than ever is your appreciation, admiration, and inspiration. Add to this, he needs …

- Your continued show of faith in him.

- An affirmation of your pride in his accomplishments.

- Ongoing encouragement.

- A sense of humor and an attitude of cheerfulness.

Knowing that you have faith in him will help your man rise to any challenge. Like a knight carrying a handkerchief bestowed on him by his lady, he can carry that faith into battle with him. If you have any doubts that your man can slay whatever his particular dragon is, keep them to yourself or share them only on a confidential basis with a friend or counselor. Just as a woman's faith magnifies a man's confidence, her doubt magnifies his vulnerability.

Uh-Oh's and No-No's

When your man's spirits are down, don't insist he be upbeat. But do be a model of resilience for him. A good general rule is, only one of you at a time is allowed to be down in the dumps.

Remaining proud of all your man has achieved in the past will also help him—and you—cope with times of hardship. Encouraging him will, literally, endow him with the courage needed to view any crisis as an opportunity. The combination of a beloved woman's pride and encouragement is a powerful elixir that has enabled many men to snatch victory from the jaws of defeat.

He Says/She Says

"A few years ago I had to shut down a company that I had built from scratch. I thought I could never do anything like that again. But my wife kept me going. She said I had always been an 'odds-beater' and always would be. The fact that she defined me that way, and believed it so strongly, is why I was able to start all over again and build another company, more successful than the first."
—Edwin, 50

Your good humor and good cheer—if not overdone and forced, that is—will help your man keep things in perspective. Without trying to coax or cajole your man out of having his feelings, do your best to see the glass as half full even if he sees it as half empty. Your optimism will permeate his consciousness subtly but surely.

Handling Disappointments and Setbacks

Although everyone's life will take a different course, it's pretty likely that at some point your man will experience one of the big three setbacks that impact most males in our society today. These issues are:

♦ Money problems

♦ Work-related problems

♦ Problems related to physical illness

These can, of course, be tough on anyone of either gender. But if you want to be able to help your man when they impact him, you should know about some of the ways in which they particularly affect the male ego.

Money and Power

All of us have emotional reactions that are tied up with money. We may equate money with many things, like freedom or security. Naturally, any kind of financial setback is bound to make us anxious.

Men, however, have a particular emotional association to money that women do not. They associate money with their, shall we say, male assets. The bigger their billfolds and bank accounts, the more virile they feel.

When your man experiences a financial setback, be it a drop in his income, an investment portfolio that went south, or a business venture that didn't pan out, he will have to deal with all the practical frustrations that the setback involves. Habits of spending and saving will have to be altered while finances are in flux. He'll be preoccupied with figuring out ways of recouping his losses. In addition, however, a man will have to endure the stress that comes with feeling as if he has lost some of his masculine power along with some of his money.

At times like these, try not to let your anxiety about the financial matters themselves cloud your affection and respect for your guy. He'll solve the problem sooner if you do all you can to affirm his continued desirability and virility. Understand that he might not be in the mood for passionate lovemaking, but nevertheless continue to be warm and affectionate and even a bit flirtatious. Make the most of opportunities to offer him praise and encouragement. But also remember to allow him enough alone time to consider and weigh various solutions to the problem. At that point, broach the subject of sitting down and coming up with a plan together.

He Says/She Says

"During our marriage, like many couples, we have had more than a few financial reversals. I quietly economized during these times, but I didn't make a big deal out if it. I have learned never to make my husband feel worse than he already does by blaming or nagging him about money troubles. I've learned that the calmer I remain, the calmer my husband is. And the calmer we both are, the more quickly problems seem to come to a resolution."
—Abigail, 51

Work and Identity

In our culture we are very interested to learn what someone does for a living. Americans typically ask a new acquaintance, "What do you do?" within minutes of meeting. In certain other counties, this might be considered intrusive, but here it is par for the conversational course.

When we know what a man's job is, we feel we know a lot about him and his traits. For us, a man's identity goes hand in hand with his occupation. Men believe this about themselves as well. Whether they're bankers or builders, fry cooks or firemen, teachers or truck drivers, they have a firm image of their skills and their overall value that is tied up in doing their best at their job. Not surprisingly, when that job is threatened, a man can be devastated.

It's not unlikely, however, that your man will face some sort of career crossroads at some time during the course of your relationship. Economic forces may change the nature of his occupation. Global competition can affect the industry in which he works. Or he may simply feel that he is ready for a change but is unsure what that change ought to be.

Career crises are tough on guys because they challenge their self-images. Now is the time to show your appreciation of him for all of the things he does that have nothing to do with his job. Find ways of letting him know that you value him for who and what he is—a strong individual, a responsible mate, a good friend, a thoughtful lover, a caring parent.

Illness and Mortality

Experiencing an illness or injury can also take a serious toll on a man's self-esteem. In fact, the more vigorous he has been in the past, the more any change in his health status will upset him. A man who is used to leading an active physical life can feel betrayed by a body that will not let him continue with that level of activity—even if only temporarily. His vanity is wounded. And he is beset with the realization that his time and youth are finite commodities.

To be human is to live in an imperfect machine. As much as he hates to think about it, every man is at risk of experiencing less than perfect health at one time or another. Even if he does not fall ill, he may become extremely distraught when close friends of his—especially those in his age group—do so. The illnesses of friends and peers can remind a man of his own mortality.

As you'll learn in Chapters 19 and 20, you can do a great deal to help keep your man healthy and fit. These chapters will also tell you how to pamper a man and give him lots of tender loving care when he is under the weather. Helping a man contend with his physical limitations and his mortality is one of most complex emotional jobs a woman can take on. Often this role does fall to her, whether she's prepared for it or not, when her man reaches midlife.

The Male at Midlife

For much of their lives, men see themselves as boys. Even though they are grown-up boys with jobs, kids, responsibilities, and more than a few wrinkles and crinkles, the image they see looking back at them in the mirror remains young—at least at heart. Then something changes. Sometimes in their mid-40s to mid-50s, men look in the mirror and see an aging man looking back. Unlike the youthful and carefree boy they usually encounter, this man is running out of time and possibilities. Facing this newly recognized image can feel like a punch right in the gut. The reaction to it can be disappointment, sadness, and fear.

Uh-Oh's and No-No's

It's a bad idea to dismiss the male midlife crisis as so much psycho-babble. This passage is a time-honored transition, described long ago by the likes of Dante and Shakespeare.

As your man comes to terms with the fact that he is no longer a strapping 25-year-old, he may well do things that try your patience and test your relationship. Responding with anger won't help. You need to be aware of what's happening to your man. He is on the threshold of re-evaluating his life and figuring out how he wants to live the rest of it. Being aware will make you less apt to blame yourself for things going awry. It will also make you less prone to trying to speed your man's passage through this time, which must run its natural course (perhaps a year or more!).

The male midlife crisis is primarily the male's problem, even when it feels like it's yours. It is up to him to find a way through it. But you can do some things—and you should not do some things—to make this phase in your relationship easier for the two of you to navigate.

Do's and Don'ts for the Midlife Wife

It is always unnerving to be married to or in any long-term committed relationship with a man in the midst of a midlife crisis. You will hear a lot of horror stories about women who were left behind as their middle-aged guys pursued 21-year-old coeds, became obsessed with body building, or sold all their possessions to trek unencumbered across Bhutan. It's easy to panic and do something to make the situation more precarious than it already is. Instead …

◆ Resist the temptation to "fix" things for him—he needs to figure things out for himself.

- Don't demand that your man "snap out of it" and "clean up his act."

- Don't attempt to explain his feelings to him—he won't hear you.

- Don't dwell on gossipy horror tales of men who left their women at midlife.

- Don't lose confidence in yourself—this is not about you.

- Give him space; don't cling.

- Give him the freedom to spend more time with his buddies.

- Work on making yourself a more independent person—do more things alone and with friends.

- Continue to treat him with kindness.

Coping with a man's midlife crisis is not easy. But it's certainly not impossible to weather the storm. As in all things, expecting a positive outcome will help you and your man attain one.

Top Props for the Midlife Crisis

One of the standard clichés about male midlife crisis is that men are apt to go out and buy some outlandish toy at this time. It's not always the case, but sometimes men actually do accessorize their midlife crises. Even if they don't buy, they may do some serious window-shopping. If your man is considering a major midlife purchase, use the handy table that follows. It will help you to understand that it's not the prop that's important—it's what it represents to his psyche.

When He Gets ...	Maybe He's Searching For ...
a sports car	his lost youth
a Harley	respect
a surfboard	freedom from responsibility
a sailboat	a challenge from the elements
skydiving lessons	immortality
a country house or farm	a simpler life
a guitar or drum set	all the parties he missed out on
exotic travel brochures	escape from everyday routine
a hair weave	a new identity
meditation cushion and T'ai Chi videotapes	the meaning of life

Chances are all your man really wants to do is explore the possibility of acquiring one of these midlife props. But if he really wants to follow through with a purchase, and can afford the item, don't try to talk him out of it. If he can't afford it but is determined, you might suggest a more modest alternative like renting his dream car for a weekend. Either way, the important thing is that you understand the emotional longing hiding underneath his consumer impulse. Knowing what your man requires will help you introduce aspects of those longed-for emotional elements into your own relationship with him.

He Says/She Says

"My husband turned 50 and signed up for karate lessons. He didn't consult me beforehand, and at first I was resentful. The lessons were expensive, and the classes cut into family time. About a year and a half later, he was on the verge of getting his black belt, and he had become a new man. He had regained the strength he felt age had taken away, and more. It was the best money and time he ever spent."
—Helene, 52

Be His Affair

It's only natural to worry, when the crisis blooms, that another woman will be your man's ultimate midlife acquisition. Yet many midlife "graduates" say that their relationships with their partners evolved during this time into even stronger bonds. To enhance the probability that when the crisis has passed you and your man will be on firmer footing than before, *you need to be the woman who understands him.*

Regardless of the ups and downs of the crisis, continue to reaffirm your love and your desire for your guy. (For a quick brush-up, revisit the A, E, I, O, U of pleasing from Chapter 1 and the flirting techniques from Chapter 6.) Evidence of your ongoing attraction to him is the best salve for the wounded vanity that accompanies the laugh lines and love handles of middle age. Tell him and show him that he is the most important person in your life. But do it without smothering, clinging, or demanding that he reciprocate on your timetable. Your serenity, fortitude, and tolerance can help him come through the crisis a better man and a better mate.

Fair Fights

No matter how patient and calm you are, it's unrealistic to assume that you and your man will always see eye-to-eye on everything. All couples in long-term committed relationships argue from time to time. Any couple that tells you they don't fight once in a while is lying.

Just because you occasionally disagree, however, is no reason to throw out your resolve to please your man. Even during an argument, you can choose to act out your worst instincts or your best. Do choose the latter, and fight fair. Doing so will help you keep from turning a minor skirmish into a major battle.

The "Is" Have It

It's a lot easier for a man to hear a message if it begins with "I" and not "you." When a woman begins a sentence with the word *you*, her man knows an accusation is sure to follow. This can lead only to defensiveness on his part. Instead, describe your feelings in the first person. Don't say, "You make me so angry when you are late." Say, "I feel upset when you are late because …"

Teasers & Pleasers

Start your sentences with "I" instead of "you." This seemingly small change is guaranteed to de-escalate any argument. It also helps you take appropriate responsibility for your own part in any problem.

Stay in the Moment

Our tendency in arguments is to drag in every grievance that we have been holding onto, even if it's not the subject of this particular quarrel. Stick to the topic at hand. Don't dig up ancient history and throw in every wrongdoing you think he's ever done. Some phrases you never want to utter are:

- ◆ You always … _____

  _____

  _____

- ◆ You never … _____

  _____

  _____

◆ What about the time you … _____

_____

_____

This kind of "kitchen sink" approach detracts from trust. Your man will feel as though you've been keeping a list and checking it twice. Instead of a win/win dynamic, you will give him the sense that there is no win for him.

Consider Your Timing

Choose the moment to say your piece. Make the time a reasonable one for you and your partner. Don't introduce a sensitive issue right before a group of dinner guests is about to descend, or just as he comes in from a long day at work. What you want is a period of time when both of you are in fairly placid frames of mind and when the two of you will have some prolonged privacy. How can you be sure it's a reasonable time for a serious discussion? Ask him.

Hands Off His Hot Buttons

Every man has his hot buttons. If you push them during an argument, you can give up all hope that your conflict will have a peaceable resolution. Hot buttons are the topics that set off a reaction that is out of proportion to what's been said. Often they have historical roots.

Your combination of intuition and experience will tell you what your man's buttons are. For example, if a woman says her man is being lazy, and he hits the roof, she may be reminding him of all the times his mother nagged him for not cleaning his room, or not doing his homework. In any case, sore spots are always sore for a reason. Don't worry about the reason, just steer clear of them. After all, you wouldn't step on *Achilles' heel*, would you?

> **Tantalizing Terms**
>
> The ancient story of Achilles tells of a great warrior immune to all mortal wounds except in the heel area that was untouched by the magic waters that protected the rest of him. Every man has an emotional **Achilles heel**—a vulnerable spot that can cause him undue hurt.

Resist Interpretations

Never tell your man what he's "really trying to say" during the course of a quarrel. Even if you're right, this will only serve to make him feel exposed and embarrassed. Keep your insights to yourself. He wants you to be his friend and lover, not his shrink.

Keep It Between You

Making a scene in front of strangers is bad enough. Doing so in front of friends, relatives, or neighbors is even worse, because now you have created a situation where those close to you may feel they have to take sides.

Besides, no one knows quite what to do with themselves when a couple starts bickering. Do they try to intervene, change the subject. Walk away? There is no good solution. Save everyone else—and your man—the awkwardness.

Make Up Sooner, Not Later

No discussion of quarrels would be complete without a discussion of reinstating peace. A committed relationship is no place to hold a grudge; that defies the very nature of commitment.

Making up after an argument is a wonderful way to re-establish the depth of your devotion and dedication to one another—rough patches or no. Besides, as I hope you already know, making up can be a lot of fun.

If you remember the movie *Love Story*, then you know it's certainly not true that "love means never having to say you're sorry." It certainly does. But there's no need to lower yourself or to grovel. Fights happen. Acknowledge your role in what occurred and remind your man of your regard and love for him. There are many inventive and endearing ways of embellishing your verbal apology as well. Try one of these ideas:

- Send a loving note or card.
- Serve a food or wine he considers special.
- Rent a movie he's been wanting to see.
- Find a way to make him laugh.
- Have some good make-up lovin'.

Above all, of course, be sincere and authentic. You would not have chosen this man if your love for him didn't transcend mundane day-to-day irritants. And you would not be so devoted to him if the bigger, deeper issues did not pale alongside your abiding, underlying admiration and affection. Apologize from the heart, and enjoy making up.

The Least You Need to Know

- Even though men are taught to play it tough, their egos are fragile, and they experience disappointments deeply.

- A man facing adversity require a woman's faith, pride, encouragement, and optimism.

- Men are especially susceptible to emotional upset when they face problems in the financial or career realm, and when they must face their own physical limitations.

- The male midlife crisis is his issue, not yours, but your tolerance and lack of clinginess can help him weather it.

- If you must fight, fight fair—describe your own feelings, stick to the topic, and acknowledge your part in the problem.

Part 7

A Man for All Seasons

Will you still need him, will you still please him, when he's 64? How about 74, 84, and more?

There's nothing more pleasing than having a healthy, happy, and hot relationship that lasts a long, long time. This part of the book will help you to keep your man fit, lively, curious, good-looking, and eager to meet each and every new day with you by his side. You'll find lots of fun-filled ideas for activities you can undertake together to perpetuate your fitness of body, mind, and spirit. This book also offers strategies for keeping the heat turned up and the connection strong between the two of you far, far into the future.

Chapter 19

Healthy Is Happy

In This Chapter

- Men's top health risks and preventive strategies
- Nutritious, tasty foods for your man's health
- Herbs and vitamins for your man
- TLC for when he's under the weather
- How to get your guy to see a doctor

When a relationship brings emotional and physical pleasure to a man, he automatically gets another benefit as well. Men who are part of a couple tend to live longer and stay healthier than those who are alone. This chapter is about how you can team up with your man to enhance his health and well being even more, so you can keep on enjoying one another for many years to come. Just as being happy contributes to health, being healthy contributes to happiness.

All About Heart ... and Some Other Parts

A woman doesn't need to go out and get a nursing degree or a physician's license to take a more active role in her man's health. But it is a good idea to be informed about men's health issues. Knowing something about factors that can contribute to illness, as well as factors that can reduce risks, is a great place to begin.

Risky Business: Men's Top Health Threat

The top health threat to men in the Unites States today is heart disease. According to the American Heart Association, men have a greater risk of heart disease and have heart attacks much earlier in life than women do. All men need to take heart disease seriously.

The good news is that fatal heart conditions often can be prevented. Healthy habits that reduce the risk of heart attacks include exercising, not smoking, controlling one's weight, and eating a healthy diet with reduced amounts of saturated fat and cholesterol. Another essential part of health is to be armed with information. Take the following brief quiz to see how much you know about heart attacks:

Answer the Following Questions TRUE or FALSE

1. Most heart attacks occur suddenly, without any warning.

2. Blood clots cause most heart attacks.

3. Heart attack sufferers require a lengthy recovery period during which they should remain inactive.

Correct Answers

1. FALSE. Advance warnings, in the form of chest pain, shortness of breath, or fatigue, affect about two-thirds of all victims.

2. TRUE. Nearly all heart attacks are triggered by the sudden appearance of a blood clot in an already narrowed vessel that supplies blood to the heart. When one of the coronary arteries becomes blocked, the flow of fresh, oxygenated blood to the heart stops. If this goes on for too long, the starved heart tissue dies. This defines a heart attack, the technical term for which is "myocardial infarction"—death of heart muscle.

3. FALSE. People recovering from heart attacks are encouraged to get back on their feet as soon as possible and to begin a mild regime of exercise.

Your man's emotional heart belongs to you, but his physical heart belongs to him. Together you can become a team devoted to keeping his heart strong. Help him start thinking about all the positive things he can do to keep his heart healthy.

More Risky Business: Threats Two to Ten

Cancer is the number two-ranked health risk to men. According to the American Cancer Society (ACS), the most common cause of cancer death for men is lung cancer, and 90 percent of these deaths are linked to cigarette smoking. Prostate cancer is the second-leading cause of cancer death among men.

About one-third of all cancer deaths are related to nutrition or other controllable lifestyle factors. Your man can reduce his risks by not smoking or chewing tobacco, by exercising regularly, and by eating a healthy diet. Avoiding excessive sun exposure helps too, as does limiting alcohol. Regular preventive health screenings can catch many cancers in time to maximize the potential for cure.

The third-ranked cause of death for men in the United States is stroke. Apart from being the number three killer of men, stroke is also one of the leading causes of disability. High blood pressure, smoking, lack of exercise, and a diet high in fat and cholesterol contribute to the possibility of having a stroke.

The fourth-ranked cause of death for men in the United States is accidents, especially motor vehicle crashes. Chronic lower respiratory disease (lung diseases), diabetes, influenza and pneumonia, suicide, kidney disease, and chronic liver disease and cirrhosis round out the top 10 health risks for men. Notice how many of the conditions can be prevented or delayed by encouraging smart choices and a healthy lifestyle.

 **Uh-Oh's and No-No's**

Lovingly remind your man to buckle up—about twice as many men as women die in car accidents.

The Way to His Health Is Through His Stomach

We've all heard the adage "the way to a man's heart is through his stomach." Its original meaning, of course, was that men love women who feed them well. There's an awful lot of truth to that. A well-fed man is a well-pleased man. Eating is not only physically satisfying, but also emotionally meaningful—because on an emotional level, food represents nurturing.

But let's take a new look at that old adage. In light of what we know today about staying healthy, the phrase takes on an additional meaning. The way to keep your man's heart—not to mention the rest of him—healthy has much to do with making sure he gets a wide variety of wholesome, nutritious foods. Of course, this may be more difficult than it sounds depending on your guy's attitude toward food.

Many men resist the advice to forego junk food in favor of healthier fare. In fact, an estimated 90 percent of American men do not eat a balanced diet. Even though they know the risks, they may stubbornly cling to a preferred diet of deep-fried doughnuts wrapped in buttered biscuits because they can't see themselves eating "girlie food."

Okay, that diet's a bit of an exaggeration, but you know what I mean. Real men want "real food." Healthy food, unfortunately, has a bad reputation. To many guys, eating healthy still conjures up visions of facing a plate containing nothing but a stalk of celery garnished with watercress. They get stomach pangs and start drooling just thinking about it.

The good news, however, is that real men can eat real food—that is, satisfying, filling, and flavorful food—and still lower their intake of saturated fat, calories, and salt (excessive salt can contribute to high blood pressure). The secret lies in wise ingredient choices.

The next few sections will cover ideas about good nutrition, healthy food preparation, and purchasing habits. No matter who in your relationship does the bulk of the cooking or food shopping, this information will come in very handy.

Lighten Up His Favorite Dishes

If you cook for your man on a regular basis and want to coax him into eating healthier, don't deprive him of the hearty Mexican and Italian dishes he loves. Don't give him the idea that he can never again enjoy the immense pleasure to be had from eating a slice of pie. Instead, make as many of his favorites as you can using substitute ingredients that enhance a recipe's health quotient without sacrificing taste. In many cases, your man will never know you've used a substitute, and if he does know, he won't care—because everything on his plate will still taste great.

Here are some top substitution tips:

- Use flavorful spices—oregano, basil, sage, rosemary—instead of salt.

- Substitute condensed low-fat milk for whole milk.

- Use low-fat yogurt in place of heavy cream.

- Cook with egg whites in place of eggs.

- Sauté with olive oil in lieu of butter.

- Bake with applesauce replacing butter.

- Start sauces from vegetable broth instead of cream.

- Mix whole wheat and white pastas.

- Use nonfat sour cream.

- When making lasagna, halve the cheese and add eggplant.

- When making casseroles, halve the cheese and add vegetables.

Teasers & Pleasers

You don't have to separate eggs to get egg whites. Liquid egg whites are readily available in cartons, right next to the eggs at the supermarket. Use the equivalent of two whites to replace one egg.

Uh-Oh's and No-No's

Men need five to nine servings of fruits and veggies per day. On average, they eat only half that amount. Fit more into his diet by including fruits with cereal, adding chopped veggies to spaghetti sauce, and including grated raw vegetables or dried fruit in batter for quick breads, muffins, and cookies.

Many cookbooks feature healthy ingredient exchanges. It's a good idea to keep a few on your shelf for new ideas. Online recipe finders can also be a great help. Of course, feel free to think up your own healthy and creative substitutions. That's part of the fun of cooking real food the healthy way.

Ten Foods to Include

Eating healthy is not just knowing what to leave out, but what to put in. Many common foods contribute to good health because of the natural vitamins, minerals, and *phytochemicals* they contain. Many of these substances are *antioxidants* that can actually help the body defend itself against disease.

Tantalizing Terms

Phytochemicals are chemicals that plants produce to protect themselves against environmental dangers. They also help us defend against harmful bacteria, viruses, and damage to DNA.

Antioxidants protect cells against the damaging by-products of oxygen. Antioxidants counteract these cellular by-products, called *free radicals*, by binding with them before they can cause damage. If left unchecked, free radicals may cause heart damage, cancer, cataracts, and a weak immune system.

A healthful diet ought to include as many of the following 10 foods as possible. Even the most skeptical guy won't resist them, provided you think of ways to incorporate them into tasty dishes. It's not as hard as you might think, because they all offer great flavorful potential.

1. Tomatoes. Pass your guy the ketchup. Studies show that cooked tomatoes found in ketchup, sauces, and soups contain the antioxidant lycopene, which can reduce the risk of prostate cancer.

2. Garlic. Add some zest to that tomato sauce and other good foods with garlic. Its odor comes from sulfur-based compounds known as allyl sulfides, which also reduce cholesterol and protect the heart. Garlic also has antibacterial and antifungal powers. To release its healthy potential, you need to smash, mash, or mince it. Just don't overcook it.

3. Blueberries. Don't let their pint size fool you. Blueberries contain more antioxidants than any other fruit or vegetable. They can help battle heart disease and cancer, and some studies show they may boost brainpower. Add them to cereals, put them in a low-fat cobbler, or sprinkle them atop a scoop of low-fat frozen yogurt.

4. Beans. If your guy likes chili, beans are easy to include in his diet. Beans stabilize blood sugar and reduce the risk of high blood pressure. They also reduce the risk of obesity and cancer. Chickpeas work, too, so try a hearty hummus dip on baked low-fat chips.

5. Spinach. No wonder Popeye ate it. It's loaded with iron and folate, an important B vitamin that lowers levels of a dangerous amino acid that irritates blood vessels. It also contains two phytochemicals, lutein and zeaxanthin, which seem to

ward off the eye disease macular degeneration. If he's not a big spinach fan, sneak some into lasagnas and stuffing. Collard greens and kale work similar wonders.

6. Nuts. A handful of nuts makes a satisfying snack. Yes, nuts have fat, but it's the good kind: polyunsaturated and monosaturated. Pecans and walnuts contain ellagic acid, which seems to trigger a process that causes cancer cells to self-destruct.

7. Soy. Soy prevents heart diseases, cancer, and osteoporosis. Don't know how to cook with soy? Don't worry. Soy is the chameleon of the food world. It can soak up all flavors and taste like just about anything. Look for soymilk, soy yogurt, soy burgers, even soy chips.

8. Oats. Oats have much to recommend them. They contain a spongy, soluble fiber that sops up substances that produce cholesterol. They also contain hard-to-find vitamin E antioxidant compounds. Serve oats raw in granola or cooked in hot, hearty oatmeal. They make a wonderful breakfast because the protein in oats helps you feel full and can help prevent overeating later in the day.

9. Green and orange veggies. They're great sources of all things healthful. Top green picks include broccoli, which is loaded with phytochemicals, beta-carotene, and vitamin C (one cup of broccoli contains more vitamin C than an orange). If your guy is really not into broccoli, offer brussel sprouts. In the orange veggie category, a top choice is pumpkin. It lowers cancer risk and promotes healthy skin. If he'll only eat pumpkin in a pie on Thanksgiving, offer butternut squash or sweet potatoes.

10. Salmon. Yes, it's a fish, not a plant. But salmon eat smaller fish, which in turn have eaten algae. The algae provide salmon with omega-3 fatty acids, which help the heart by preventing plaque formation on arteries. They also reduce cholesterol and may even protect against Alzheimer's Disease.

What to drink with all this healthful fare? A glass of red wine per day may actually be good for your man, because the grape skins it is made from work against hardening of the arteries. Green or black teas are also an excellent beverage choice. They're *loaded* with antioxidants, and many scientists think that these teas may even help us prevent cancer. If your man doesn't like hot tea, try it iced.

Labels Versus Fables

Even if you're unable to do a lot of home cooking, you can help your man eat healthier by keeping an eye on what you both buy. Reading labels on prepared foods is a great first step in elevating your food awareness. Food labels can provide useful information about the amounts per serving of calories, fat, cholesterol, dietary fiber, and several important nutrients, like vitamin A, vitamin C, calcium, and iron. They can also help you compare different brands in terms of their overall nutritional content and their compatibility with your dietary goals. For example, if you're looking to reduce fat, you can opt for a yogurt that has 1 gram of fat per serving over a rival brand that has 5 grams. Beyond noting fat grams per serving, food labels also contain information on what *kinds* of fat are in the food. Monounsaturated fats are "good fats"—some of which we all require to maintain robust health. Saturated fat is the kind to avoid because it can raise the level of artery-clogging cholesterol in the blood.

CAUTION
Uh-Oh's and No-No's
Check out those chips! Trans fat, which can increase the risk of heart disease, is often found in snack foods like chips and crackers, as well as in vegetable shortenings, some margarines, and other foods made with or fried in partially hydrogenated oils.

A recent common addition to food labels (and soon to be a required one) is information on trans fat, or trans fatty acids. The Food and Drug Administration (FDA) has directed manufacturers to list trans fat on the nutrition facts panel of foods and some dietary supplements. Basically, trans fat is made when manufacturers add hydrogen to vegetable oil—a process called hydrogenation—to increase shelf life and flavor stability. The FDA has confirmed that trans fat, like saturated fat and dietary cholesterol, increases the risk of coronary heart disease.

Supplements to Energize Your Man

Even a really good diet can leave a few gaps, so it's a good idea to encourage your man to take a few dietary supplements. One thing you'll want to leave beside his cup of tea or glass of orange juice in the morning is a good multivitamin. Make sure it includes the antioxidants E, C, and beta-carotene, as well as vitamin B_6 and the mineral zinc (both of which are beneficial for prostate health). Don't forget a supplemental dose of calcium, too. Men need it as much as we do to prevent osteoporosis.

If your man needs an additional boost, consider some herbs that are believed to contribute to male well-being. Some are meant to treat specific male problems. Many are generally useful for men who are beset by stress and often on the run. Some herbs frequently recommended for men include the following:

- ◆ Saw Palmetto. This herb is from a small palm tree native to the Atlantic seaboard. It is the most popular and researched prostate herb. Studies show that saw palmetto shrinks enlarged prostates and relieves urinary problems.

- ◆ Red Clover. Red clover is a member of the pea family and contains powerful antioxidants that fight off cancerous growths. Red clover inhibits enlargement of the prostate gland and the symptoms that accompany it.

- ◆ Tongkat Ali (Eurycoma longifolia). Tongkat Ali comes from the root of a shrub that grows in Southeast Asia. Its name means "walking stick" in reference to its effects on male sexuality. Research has shown that this substance contains several plant chemicals that support healthy testosterone levels required for the male sexual functions. It also supports healthy sexual organs, mental alertness, general energy level, and good blood circulation.

- ◆ Ginkgo Biloba. This herb comes from a tall, hardy, deciduous tree, and has been used in Chinese medicine for years to enhance the health of the brain, circulatory system, and respiratory tract. In recent decades, hundreds of studies have confirmed many of ginkgo's ancient traditional uses. Gingko stimulates the mind, helps concentration, and can act to alleviate the symptoms of depression. It also enhances circulation, including circulation to the penis.

- ◆ Muira Puama. Muira puama is a shrub that grows in the Amazon jungle. Known as "potency wood," it has been shown to increase both male and female sex drives, as well as to help men maintain erections. Muira puama may also help balance sexual hormone levels.

> **CAUTION**
>
> **Uh-Oh's and No-No's**
>
> Men and women need the same amount of calcium each day to help prevent osteoporosis—a disease that makes bones brittle and more likely to break. Everyone needs 1,000 milligrams (mg) of calcium between the ages of 19 and 50 and 1,200 mg if you're 51 or older. Believing osteoporosis is only a women's disease, men may ignore simple steps they can take to prevent it.

Herbs are natural substances and have been used medicinally by countless societies for millennia. However, herbs are unregulated substances; it's wise to do your own research, to use caution with regard to amounts, and to obtain any herbs from a reputable source.

Poor Baby: Caring for Your Sick Guy

Even the well-cared for man finds himself under the weather every now and again. When that happens to your guy, there's one important principle to bear in mind. No matter how much of a tough-guy front he puts up at any other time and for any other person, when he's sick at home he wants you to pamper, pamper, pamper him—and then some.

Don't join the ranks of women who complain about how "men are such babies when they're sick." Everyone needs to be coddled sometimes, and everyone needs to offer TLC sometimes. Caring for your sick hubby or boyfriend can give you a chance to enjoy babying him. Indulge your guy and satiate your nurturing instincts by doing some of the following:

◆ Put his blanket in the dryer to warm it up for him.

◆ Rub his back.

◆ Rent a video for him and watch it together.

◆ Play checkers or cards with him.

◆ Get him tissues with lotion so his nose won't chafe.

◆ Make him a get-well card or banner.

◆ Bring him simple comfort foods like gelatin and soup with crackers.

◆ Turn off the news and let him watch old sit-coms and movies that make him laugh.

◆ Buy him a book of sports trivia.

◆ If there are kids around, bribe—er, encourage—them to stay quiet.

It may not always be possible for you to be by your guy's sickbed 24/7. If that's the case, check in by phone with lots of sympathetic cooing. Sending a festive get-well basket is also a great idea.

Getting Your Guy to the Doctor

When your guy is really sick you might want to encourage him to go to the doctor. In fact, you would probably like to get him to go to the doctor for regular check-ups. But will he? If he's like most men, you'll have an uphill battle here.

Study after study has shown that men resist going for medical check-ups far more than do women. Their reasons are many. Men, in general, exhibit less support-seeking behavior than women (it's the reason they hate to ask for directions even if they've spent the day going in circles). They also have an "if it ain't broke, don't fix it" attitude. Besides, even if they suspect there *is* a problem, they may fear having their worst suspicions confirmed.

Another reason men don't like to visit the doctor is embarrassment. They feel emasculated by some of the procedures involved in a medical exam. To make matters worse, if they are overweight or out of shape, they dread being reprimanded.

Finally, many men say they hate to take time off from work for a routine check-up. A "real man" wouldn't do any such thing! It might seem silly to us sensible female types, but remember, when boys complain of feeling less than great, they're often told to suck it up, shake it off, and get on with important things— like Little League games. You can't totally blame men if this early conditioning stuck.

> **Uh-Oh's and No-No's**
>
> One-third of American men have not had a check-up in the past year. Nine million men haven't seen a doctor in five years. Every year, men make 150 million fewer trips to doctors than women.

The price of denial, however, is high. For example, one in nine men will be diagnosed with prostate cancer, yet few will have the easy and painless digital rectal exam and prostate-specific antigen blood test to detect it. Men need to get appropriate screenings done. Each visit gives them an opportunity to talk with their doctors about their health behaviors and to establish a working relationship with a physician in the event a condition is discovered.

Will nagging help get your man to an exam? If it would, this would be the one instance where I would make an exception and heartily recommend it. But nagging your guy to see a doctor probably won't do much except strain your relationship and get him to dig in his heels. Instead, try these strategies:

◆ Find out about any wellness-at-work programs offered by your man's employer. (This is easy to do if you two share a healthcare plan.) More and more companies are stressing the importance of preventive care for their employees. Some even offer wellness medical exams onsite during work hours. These check-ups may not be as exhaustive as one your man would get from his personal physician, but they're a good start. What's more, your man might well find this dose of preventive medicine easier to swallow if he doesn't have to miss work and if he knows his colleagues are doing it, too.

◆ Encourage another guy to talk to your guy about the importance of regular check-ups. He might be more receptive when a friend broaches the idea, especially if that friend has had a positive experience. In the same vein, try to expose your man to media coverage of or public service announcements by male athletes or other celebrities who speak out about the importance of early detection and prevention.

He Says/She Says

"I got my husband to get a check-up by collecting quotes from athletes who encouraged that sort of thing. He loved the Mickey Mantle quote: 'If I'd known I was going to live this long, I would have taken better care of myself.'"
—Georgia, 45

◆ Make an appointment for him. In many cases, a man will strenuously resist making the actual phone call to set up an exam. Funny enough, however, once someone makes the appoint-ment for him, that hurdle is overcome. He might decide it's just as easy to go ahead as to cancel it.

If a chosen strategy doesn't seem to be working, back off for a while before trying another. It won't help your man's well being for you and him to turn this into an ongoing argument. But do commit yourself to giving your man an important message when it comes to his health: "I love you so much, I want to keep you around."

Finally—and very importantly—remember always to take good care of yourself. This way you'll be a wonderful role model, and also be able to give your man the gift of your vitality and loving companionship for a long time to come.

The Least You Need to Know

◆ Healthy lifestyle choices can prevent or lessen many of the major health threats facing men today.

◆ Real men want real food—but flavorful food can be healthy, and healthy foods can be flavorful.

◆ Read labels on prepared foods and try to get your guy to do the same—food manufacturers have a mandate to tell you exactly what's what.

◆ No matter how balanced the diet, a few good supplements—like multivitamins and calcium—can help fill in any gaps.

◆ Pampering your guy when he's under the weather can be satisfying to you both.

◆ Encourage your guy to have regular medical check-ups; the price of avoidance can be high.

Chapter 20

Fit Is Hot

In This Chapter

- Reaping the many benefits of exercise for your man
- Making exercise fun for two
- Enjoying the aerobic benefits of sex
- Planning fitness-oriented getaways
- Lessening stress together

Unless your man has been living in a sealed-off bubble without contact from the outside world, he already knows that exercise—in theory—is a good thing. Its many proven merits are hard to ignore. But your man may need more convincing if he's going to agree that he actually ought to get more exercise himself. That's especially true if he's used to doing nothing more strenuous than power lifting a bowl of pretzels and a *TV Guide*.

It's worth your while to try to get your guy moving. Doing so will improve his body, his mood, his energy level, his sex drive, and his prospects for longevity. This chapter will look at the many ways exercise can positively impact your man's health and offer ideas for how you and he can tighten, tone, and burn some calories together in pleasurable ways.

When His Get Up Gets Up and Goes

I once knew a man who refused to start an exercise program because he said it sounded dangerous. "Why else," he asked his wife, "do they always tell you to consult a physician before you start?" His wife commented that it was too bad no one advised consulting a physician before becoming a couch potato. Her comment hit home. Her husband did end up seeing his doctor, who heartily endorsed getting up off the sofa and beginning a sensible exercise program.

After this man started working out on a regular basis, he thanked his wife for her encouragement. He felt great, he said. His get up and go—which had long since gone—was back. He even started encouraging his wife to exercise more, and the two of them began enjoying new activities together.

This man's reaction was typical. More often than not, the hardest part of exercising is deciding when to start. After you begin, though, exercise can be self-reinforcing. The more you do it, the more you want to do it. That's because you get a bonanza of benefits, including the following:

♦ **A healthier heart.** When you exercise regularly, your entire cardiovascular system benefits. This is because exercise prevents the onset of high blood pressure if you're at increased risk of developing it and lowers your blood pressure if it's already high. Exercise also increases the concentration of high-density lipoprotein (HDL) cholesterol (the "good" cholesterol) and decreases the concentration of low-density lipoprotein (LDL) cholesterol (the "bad" cholesterol) in your blood. It strengthens your heart so it can pump blood more efficiently and bring much-needed oxygen and nutrients to the rest of the body. This is one of the main reasons why you generally feel refreshed and energetic after exercising.

Teasers & Pleasers

Say good-bye to his two left feet. Bones respond to the force of muscles at work. Exercise can help your bones build calcium reserves and improve agility, balance, and strength—all of which reduce the chances of falling and breaking a bone.

♦ **Better breathing.** Your respiratory system also benefits, because regular exercise promotes rhythmic, deep breathing. Your lungs actually develop greater capacity, so you're better able to take in oxygen to nourish your cells.

♦ **Strong bones and muscles.** Regular exercise prevents the bone-weakening disease osteoporosis. Strength-training exercises—such as lifting weights or working with resistance tubes—are particularly beneficial for bones, as are exercises that bear your body's weight, such as walking and jogging. Strength-training and weight-bearing exercises help preserve bone mass and may even increase bone density.

◆ Better balance and coordination. By strengthening your muscles and bones, you can also improve your balance and coordination, reducing your risk of falls.

◆ A stronger libido. Need I say more?

◆ Weight control. If you exercise, your body works harder and requires more fuel (calories). And here's a bonus: Even after you stop exercising, the body continues to burn calories at a somewhat increased rate for a few hours. The more intense the exercise, the more calories you burn. By burning more calories than you take in, you can reduce body fat.

> **CAUTION**
>
> ### Uh-Oh's and No-No's
> When a man gains weight, he tends to accumulate fat around his waist in the abdominal area. Having a waist size greater than 40 inches correlates with a man's risk of high blood pressure, diabetes, heart disease, and stroke.

◆ Lower blood sugar levels. As muscles contract during exercise, they use sugar for energy. To meet this energy need, sugar is removed from your blood during and after exercise, which lowers your blood sugar level. Exercise also reduces blood sugar by increasing your sensitivity to insulin—allowing the body to use available insulin more efficiently to bring sugar into your cells. Lower blood sugar levels can help prevent or control adult-onset diabetes (Type II diabetes).

◆ Uplifted spirits. Exercise can take the proverbial weight off your shoulders as well as the literal weight off your waist. Exercise counters depression by activating the neurotransmitters (brain chemicals used by nerve cells to communicate with one another) serotonin and norepinephrine. The levels and balance of those neurotransmitters play a role in how you respond to daily events. When you are depressed, the level of serotonin, norepinephrine, or both may be out of sync. Exercise can help synchronize those brain chemicals. It also stimulates the production of endorphins—other neurotransmitters that produce feelings of well-being.

◆ Longer life expectancy. In a study of Harvard graduates, men who burned 2,000 or more calories a week by walking, jogging, climbing stairs, or playing sports lived an average of one to two years longer than those who burned fewer than 500 calories a week by exercising.

Teasers & Pleasers

Thirty minutes of physical activity on most days is the minimum needed to improve fitness and enjoy all the benefits of regular exercise.

Exercise will help your man not only live longer, but also live better. His entire quality of life will improve. The stamina and strength gained with regular exercise make daily tasks—from going up and down stairs to mowing the lawn—much easier on the body. He'll feel more relaxed overall, and sleep better at night. He'll also feel proud of himself, as well he should, and enjoy more confidence and self-esteem.

Adventures in Exercise

Another woman I know tried to get her man to exercise by telling him she had heard that if exercise were a pill, it would be the most powerful medication known to humans. Her information was correct, but her strategy backfired. Her boyfriend didn't care for the analogy at all. He said, "Yuck. Who wants to take a pill? What fun is that?" The truth is that for some men, the prospect of exercising seems boring, and doing it solo seems like a lonely prospect.

Even those who do pursue fitness alone might enjoy a change of pace and some good company now and again. Happily, there are many fun ways to stay fit as a couple. Exploring a few of them will afford you opportunities not only to keep in great shape but also to have more fun together.

Bicycle Buddies

Remember how free you felt when you first learned to ride a bike? No doubt your man felt the same. Riding a bike is a rite of passage, a ticket to the world that lies beyond the confines of the backyard.

Even for grown-ups, bikes still conjure up associations with freedom, fresh air, and fun. Taking a long bike ride on a lovely day can be downright exhilarating. Biking is also an incredibly healthy pastime that develops heart strength and lung capacity. It tones muscles without impact and cultivates balance as well as overall fitness.

People of all shapes, sizes, and ages can enjoy bicycle riding, so it's a great way to get started getting fit together. If you don't own bikes, try renting for starters. It's a great way to go!

Sexy Swims

Swimming is one of the best forms of exercise there is. It promotes strength, stamina, and mobility and improves cardiovascular fitness. It's especially great for upper body tone. The more you swim, the better you'll both look in your bathing suits.

The thought of swimming together might never have crossed your mind, simply because you don't know where to get access to a pool. But access is more readily available than you might think. Try your local "Y" for starters, or explore the possibilities of municipal pools. Many towns have them. In summer, explore nearby beaches, lakes, or ponds. Hiking to a secluded swimming venue can offer excellent warm-up exercise as the swim itself.

Don't know how to swim? Everyone should. Take lessons together and enjoy a great sense of accomplishment. To get your feet wet, so to speak, you can try water aerobics at a local gym. Exercising in the water is safer than working out on land because water supports your weight and doesn't strain your back or knees.

Dance with Me

Many people believe that dance is the ideal exercise. After all, it's a mild aerobic workout, minus any boring parts. When you take dance lessons with your man, you make exercise a fun and enjoyable social event. Your dance workout takes place to music that puts everyone in a good mood.

Olympic athletes often include dance in their training to sharpen their control, agility, speed, and balance. No wonder. Dancing increases your flexibility and stamina and encourages gentle stretching. It's great for posture and body alignment. Finally, learning to dance is as great for self-confidence as it is for physical fitness.

Teasers & Pleasers _____

Many people take up ballroom dance when more traditional exercise programs fall by the wayside, either because of injuries or boredom. The International Olympic Committee gave ballroom dancing provisional recognition, and as a result it's been getting a lot of attention as a bonafide athletic pursuit. The physiques of professional ballroom competitors, trainers, and dance teachers provide all the evidence you needed in terms of results.

Walking the Walk

If your guy—or you—are befuddled by the array of choices for fitness, or if you're intimidated by hard-core gym offerings like kickboxing or spinning, don't despair. Many experts say that one of the best exercises of all is one of the most basic: walking.

Walking for fitness is not to be confused with running or jogging. Simply walking at a brisk three- to four-mile-an-hour pace for 30 minutes or so five or six days a week can do a tremendous amount of good. Walking can lower the risk of stroke, osteoporosis, and diabetes, and help treat conditions like arthritis and high blood pressure. Walking aids weight control. It also helps defend against depression. Devotees say that nothing is as apt to change one's attitude in a hurry as a nice, vigorous walk.

Walking is easy, and it's free (though a good pair of shoes that have been fitted by a professional is strongly recommended). You and your man can do it anywhere, anytime—enjoying the opportunity to be alone together, take in the scenery, and do yourselves a world of good.

> **Teasers & Pleasers** _____
>
> Want to know how far you've walked? A *pedometer* is a pager-sized device worn on your belt that records the number of steps you take based on your body's movement. Some pedometers are analog devices that simply measure steps. Some are fancier digital models that track the distance you walk, plus the calories you burn.

Sex for Exercise?

Believe it or not, another wonderful thing you and your man can do together to gain and maintain aerobic fitness is to have more sex. The act of intercourse burns about 200 calories, the equivalent of running vigorously for 30 minutes. During orgasm, both heart rate and blood pressure typically double, all under the influence of the hormone oxytocin.

Researchers believe it would be logical to assume that sex, like other aerobic activities, can protect against heart disease. A study conducted in Wales in the 1980s showed that men who had sex twice a week or more experienced half as many heart attacks after 10 years as men who had intercourse less than once a month.

> **Teasers & Pleasers** _____
>
> Studies are showing that sexual arousal and an active sex life may contribute to longevity, heart health, an improved ability to ward off pain, a heartier immune system, and even protection against certain cancers. Sex also lowers rates of depression.

Toning Travel

Another great way to pursue fitness is to plan vacations that incorporate healthy exercise activities. A fitness-oriented getaway can be a weekend break or a longer excursion. Either way, it can be a great way to break in new habits and get a fresh new start on fitness.

Fitness travel is growing in popularity by leaps and bounds, as more and more vacationers weary of being poolside potatoes. The sky's the limit on what activities you can choose. The sections that follow detail some suggestions.

Fitness Spas

Work out with a trainer, get a fitness evaluation, take low-fat cooking classes, get a massage, and learn all kinds of wellness strategies in an environment devoted exclusively to facilitating guests' well being. Most fitness spas make it a point to encourage visitors to continue their newly adapted good habits at home. For more info, visit www.spafinders.com.

Walking Tours

Walks across every possible venue on the planet are offered for walkers of every level and preferred pace. Traverse the Scottish moors, trek the foothills of Bhutan, or hike the back roads of the American countryside. The venue you choose is up to you, but the benefit is the same. Look for a walking tour operator that offers flexibility, daily route options for all levels, knowledgeable guides, and the support you need when you're ready for a break. For ideas, visit www.grandex.com, www.trekamerica.com, and www.theworldoutdoors.com.

Bicycling Tours

You can bike anywhere and everywhere from the South of France to Tuscany to Nova Scotia to California's wine country. Tour operators offer everything from easy explorations to challenging epic journeys. A good organization will be sure to match your fitness level to your trip—and will always have a backup van available if you want to take a day off from more difficult stretches of road. For more info visit www.bicycletour.com, www.eurobike.com, and www.CarolinaTailwinds.com.

Multisport Tours

You can mix hiking, biking, kayaking, and water sports in many diverse locales that include the coast of Maine, the Shenandoah Valley, the Rocky Mountains, and more exotic places like Costa Rica and Switzerland. These comprehensive tours are great for families because everyone gets to pursue their favorite activities. Check out www.active4.com, www.experienceplus.com, and www.amazonadventures.com.

Yoga Retreats

Yoga retreats are great for restoring the heart and soul as well as enhancing flexibility, balance, and strength. Retreats are offered in every style of yoga (some styles stress breathing techniques, some more strenuous postures, and some a more rapid pace). You don't need to head off to India or Katmandu, either. Yoga retreats are found all over the world. There's probably one close to your own backyard, for those who feel there is no place like "om." For ideas, visit www.retreatfinder.com and www.retreatsonline.com.

He Says/She Says

"My wife and I used to come home from vacations feeling overweight and bloated. We'd feel like we had to pay for our indulgence by going on a strict diet. Now we only take vacations where we stay active and eat well. We come home feeling more energized than when we left, which is the whole point, isn't it?"
—George, 52

Add-On Activities

Even if you and your guy are not quite ready for an entire vacation devoted to fitness, think about integrating some more activity into your upcoming travel plans. These days even cruise ships—once known as opportunities to chow down at six-times-a-day buffets and nap on deck chairs—now offer state-of-the-art workout centers and numerous active shore excursions. There are all-day and half-day trips spent kayaking, canoeing, snorkeling, scuba diving, parasailing, and even glacier trekking. Skip the midnight snacks and stroll the promenade deck, or make a little calorie-burning whoopee in your cabin.

Mind and Spirit Fitness

Exercise is a wonderful tool for stress management. Physical exertion is an antidote to many of the physical, mental, and emotional symptoms of stress. These symptoms include everything from indigestion, teeth grinding, and neck and back pain, to irritability, fatigue, and the inability to concentrate.

After your man gets used to physical activity, he may find himself especially eager to engage in it after facing frustrations. Many people believe there's nothing better than an hour at the gym to counteract the negative impact of deadline pressures, challenging encounters with the boss, or even daily commutes fraught with traffic.

There is, however, something more that you and your man can try together to counter the impact of stress. It's not something to try *instead* of exercise, but something to try along with it. It's called the *relaxation response*—a very basic kind of meditation technique.

The relaxation response involves taking just 20 minutes a day to conduct a practice that can be beneficial to both your physical and mental health. This practice has existed in other cultures for millennia, and it has gained wider and wider acceptance in the United States since the 1970s. In that decade, when many people were taking up the practice of meditation, a group of doctors at Harvard and at Beth Israel Hospital in Boston conducted studies on the effects of meditation on people who had high blood pressure brought on by everyday stress.

Tantalizing Terms

The **relaxation response** is a learned self-calming technique that reduces tension through focused stillness. It engenders the opposite of the "fight or flight" response to stressful or threatening situations, which over time may produce hypertension and cardiac and other health problems. The concept of the relaxation response was first popularized in the United States in Dr. Herbert Benson's book of the same name.

The relaxation response can be practiced by anyone, at any time. Here how to do it:

1. Find a quiet environment. This can be a quiet room at home an outdoor spot in a garden, or at a park or beach. Just make sure there are no distractions.

2. Assume a comfortable position. Sitting with a straight spine is preferable, although you can also sit cross-legged. Lying down isn't recommended, because you might fall asleep.

3. Find a point of focus. This can be a special word or phrase, such as "one" or "peace," that you repeat throughout the session. You can practice with your eyes closed or focus them on an object, such as a candle or a flower.

4. Take an objective attitude. Don't be concerned with your thought processes during a relaxation session. Distracting thoughts are hard to eliminate. Allow them to occur, but when they do, simply notice them and return to your chosen point of focus.

A variety of similar methods are available to relieve stress. The two of you may need to explore different techniques to discover which one best suits you both. When you have found a technique that works, encourage one another to practice it routinely. Benefits of the relaxation response include the following:

- Lower blood pressure

- Decreased stress hormone production

- Reduced anxiety

- Improved concentration

- Reduced tension headaches

- Improved sleep

- Reduced vulnerability to depression

Best of all, with continued practice, these benefits compound over time.

The Least You Need to Know

- Regular exercise contributes to cardiovascular health, strong bones and muscles, weight control, and control of blood sugar—as well as helping men to beat the blues and counter stress.

- If your man finds solo exercise a dull prospect—or if he would just like to spice up his workout routine—explore ways of getting fit as a twosome (including more sex!).

- Vacations don't have to be excuses to overeat and laze around; they can be a way to immerse yourself in healthy habits that will last after you return home.

- Stress is the basis of many dangerous medical conditions; try alleviating stress by practicing simple relaxation and meditation techniques together.

Chapter 21

Gorgeous Is Great

In This Chapter

- ◆ Why help your guy get more gorgeous?
- ◆ His clothes closet essentials
- ◆ Colors and patterns for men
- ◆ Care for his hair
- ◆ Good skin for guys
- ◆ Keep him inspired

Keeping your guy healthy and fit will help him not only feel good, but look good. But you can do even more to help your guy improve his appearance. Will this please him? Yes, indeed, so long as you do it tactfully and lovingly.

This chapter will help you keep your guy well groomed and well dressed while still letting him look and feel like the real man he is.

Why Help Your Guy Look His Best?

Whether they admit it out loud or not, most guys are pretty clueless about the art of pulling themselves together so that they look their most attractive and appealing. Unlike females they were not coached in the art of looking their best by their moms or their friends. Additionally, men had few fashion options until recently and only a small number of appearance-enhancing products were even developed specifically with men in mind.

Some guys pretend simply not to care about their looks. They might profess indifference with a kind of "take me or leave me" attitude. Some even act as if any concern with their appearance might brand them as some kind of sissy. And some pretend to know exactly what they're doing—even though it's somewhat obvious that they don't. Deep down, what they would really like is for a woman who already appreciates and admires them (and, therefore, has good taste) to gently steer them in the right direction.

Of course, you might be wondering whether it's really such a good idea to help your guy look hotter than he does right now. What if that makes him more desirable to other women? Well, fear not. Helping your guy in the looks department will please him so much that he'll be even more devoted to you than ever. Sure, other women can look—but he won't be tempted to let them touch! Besides, you'll have the satisfaction of being envied for being on the arm of that handsome hunk.

One thing your man is sure to gain along with an improved appearance is a boost in confidence and self-assurance. When a man knows he looks good, he stands tall and proud. He shakes hands firmly, and he looks people in the eye. His confidence, in turn, makes others feel confident in him.

Teasers & Pleasers

Help your guy look great for that important job interview. When two job applicants with similar experience and abilities compete, the one who wins out is most often the one who has a nicer appearance.

Not surprisingly, good grooming and a pleasing appearance correlate with worldly success and financial advantage. A review of experimental studies clearly shows that physical attractiveness is of considerable significance in the business world. Overwhelmingly, attractive people fare better in terms of perceived job qualifications, personal recommendations, and predicted job success. In fact, the scale-tipping factor in hiring decisions is often good looks.

In addition to boosting your man's confidence and quite possibly contributing to his increased success, your well-meaning attention to his appearance can make him feel truly loved. That's because grooming someone is a natural, instinctive expression of affection. Throughout the animal kingdom, creatures rub, scratch, lick, and stroke one another's body surfaces—using grooming to signal courtship behavior, coalition building, and peacemaking. Horses groom one another, and so do impalas. Bees do it, and birds do it.

In monogamous bird species, such as parrots, grooming becomes a big part of domestic life. When a mating pair of parrots is reunited after a separation, the rate at which the birds preen one another jumps dramatically. Monkeys groom one another as well and put a great deal of time and effort into doing so. Chimpanzees may spend more than an hour a day grooming each other by moving their fingers through each other's hair.

So, once again, let Mother Nature be your guide. Groom your guy to say how much you care. It's a win/win situation. He'll look better than ever and feel prized and adored. And you will have in him even more of a prize than you did before.

411 or 911: How Much Help Does He Need?

Before you help your man out in the fashion and grooming departments, you should assess just how much help he needs. While men, in general, don't pay as much attention to their appearance as women, they still display a wide range of attitudes in this area. Some men are pretty persnickety about their personal appearance; some make a half-hearted stab at looking acceptable. Some seem genuinely oblivious. Where on the spectrum does your guy fall? Take this quiz and find out.

1. The last time your man got a haircut was …

    A. Last week

    B. Last month

    C. Sometime last year

2. His idea of great footwear is …

    A. Stylish leather loafers

    B. Scuffed sneakers

    C. Flip-flops

3. For an evening out he would typically wear…

    A. Casual but stylish pants and a dressy sport shirt

    B. Jeans and a T-shirt or sweater

    C. Sweat pants and a sweatshirt

4. If you asked your guy to attend a black tie dinner, he'd...

   A. Agree happily

   B. Agree reluctantly

   C. Laugh, or cry

5. In general, his wardrobe is...

   A. Up-to-date

   B. Somewhat dated

   C. Prehistoric

6. When it comes to matching colors and patterns ...

   A. His choices are impeccable

   B. His approach is haphazard

   C. He sometimes induces motion sickness

7. The insides of his clothes closet is ...

   A. Meticulous

   B. Disorganized

   C. Empty—all his clothes are on the floor

8. His medicine cabinet contains ...

   A. Numerous quality hair-styling products and skin creams

   B. Soap, shampoo, shaving cream

   C. Medicine

9. If the house caught fire, the one item of clothing he would try to save would be ...

   A. A designer suit

   B. His most comfortable jeans or khakis

   C. His bowling jersey

10. His self-assessment of his clothing and fashion sense is …

   A. I know I'm looking good

   B. I hope I look okay

   C. Huh?

If you answered mostly As, your guy is definitely keen on looking his best. That's good. He'll be receptive to ideas you have for making a good thing better—so long as you are positive and diplomatic.

If you answered mostly Bs, your guy falls into the same category as the majority of males. He needs 411—lots of information. He's so flummoxed by making choices about his appearance that he'll be truly pleased with your wisdom and taste—just don't overwhelm him with too may details at once.

If you answered mostly Cs, you have your work cut out for you. This man needs 911—emergency assistance. But don't take his serious level of need as an invitation to nag him into better dressing and grooming. Be gentle, be patient, and be content with small successes. Although part of him may be crying out for help, part of him likes things just as they are. The best way to please this fellow is to accept the fact that he'll never be Hugh Grant in white tie. But, remember, a little improvement can go a long way. When he finds out it is painless to incorporate a few style options other than his usual full-out Animal House look, he *will* thank you.

Stroking Him Toward Gorgeousness

The key to helping any type of man look his best is to begin and end every conversation by accentuating the positive. It is essential that your guiding principle be not to hurt his feelings. Remember *your man wants to feel that he is desirable to you.*

Want to have a conversation about your guy's appearance? Always begin that conversation with a compliment. Then offer a gentle suggestion. Then follow up with another compliment. Think of this as a kind of suggestion sandwich. Here's how it works:

1. First, notice something about his looks that you genuinely find appealing and flatter him. For example, "Wow, honey, look how blue your eyes are when you wear that shirt."

2. Now he will be in a receptive mood, and you can offer a tiny nudge in the form of a suggestion. Whenever you can, try offering that suggestion in question form. This will inspire him to do some thinking about the topic and to keep talking. For example, "Hey, have you ever thought about trying contact lenses?"

3. Finally, wrap up your suggestion sandwich with another compliment. "I love being able to look right into your eyes, like I can when we're in bed."

So garnish, add some flirty fun and variety to your suggestion sandwiches by embellishing some of the compliments with nonverbal reinforcement. Do you like the way his butt looks in those jeans (despite the jeans' multiple knee holes)? Try, "Mmmm, I like the rear view of you in these jeans (goose, goose). Do you think they still make that style? Because I see these are looking a little worn in the knees. I don't want to lose this fabulous view."

The Clothes That He Knows—And Doesn't

Speaking of worn jeans, does your man's wardrobe need some updating and expansion? I'm not surprised. For many of us women, shopping for clothes is a sport. For men, it's a chore. Why do you think men's clothes are always on the first floor of a department store? It's because retailers know that men want to get in and out of a store as quickly as possible. We like to browse; they like to blitz.

Yet many people adhere to the philosophy that clothes make the man. The idea that what a man wears says lots about who he is is hardly a new belief. In fact, the original line "The apparel oft proclaims the man" dates back to Shakespeare's *Hamlet*.

Tantalizing Terms

The term **clotheshorse,** referring to someone who cares a great deal about what they wear, dates back to around the middle of the nineteenth century. It originally referred only to a wooden frame upon which clothes were hung to dry.

But, let's face it. If your man has nothing in his closet (or strewn across his floor) except a few overworn staples, nothing you do is going to turn him into a *clotheshorse*. You can, however, use your suggestion sandwich method, combined with some judicious special occasion gift giving, to expand his options.

Of course, if you're like me, you probably spent much of your life *not* thinking all that much about men's clothing. Until we have men in our lives who need a "wardrobe mistress," we women tend to race through that first floor of the department store on the way to all those cute outfits on the upper levels. Yet we do notice those men who look put together. What do they have that your man may not have? Here are some essentials that style mavens say every man ought to have in his wardrobe:

1. Two pair of flat-front khaki pants—a warm gold or brown shade for fall and winter; a sand or putty shade for spring and summer.

2. A few well-fitted fine cotton T-shirts in solid dark colors.

3. A couple of fine wool pullovers.

4. A black turtleneck.

5. A lightweight, high-quality nylon windbreaker.

6. A pair of great-fitting jeans.

7. A navy gabardine three-button jacket—goes with everything all-year round.

8. A white dress shirt.

9. A couple of silk ties in solids or discreet patterns.

10. One staple gray or navy suit—splurge on a classic that fits exceptionally well.

> **CAUTION**
>
> **Uh-Oh's and No-No's**
>
> How can you tell whether his jeans fit well? If you can see any of his up-front anatomy through them, they're too tight. If you can see any of his rear end anatomy above them, they're too loose.

If you think your guy might resist some of these items, break the list into two parts. Items one through six usually don't raise too many male hackles, even for the most relentlessly casual guy. Besides, with the exception of the jeans and khakis, which must be tried on, all these items are easy to give as gifts. After he's become accustomed to looking a bit more dapper, then you and he can gradually work your way up to items seven through ten.

Matching Him Up

One clothing dilemma that seems to plague a lot of guys when it comes to dressing is the issue of colors and patterns. We women love to learn about the colors that flatter us, and many of us know right off the bat whether our skin tone suits us to a "winter" or a "spring" palette. Trust me, no guy knows or cares whether or not he is a "winter," and if you broach the subject with him that way, you deserve the blank stares you will get in return.

Nevertheless, skin tone does matter when selecting the right shades to wear. Colors too close to a man's skin tone will wash him out. Like us, men need contrast. Tell your tan or naturally dark-skinned man how handsome he looks in bright colors and whites. Praise your fair-skinned boy when he sports soft pastels and earth tones. When in doubt, get him a shirt that matches his eyes. For some reason, men always look great in those!

In general, another color rule for men, more so than women, is to keep it simple. Male peacocks attract positive attention with their magnificent multicolored tails, but somehow this strategy doesn't work out well for human males. In their case, a bright color should always be paired with a neutral, such as black, beige, or denim.

As for patterns, one per outfit is usually a good rule of thumb. If he's considering a sports coat or suit with a pattern, make sure that the pattern matches up where the seams meet (the way you would with wall paper). If the patterns don't match up, the quality of the garment is suspect.

Playing Footsie

Clothes may make the man, but bad shoes can break even the most well-dressed gentleman. Tell the truth ladies, haven't you ever met a guy who you thought was kind of neat and then made a run for it the moment you looked at his feet? Well, others do the same. Prospective employers, clients, business associates, and virtually any new acquaintance can be instantly put off by the sight of beat-up, low-quality footwear. Somehow, it seems to proclaim that their wearer is not a guy with a high self-opinion.

Sure, every guy has his favorite pair of beat-up sneakers. There's no shame in that. Don't ask your man to throw them out. They're there to stay, and you'll simply have to make peace with them. But if the occasion calls for anything more—and let's face it, most do—he'll need a few pair of classic shoes to see him through.

The easiest kind to coax him into will probably be a penny or tassel loafer. He can wear a good leather loafer with jeans, with casual sportswear, and even with a sport coat. After he's comfortable in his loafers, see whether you can nudge him toward a pair of wingtips (these are sometimes called "brogues").

Wingtips never, ever go out of style. They were designed decades ago, and they'll be here decades from now. A pair made of good quality leather will retain their shape indefinitely, so they're worth a splurge. Wingtips are also extremely versatile. Like loafers, they can also go casual and be worn with jeans. Unlike loafers, however, wingtips can also be worn with a suit.

Now your guy is set from top to bottom. In a way, you might be a bit envious. Don't you wish shopping for women's shoes was as simple?

Farewell Bad Hair

The head is your man's crowning glory. But troubled hair can be his grooming Waterloo. The good news is that nearly all men are vain about their hair, whether they admit it or not. So they're often open to a little assistance in this area. The bad news is that his very vanity can make hair a touchy subject between you and him, so you will need reinforcements. The first thing you should address when helping your man with is hair is the question of *who else helps him?*

Is your guy's hair guy a barber or a stylist? The difference can be critical. Barbershops are good for the basics: Haircuts 101. Stylists are skilled at choosing a hairstyle that fits a client's face and hair type. If your man has always gone to the barbershop, he may be amazed at what a good stylist can do for him.

Many men, however, are initially resistant to the idea of a hair stylist. They consider it an expensive indulgence, and besides, they're loyal to their barber, with whom they've traded jokes, sports talk, and philosophical insights throughout the years. Happily, it's possible to have the best of both worlds. If you can coax your guy into seeing a good stylist (ask around for personal recommendations) a couple of times a year, his barber can handle the basic trims in between.

> **Teasers & Pleasers**
>
> Does your man have a cowlick—a rogue tuft growing in the wrong direction, as if a cow licked it? Have him ask his stylist about hitting it with the kind of hair relaxer that's used to straighten curls. It only needs to be left on for five to ten minutes, and reapplied every three months or so.

Another service that an able stylist can offer is to guide your guy through the thicket of hair care products that are now available for men. Your guy will need a shampoo and conditioner suited to his hair type (thick, fine, oily, or dry). He'll probably also need a styling product, like gel or mousse, along with instructions on how to use it without looking like "the Fonz."

But, wait a minute, suppose that your guy has a lot less hair than he used to have? Men often commit their worst hair bloopers when they begin to lose some of their locks. Bad comb-overs and ill-fitting toupées look silly and don't fool anyone. Think of it as a personal and public service to get your guy to give up either of these misguided strategies.

First—and very importantly—let him know that losing his hair does not correlate with the loss of any of his attractiveness. It really doesn't. We can all think of guys with little or no hair that turn us on, from Bruce Willis to Ed Harris to Patrick Stewart to Damon Wayans to, well, you fill in the blank. Next, have your guy consult his fabulous stylist for better options. These include the following:

♦ Cutting his hair shorter and styling it more naturally (think Gene Hackman).

♦ Adding some facial hair (Sean Connery).

♦ Shaving it all off and showing off that shiny scalp (Vin Diesel).

Teasers & Pleasers _____

Want him to trim those hairs in his nose? Tell him they tickle when he kisses and buy him a trimmer. After all, you don't want to be distracted! Want him to address his ear hair? Tell him it interferes with your whispering sweet nothings.

In many cases, the secret of good hair is that *less is more*. But do be sensitive to a man's initial reluctance to see it this way. Your man may be emotionally wed to the hairstyle of his youth, even though it is no longer suitable and only serves to date his look. Leave it to his stylist to offer him some tough love in this area. You keep running your fingers through his hair—regardless of how much of it there is or isn't—and letting him know how much he turns you on.

Good Skin Is Always In

No doubt, your man's kissable face was one of the things that attracted you to him. Who knows what feature was, and is, your favorite? Perhaps his soulful eyes, his rugged chin, his magnetic smile, or his jaunty mustache. Well, framing all those features is about 30 square inches of epidermis. And it requires tender loving care.

When a man's skin looks clear and fresh, it will automatically show the rest of his facial features off to their best advantage. Because a man's face is his visual calling card, a well-cared for visage will mark him as an individual brimming with health and vigor. Unfortunately, skin care is one of those areas of knowledge to which most men have had little or no exposure.

His Skin Care Basics

Once again, it's up to you to offer a bit of knowledge and assistance in this area. As always, start with a complimentary stroke. Tell him what it is about his face you've always been drawn to. Ask him whether he would consider protecting his skin so that he continues to look great. Now give him a literal stroke by gently caressing that charming face.

Chances are he will be agreeable but dismayed by not knowing where to start. And unlike we ladies—who can think of few things more entertaining than a nice chat with the salesperson at a department store cosmetics counter—most men will probably be reluctant to consult a pro in public. No problem. You can pick up a few basic products and leave them lying around for him to experiment with.

Start slowly, with three skin care fundamentals:

- A moisturizer will keep his face hydrated and give his razor a smooth surface to glide over.

- A mild cleanser, unlike soap, will clean skin without stripping it of its natural oils. (Make sure the cleanser matches his skin type. If his skin is oily, make it an oil-free cleanser formulated to help prevent breakouts.)

- Sunscreen, to protect his skin from damaging sunrays that cause premature aging and, in the worst case, skin cancer. (Even if his moisturizer has sunscreen in it, it's best if he applies extra protection when he's, say, out on the golf course.)

He Says/She Says

"Since I was a girl, my mother wisely cautioned me not to use soap on my face, because it would dry out my skin. My husband jokes that when he and his brothers were boys his mother was so grateful when they used soap that she never discussed its limitations."
—Lauryn, 32

Uh-Oh's and No-No's

Don't worry about your man's not wanting to exfoliate, i.e. using a product that will scrub off the skin's dead surface layer. Men typically don't need to do this because they shave daily.

Even though some skin care products for men and women can have near-identical formulas, this is an area in which packaging and marketing may play an essential psychological role. Don't be tempted to advise your guy to use your skin care products, even if you feel they will serve the same purpose. Get him a dedicated "men's" moisturizer and cleanser. And although sunscreen tends to be generic, be generous and get him his very own tube.

His Skin Conditions

After you've got your man used to the idea of caring for his skin, you can encourage him to address any special problems he may have in this area. Like women, men may be prone to certain skin problems simply because they have skin that is naturally oily or dry. They may have special issues too, because the poor fellows have to take a razor to their face every day. Finally, certain skin problems can arise as men age. Chief among skin problems that may affect your guy are the following:

- Acne. If your man is pimple-prone, it could be attributable to testosterone. This hormone can trigger overproduction of a pore-clogging oily substance called sebum. When this mixes with bacteria, the result is an eruption.

- Ingrown facial hairs. If his facial hair is curly, what's left behind after shaving can grow back into his skin instead of growing out. The result is *pseudofolliculitis barbae*—hard, red, infected bumps that resemble mosquito bites.

- Dermal dandruff. This could be what your guy has if he's got itchy, flaking, reds patches along his eyebrows, around his nose and mouth, and even under his beard. Technically, skin dandruff is called *seborrheic dermatitis*. It occurs when a skin fungus called *pityrosporum* starts multiplying out of control.

- Age spots. If your guy is sporting little brown spots on his face, it's likely the result of having gone without sunscreen too many times. Commonly known as age spots—but you don't need to call them that in front of *him*—these markings are really small piles of sun-damaged skin that have clumped together with the passage of time.

- Rosacea. Although more common in women, an estimated five percent of men over 40 have rosacea. Hyperactive blood vessels produce a red-faced effect. At first, the blush comes and goes. But if untreated, the blushes last longer, and bumps and pimples start to crop up.

A dermatologist can correctly diagnosis any of these conditions and recommend treatment. I know; your guy doesn't like doctors—but as medical exams go, a dermatological one is pretty noninvasive. If he's resistant, keep in mind that simply taking better basic care of the skin—with good moisturizer, skin cleanser, sunscreen, and perhaps a mild astringent to close the pores—can have a positive initial impact on the management of some skin conditions.

Keeping Him All Together

You don't need to wait until your man is totally together from head to toe to start giving him all kinds of wonderful positive reinforcement for any improvement in his fashion and grooming repertoire. Be sure to flatter, flirt, and ogle in sincere appreciation of every improvement. Even attempts that don't quite work out as end results should be applauded. He's trying, right? And that alone makes him more appealing than ever.

The Least You Need to Know

- Helping your man look his best will boost his confidence and, very likely, his level of worldly success.

- The secret to helping your guy with his appearance is to always accentuate the positive—make a "suggestion sandwich" by beginning and ending every such conversation with a compliment.

- Clothes say a lot about a man, but most men aren't too talkative with their wardrobes—help him assemble the basics as a start.

- Quality shoes proclaim that their wearer is a quality guy—and men's classic shoes can last a long time, so they're worth a splurge.

- Nearly all men are sensitive about their hair, whether they say so or not—so helping him find a good stylist is critical.

- When it comes to his appearance, never let the smallest improvement go by without reinforcing it with praise.

Chapter 22

Monogamy Without Monotony

In This Chapter

- The chemistry of falling, and staying, in love
- The power and passion of new experience
- Young-at-heart makeovers
- The myth of complete compatibility
- Your shared mission and legacy
- The three aspects of lasting love

When you fall in love, everything seems fresh and new. You feel so happy, so lucky, so consumed with this new experience that you might even forget to eat and sleep. But one of love's great paradoxes is that the better the relationship goes, the more the initial excitement fades. The good news, however, is that passion can be periodically rekindled, even as intimacy and commitment grow. That's the subject of this final chapter.

Loving After the Lightning Stops

Love between each man and woman is a beautiful, unique experience. But for each couple, the emotional and biological pattern that love follows is remarkably similar. Lust and longing inspire us to hunt for a mate. Romantic love, the craving to bond with a special person, gets us to narrow our search and focus our energies on one exceptional individual. Once we have found a suitable mate, we stay with them because we are also driven to seek lasting familial attachments.

At each of these stages, various brain chemicals shape our behaviors and responses to our beloved. When we are initially hit with love's *lightning bolt*, as the French put it, our levels of dopamine and norepinephrine soar. Turning on these chemical switches causes us to experience feelings of elation and exhilaration. We are so consumed with and preoccupied with our loved one that our very need to sleep and eat is diminished. And when we sense our feelings are reciprocated, we are cheerful to the point of near-giddiness.

But these happy-making brain chemicals do not work their magic indefinitely. Their surge is, by nature, impermanent. That is because the chemicals are released at this intense level only when we have an experience that is new and previously *unknown*.

When we get to know the object of our affections better, the chemical rush subsides. Dopamine and norepinephrine are then replaced with hormones that some researchers call *cuddle chemicals*. These cuddle chemicals are neurotransmitters that stimulate the bonding required to start and raise a family.

Cuddle chemicals are very nice, thank you, but let's face it: Their effect is not as thrilling as the chemicals that accompanied love's lightning bolt. So, what's our next step? Sure, we could go out and find someone new. But if we really value the relationship we're in—and the person we're in it with—that's not such an appealing prospect.

This is the situation in which all long-term lovers find themselves. Are we going to stay and cuddle, or go off and cavort? And if we stay, can we ever recapture the kinds of thrills that started our relationships off with a bang?

Tantalizing Terms

The French refer to the phenomenon of falling in love as *le coup de foudre*, literally, the **bolt of lightning**.

Sometimes we refer to this emotional phase of love as lovesickness. Researchers say that **cuddle chemicals,** the hormones vasopressin and oxytocin, are released during sex, facilitating the drive for long-term attachments.

An Ever New You—And Him, Too

The solution to this age-old dilemma is being answered by modern science. To happily blend comfort and cuddling with periodic elation, keep the familiar relationship and, at the same time, enhance it with new experiences. Novelty drives up those levels of happy-making brain chemicals all over again.

Several studies show that couples who make it a point to step outside their routines to shake things up and embrace new adventures report a higher level of satisfaction with their partners and their relationship. They also report more romantic feelings than do those couples who do the same things day in and day out.

Which kind of couple are you and your man? Take this quiz and see:

How Often Do You Do Something new?

On a scale from 1 (never) to 5 (very often) how often do you and your man do the following?

1. We try new sports or fitness activities together.

   1   2   3   4   5

2. We cook and eat new types of food.

   1   2   3   4   5

3. We go to restaurants we have not tried before.

   1   2   3   4   5

4. We take a class together.

   1   2   3   4   5

5. We socialize with new people.

   1   2   3   4   5

6. We tell each other about new books we've read.

   1   2   3   4   5

7. We discuss current events.

   1   2   3   4   5

8. We listen to new music.

   1   2   3   4   5

9. We try out a new type of technology.

   1   2   3   4   5

10. We take a vacation to somewhere we've never been.

   1   2   3   4   5

How did you do?

10—20 You two are in a rut. You need a happy-making chemical infusion.

21—30 You're somewhat game for new adventures, but could do much more.

31—40 You're pretty adventurous. Keep it up.

41—50 You'll never be bored—or boring! Your relationship will be all the better for it.

Seeking out new and novel experiences may seem like a very simple prescription for revitalizing romance. It *is* simple. The hard part is to remember to do it! Whenever we get used to a certain way of being, inertia sets in. It takes energy to change, and we resist changing what is working just fine. But remember, in the long run, getting into a rut will not work for your relationship but against it. Sure it's nice to do what's familiar, but a tipping point occurs when the familiar becomes monotonous.

Each time you notice that you and your man haven't tried something new in a while—30 days is long enough to stick with the familiar—do something different.

   ◆ Do it in the great outdoors (take a hike, learn to kayak).

   ◆ Do it in the kitchen (cook a new cuisine, add exotic spices to the spice rack).

- Do it at school (take an adult education class in anything from square dancing to Spanish).

- Do it in the bedroom (see Chapters 11—15 for inspiration).

The important thing is—just do it.

A good way to make sure you are trying new things is to keep a New Adventure calendar. Note every time you and your man try something you've never tried before. If a month has gone by without noting something new, put your heads together and come up with a plan.

Your new adventure can be something that is purely for fun, or it can involve more serious goals. In the latter case, talk about what's important to you both. What are your shared concerns about the world, peace, the environment? Get passionate about an issue you agree on. Volunteer to feed the hungry, work at a shelter, raise funds for a good cause, or work to support a political candidate.

He Says/She Says

"I have to admit I thought my wife was off her rocker when she suggested we go back to school at night and take Italian lessons. But we had a blast and met some great people, too. The next summer we took a trip to Italy. Now we're taking French lessons; I can only imagine what will happen. But, you know what? This kind of thing has really put the fun back in our relationship. Sometimes we pick a night when we try to have a conversation completely in Italian or French. We cook food to go along with the language. We often mess up the recipes and mispronounce all the words. Then we laugh our heads off. That's the best part."
—Roger, 54

His and Her Makeovers

Another way to help each other feel fresh and new is to encourage one another to look as renewed on the outside as you feel on the inside. Certainly physical attraction played a big role in your initial attraction to one another. A new look—or even a little tweak to a familiar look—can help reignite those sparks.

Where can you start?

- Go on a sexy shopping spree together.
- Buy him something elegant he'd never buy himself.
- Let him pick out a daring outfit for you.
- Try washable hair dyes (you can go permanent if you like the look).
- Stick some washable tattoos on one another.
- Talk him into getting a facial.
- Buy him some eye cream and moisturizer.
- Give him a manicure.
- Let him pick out a hot shade of toenail polish for you.
- If he's never grown a mustache or beard, talk him into trying.
- If he's always had a mustache or beard, talk him into shaving.
- Try straightening hair that's always been curly.
- Try curling hair that's always been straight.
- Try Pilates and straighten your posture together.

CAUTION

Uh-Oh's and No-No's

Never give your partner the idea that he should change his appearance because you don't find him attractive. Let him know it's because you find him *so* attractive that you would like to see how hot he would be if he tried something new.

None of these things is going to magically take 10 or 20 years off your man's appearance, or yours. But that's not the point! Periodic makeovers can serve to keep you and your partner young at heart. Often even the tiniest change can give us a mental and emotional lift. That lift enhances our confidence and—presto!—that truly makes us more attractive than we were before.

It's Okay to Be Different

Togetherness is great, but don't forget that separateness has its place in a long-term relationship as well. Seeking out new adventures together should be complemented by seeking out new adventures as individuals. If you discover a new aspect of yourself, you will be able to share that more energized and interesting self with your lover. You will also be able to learn from each other and appreciate one another's accomplishments.

One of the myths we have about long-term relationships is that couples have to be compatible in all ways, and like to do all of the same things. But think back to when you first felt love's lightening bolt. Sure, you were happy to discover similarities between the two of you. You both liked to ski. You both liked Chinese food. You both liked country music. You both had a great sense of humor. You both wanted three kids and a golden retriever.

But weren't you really intrigued by the ways in which you and your man were different? There is something to the old cliché that tells us "opposites attract." We are fascinated by people who in some ways embody the traits we lack. Perhaps your guy was funny and outgoing, while you were more quiet and reserved. Perhaps you were a great gardener, whereas he had a "black thumb."

There is no reason to let such differences recede into the background of your lives after you decide to share those lives. Let him exercise those traits you found so appealing and exciting. Encourage him to do those things that he's always wanted to do. Cheer him on as he …

- Hikes the Appalachian trail.
- Joins a singing group.
- Enters a sailing regatta.
- Takes tap dancing lessons.
- Takes flying lessons.
- Writes some poetry.
- Tries out as a game show contestant.
- Takes up piano.
- Learns to scuba dive.
- Joins a softball or soccer league.
- Runs for the local School Board.
- Volunteers at Habitat for Humanity.

As for you, the same holds true. Confess it: There are some things you always wanted to try that you *still* haven't tried. Perhaps you never had anyone willing to do these things with you and still don't. Never mind. Do them anyway.

There's no need to worry that the two of you pursuing some new experiences on your own will detract from your relationship—so long as you remember to do two important things. First, don't neglect to pursue *some* new experiences as a couple. Second, always take the time to update your knowledge of your partner. Show an interest in what he's been pursuing and be sure to let him know what it is about *your* activities that excite you.

Don't ever worry about what other people say. Sometimes other couples—especially ones who might be insecure about their own relationships—see a man and a woman pursuing separate hobbies and decide they are "going their separate ways." But true compatibility is born not of always *acting* alike, but of *interacting* well.

He Says/She Says

"My husband and I had been together for over 15 years when he finally confided to me that he always had a dream of being a stand-up comic. He didn't want to do it for a living. He just wanted to try it at a local club on their amateur night. This would be the sort of thing I would never do myself in a million years. It terrified me just to imagine it, and I was even scared for him. I know those audiences can be tough. But I always thought he was hilariously funny, and I told him to go for it. He worked so hard and so long before he was ready. I got kind of bored in the evenings and so I started a book group. Late at night, he'd tell me jokes, and I would tell him about the books we'd read. He worked in a bit about book groups in his comedy routine, by the way. I have to say we both had fun, and we both appreciated our time together more."
—Cassie, 45

Looking in the Same Direction

What about your goals for the future? Do they match up with your partner's? And how well do they need to? Antoine de Saint-Exupery, the author of *The Little Prince* (Harvest Books, 2000), said, "Love does not consist in gazing at each other, but in looking together in the same direction." Those are wise words indeed. If your vision of the future is that the two of you will remain unchanged and that your relationship will stay frozen in time, think again.

Over the years, you and your man will have your challenges, both as a couple and as individuals. You will endure tests and triumphs, setbacks and renewals. You will each have to modify certain dreams and come up with new aspirations as you move forward.

Some parts of the journey you will have to make alone, but the support of your partner can be carried with you, and serve as an ever-present source of strength. After the solitary struggles, you can fall into each other's arms again, thrilled to see how each other has grown. How do you know when it's all going as it should? You will fall in love with your man over and over again—and he with you.

Your Mission Statement

Today most business enterprises have what is known as a mission statement—a succinct formal declaration that states the aims of the organization. Without ever having formalized it as such, you and your partner have most likely had a series of evolving mission statements as your relationship progressed. Your initial mission may have been to create a loving partnership and make a home together. Later it may have been to build your careers while supporting one another, to raise a family, to participate in your community, to launch your children into the world. What is your mission statement now?

As long-term partners you will need to continually re-evaluate your mission as a couple. Will you support one another as children leave the nest? Will you be there for one another as your own parents age? Will you strive to keep one another vital and healthy? Will you work to enhance the world in some way for the next generation? Deliberately addressing and revising your mission statement is something you and your man should do at regular intervals, to make sure that your general goals for the future coincide. Having shared goals is key, even if each of you contributes to them in your own individual way.

Another thing you'll want to discuss is what kind of legacy you want to leave. Maybe you want to leave the world the legacy of well-adjusted children, or a well cared for home, or a solid family business. Maybe you want to leave spiritual traditions that will be honored and carried forth by your descendants. Maybe you simply want to be remembered as role models—good parents, good neighbors, good friends—for those who come after you. It is your conscious decision to leave a legacy that matters.

But along with goal setting and crafting a legacy, don't forget to do the most important thing of all. Enjoy your man and let him enjoy you. Play together and do it often. Play the way little children play: Do things for the sheer joy they give the two of you. Throw out the rulebook. Forget about what you're going to get out of it. Just relish the moment and have fun.

The Three Aspects of Love

Lasting love consists of three elements:

- ◆ Intimacy
- ◆ Commitment
- ◆ Passion

Each component is invaluable and indispensable if a relationship is to endure.

The word intimacy comes from a Latin root meaning "innermost." That makes sense, because intimacy is love's deep emotional component. Intimacy involves having warm, friendly feelings for another. It involves disclosing our feelings, listening to our partner's feelings, and believing that it is safe to do both. It involves the ability to be empathic, to see the world from our partner's points of view. Somewhat paradoxically, it also involves the ability to give other people enough space to be themselves and to evolve as individuals.

Commitment is love's glue. It keeps us around even on those days when our feelings may not be so warm and fuzzy. Commitment is a decision made and honored—a decision to stay at someone's side even when immediate gratification might be found elsewhere. We stay because we have made a promise, and we stay because the long-term rewards of staying outweigh those of making a change.

Intimacy and commitment are the meat of any relationship—the thick, juicy steak. But passion gives the steak its sizzle. No one wants passion to fall by the wayside; yet many who have studied love talk matter-of-factly of passion's passing and the fact that mature love must endure its loss.

Refreshingly, noted Yale psychologist Robert Sternberg, who came up with the "triangular theory" of love's three components, notes that intimacy and commitment without passion yield only a comfortable, companionable love—like the love of best friends. But passion, he says, is required for consummate love to be complete.

There are times during any long-term relationship when one element or another takes the lead position. There are times when the level of intimacy might be high, with passion simmering almost imperceptibly on the back burner. There are instances when there is more distance between our partners and us than we would like, yet commitment sees us through. These shifts are normal and natural. But don't let your relationship get stuck in any one mode. And don't let anyone tell you that passion is not important, let alone not possible.

Anything is possible when you love your man for who he is and when you love yourself for who you are. Never stop appreciating all the wonderful things your guy brings to your life and never stop bringing wonderful things into his. Then the two of you will never stop pleasing one another in every way that counts.

The Least You Need to Know

- Powerful brain chemicals that make us feel elated when we fall in love can be restimulated by sharing new and novel experiences.

- Couples can help each other update their outsides as well as their insides—so both will feel more attractive and attracted.

- Compatibility is more about the way we interact than the way we act; we celebrate our diverse strengths and skills and learn from one another.

- A couple should have evolving goals and missions and should agree on the legacy they will leave—but none of this should take precedence over simply enjoying one another.

- Love consists of intimacy and commitment (the steak) and passion (the sizzle); all are important for long-term satisfaction.

Pleasing Toys Resources

007 AdultSextoys.com
www.007adultsextoys.com
e-mail through site

123 Sex Toys.com
www.123sextoys.com
e-mail through site

1-sex-toys-and-adult-toys.com
www.1-sex-toys-and-adult-
toys.com
e-mail through site

1Toy.com
www.1toy.com
1-800-532-2035

AdamEve.com
www.adameve.com
1-800-293-4654

Adultdvd.com
www.adultdvd.com
1-877-878-0966

Adultshop.com
www.adultshop.com
1-866-833-3339

Amour on the Boulevard
www.amourblvd.com
e-mail through site

Ashardaswood
www.ashardaswood.com
sales@ashardaswood.com

AshleySexToys.com
www.ashleysextoys.com
845-463-0035

Bedroomsports.com
www.bedroomsports.com
1-877-891-6529

Bedroomtoys4u.com
www.bedroomtoys4u.com
e-mail through site

Bedtime Boutique
www.bedtimeboutique.com
610-351-1456

BetterSex
www.bettersex.com
1-800-955-01-888

BigSexToyStore.com
www.bigsextoystore.com
e-mail through site

Blowfish.com
www.blowfish.com
415-252-4340

BlueTrouble.com
www.bluetrouble.com
e-mail through site

Canadian Sex Toys
www.canadiansextoys.ca
sales@canadiansextoys.ca

ClassyAdultStore
www.classyadultstore.com
gg@classyadultstore.com

Drugstore.Com
www.drugstore.com
1-800-378-4786

E-adult-sex-toys.com
www.e-adult-sex-toys.com

Early To Bed
www.earlytobed.com
1-866-585-2BED (2233)

Eden Fantasys
www.edenfantasys.com

Eve's garden
www.evesgarden.com
1-800-848-3837

Gigglesworld.com
www.gigglesworld.com
845-463-0035

Glassfantasy.com
www.glassfantasy.com
919-630-4895

GlassSexToy.com
www.glasssextoy.com
1-877-371-3862

Good Vibrations
www.goodvibes.com
1-800-289-8423

Holistic Wisdom.com
www.holisticwisdom.com
1-800-490-8165

Home Made Sex Toys
www.homemade-sex-toys.com

Intimate Toys Online
www.intimatetoysonline.com
1-800-728-5285

Jennasextoys.com
www.jennasextoys.com
1-800-532-2035

JT's Stockroom
www.stockroom.com
1-800-755-TOYS

Kittenstoyroom.com
www.kittenstoyroom.com
e-mail through site

Likitystix.com
www.likitystix.com
e-mail through site

Luckysextoys.com
www.luckysextoys.com
440-567-9221

My Pleasure.com
www.mypleasure.com
1-866-697-5327

Mybodytoys.com
store.mybodytoys.com
1-866-833-3339

Mybodyvibes.com
www.mybodyvibes.com
1-925-934-4257

Myla
www.myla.com
212-237-2676

MySecretToys.com
www.mysecrettoys.com
1-800-256-2145

MySexShop.com
www.mysexshop.com
718-896-0699

NaughtyNovelty.com
www.naughtynovelty.zoovy.com
1-800-351-8669

PassionShops.com
www.passionshops.com
239-243-4623

Philida
www.philida.com
1-877-584-0631

Pjur Lubricants
www.erosusa.com
1-877-628-7100

Rainbowtoys.com
www.rainbowtoys.com
1-888-660-8970

Safesexmall.com
www.safesexmall.com
cs@safesexmall.com

Seeking0.com
www.seekingo.com
1-866-937-7255

Sensationsextoys.com
www.sensationsextoys.com
e-mail through site

SensualLuxuries.com
www.sensualluxuries.com
info@sensualluxuries.com

SensualSampler.com
www.sensualsampler.com
1-800-242-2823

Sex Adult Toys
www.sexadulttoys.com
e-mail through site

Sex Toy Clearance.com
www.sextoyclearance.com
1-866-538-3599 ext. 5833

SexProducts.com
www.sexproducts.com
service@passionshop.com

Sextoys.org
www.sextoys.org
253-351-5001 ext. 146

Sex-toys-next-day.com
www.sex-toys-next-day.com
718-786-1460

SexToysPlease.com
www.sextoysplease.com
1-800-570-4869

SexToyX.com
www.sextoyx.com
e-mail through site

Sexy Toy Warehouse
www.sextoysex.com
617-666-7826

SexyToyVibes.com
www.sextoyvibes.com
1-866-833-3339

Spicygear.com
www.spicygear.com
1-800-871-4421

Stockroom.com
www.stockroom.com
1-800-755-TOYS

Sunsetsextoy.com
www.sunsetsextoy.com
1-866-833-3339

Sweet and Sassy Boutique & Women
Fun Parties
sweet-and-sassy.com
1-800-98-SASSY

The Kama Sutra Company
www.kamasutra.com
1-800-216-3620

The Marriage Bed
www.themarriagebed.com
667-761-7231

TheErogenousZone.com
www.theerogenouszone.com
customerservice@snjllc.com

ThePlayboyStore.com
www.playboystore.com
1-800-993-6339

TooTimid.com
www.tootimid.com
1-888-660-8970

Torridtoys.com
www.torridtoys.com
1-800-833-8339

Toys in Babeland
www.babeland.com
1-800-658-9119

Toys of the Night
www.toysofthenight.com
1-877-33-BOGEY

ToysSexShop.com
www.toyssexshop.com
1-877-969-8697

Tweeker.com
www.tweeker.com
1-888-393-8697

WestMarket
www.dearlady.com
1-800-7-SEXTOY

Xandria Collection
www.xandria.com
1-800-242-2823

Pleasing Apparel Resources

1 Lingerie Store
www.1lingeriestore.com
1-800-206-7230

3 Wishes.com
www.3wishes.com
919-844-8515

Angel BodyWear.com Lingerie
www.angelbodywear.com
No phone, only e-mail

Ascanty Lingerie
www.ascantylingerie.com
760-480-7439

Big Gals Lingerie.com
www.biggalslingerie.com
1-866-501-6355

Biggerbras
www.biggerbras.com
1-877-475-8110

Blakelogan
www.blakelogan.com
312-733-0700

Body Body
www.bodybody.com
jennifer@bodybody.com

Cameo Lingerie
www.cameolingerie.com
1-800-808-2141

Carabella Lingerie
www.carabella.com
1-800-Carabella

CornerFashion.com
www.cornerfashion.com
support@cornerfashion.com

Davidscloset.com
www.davidscloset.com
972-475-8110

Dimout.com
www.dimout.com
1-866-346-6880

Discover Lounges.com
www.discoverlounges.com
1-866-697-2629

The Diva Splendorium
www.divasplendorium.com
1-800-546-3482

Electrique Boutique
www.electriqueboutique.com
1-800-461-8554

Elingerie Plus
www.elingerieplus.com
609-548-1473

Feeling USA
www.feelingusa.com
1-877-293-3393

First Fantasies Costume Cuzzins
www.theinternetdepartmentstore.com
1-866-9-Themes

Fredricks of Hollywood
www.fredericks.com
1-800-323-9525

Funwear-lingerie.com
www.funwear-lingerie.com
713-944–3223

Heavenly Lace
www.heavenlylace.com
CustomerService@
HeavenlyLace.com

Inchant.com
www.lingerie.inchant.com
1-888-446-2426

Jaded Clothing and
Sexy Lingerie
www.jadedclothing.com
504-259-3001

K.M.A. Lingerie, Inc.
www.kmalingerie.com
customerservice@kmalingerie.com

La Redoute Paris
www.us.redoute.com

Lavishwear
www.lavishwear.com
423-477-0469

Lingerie Avenue
http://lingerieavenue.com
service@lingerieavenue.com

Lingerie of Hollywood
www.lingerie-of-hollywood.com
1-877-473-3070

LingerieGifts.com
www.lingeriegifts.com
1-877-863-GIFT (4438)

Lingerie WebShop.com
www.lingeriewebshop.com
sales@lingeriewebshop.com

Lollipop Lingerie
www.lollipoplingerie.com
732-901-8263

Love Fifi
www.lovefifi.com
1-866-LUV-FIFI

Memory Impression Lingerie
www.memoryimpression.com
1-877-815-9790

Mystical Lingerie
www.mysticallingerie.com
webmaster@mysticallingerie.com

Oh Baby Lingerie, Cathy Williams
NYC Collection
fashion.ohbabylingerie.com
ohbabylingerie.com

Orchard Corset
orchardcorset.com
1-877-267-2427

Pajama World
www.pajamaworld.com

The Playboy Store
www.playboystore.com
1-800-993-6339

Seductive Apparel.com
www.seductiveapparel.com
1-888-666-0111

Seductive Lingerie Shop.com
www.seductive-lingerie-shop.com
sales@seductive-lingerie-shop.com

The Sensual Woman.com
www.the-sensual-woman.com
1-877-886-5576

Serge-lingerie.com
www.serge-lingerie.com
e-mail at site

Spicy Nights.com
www.spicynights.com
0845 129 8328 (UK)
info@spicynights.com

Sunup/Sundown
www.sunupsundown.com
954-238-3289
1-866-9THEMES

SurpriseHim.net
www.surprisehim.net
562-307-7253

Venus Fashions
www.venusfashions.com
916-781-9839

Victoria's Secret
www.victoriassecret.com
1-800-411-5116

Wicked Promises
www.pagewave.com
410-768-3184

Wicked Temptations
www.wickedtemptations.com
1-800-883-9693

Glossary

Achilles heel   The ancient story of Achilles tells of a great warrior immune to all mortal wounds except in the heel area, which was untouched by the magic waters that protected the rest of him. Every man has an emotional Achilles heel—a vulnerable spot that can cause him undue hurt.

antioxidants   These substances protect cells against the damaging by-products of oxygen, which are called *free radicals*. Antioxidants counteract these cellular by-products by binding with them before they can cause damage. Left unchecked, free radicals may cause heart damage, cancer, cataracts, and a weak immune system.

aphrodisiac   Named for Aphrodite, the Greek goddess of sexual love and beauty, an aphrodisiac is anything that arouses or intensifies sexual desire and enhances sexual performance.

bolt of lightening   This is a term the French refer to as the phenomenon of falling in love: *le coup de foudre*. We sometimes refer to this emotional phase of love as lovesickness.

chi   Named by the Chinese, this is the life force—the vital energy that runs throughout the human body along paths known as meridians. Those who believe in the concept of *chi* say that an imbalance in this energy can lead to fatigue, listlessness, and even illness. Massage is one of the methods the Chinese have long used to balance *chi*.

clitoris   Derived from a Greek word meaning "little hill," it's been recently discovered that this small erectile organ found in females is much bigger than previously thought. It extends in two arms, about nine centimeters back into the body and high into the groin.

clotheshorse   Dating back to around the middle of the nineteenth century, this term refers to someone who cares a great deal about what they wear. It originally referred to only the wooden frame upon which clothes were hung to dry.

cuddle chemicals   Researchers say that the hormones vasopressin and oxytocin are released during sex and facilitate the drive for long-term attachments.

deep throating   A term that has evolved into a verb, it comes from the title of the randy 1972 film, *Deep Throat*, in which adult film star Linda Lovelace played a woman who discovers that her clitoris is located in the back of her throat.

doggie style   Commonly known as the man-from-behind position, this term is derived from the rear-entry mating position dogs and most mammals use to mate. While some people don't like this terminology due to its animalistic connotations, it's exactly what others love about the term. The idea of being "an animal" to them during sex can be quite stimulating.

eating units   Nutritional sociologists define couples as eating units because their dietary choices and exercise habits are mutually influential. Couples who support each other in healthy eating and exercising regularly will contribute to the health of one another and to the overall health of their relationship.

empathy   This is the action of understanding and entering into another's feelings. Empathy provides us with a window into someone else's point of view.

full body orgasm (FBO)   This is the sensation that every part of your body—not just your genital area—is vibrating when you climax. FBOs are said to be attainable by prolonging foreplay, controlling your breathing, and becoming more aware of your partner's energy and of all your bodily sensations.

geisha   This literally means "art person" or "artisan." Geishas were very common in the eighteenth and nineteenth centuries and are still in existence today, although their numbers are dwindling. The geisha tradition evolved from the Japanese equivalent of court jesters, hence the emphasis on wit and entertainment.

ginseng   Meaning "man root," this plant's reputation as an aphrodisiac probably arises from its marked similarity to the male anatomy. For centuries, ginseng has been seen as an energizing and rejuvenating agent in China, India, Korea, Indochina, and Tibet. Although there have been some experiments reporting a sexual response in animals treated with ginseng, no evidence exists to prove that it has an impact on human sexuality. For us, ginseng acts as mild stimulant, like coffee.

hormone   A hormone is a chemical substance produced in the body's endocrine glands. Its function is to stimulate or regulate metabolism. Derived from the Greek language, the word literally means it means "to excite" or "to stir up".

macho   Derived from Spanish, macho when used as a noun means "virile man". When used as an English adjective, it means "strongly masculine".

masculinity ideologies   These are ideas and concepts that individual men hold about what it means to be a man.

muse   Related to the English word "mind," this term means "memory" or "reminder." Ancient poets, having no written texts to rely upon, had to call upon their *muse* in order to recite the lines they had authored.

oral sex   Oral sex is an act which uses the mouth and tongue to stimulate a partner's genitals.

phytochemicals   These are chemicals that plants produce to protect themselves against environmental dangers. They also help us defend against harmful bacteria, viruses, and damage to DNA.

placebo (Latin for "I shall please")   This is a medication or treatment believed by the administrator of the treatment to be inert or innocuous. In controlled scientific experiments, placebos are often sugar pills or starch pills.

relaxation response   The relaxation response is a learned self-calming technique that reduces tension through focused stillness. It is the opposite of the "fight or flight" response, which over time may produce hypertension and cardiac and other health problems. The concept of the relaxation response was first popularized in the United States in Dr. Herbert Benson's book titled *The Relaxation Response*.

self-fulfilling prophecy   This means that when we expect someone to act a certain way, they tend to act out our expectations. Expect the best of someone, and that's what you get.

sixty-nine (69) position This position's name is derived from the way lovers position themselves with one partner upright and one inverted, leaving them thus upside down relative to one another (like the numbers "6" and "9"). This position is also known by its French numerical moniker, *soixante-neuf*.

Spanish fly (cantharides) This is a substance made from pulverized emerald-green beetles found in southern Europe. Spanish fly mimics arousal—badly—by irritating the urogenital tract and causing the genitals to burn, itch, and swell. Side effects can include pain, nausea, and vomiting. In some cases, it has proven to be lethal.

yin and yang From the Chinese Taoist tradition, yin energy, representing the female, is necessary to balance yang energy, representing the male.

Index